Sex:

Does It
Make a Difference?

Sex Roles in the Modern World

Sex:

Does It
Make a Difference?

Sex Roles in the Modern World

Jean D. Grambs
University of Maryland

Walter B. Waetjen
Cleveland State University

 Duxbury Press

North Scituate, Massachusetts

A Division of Wadsworth Publishing Company, Inc., Belmont, California

DUXBURY PRESS

A DIVISION OF WADSWORTH PUBLISHING COMPANY, INC.

Sex: Does It Make a Difference was edited and prepared for composition by Maryellyn Montoro. Interior design was provided by Jane Lovinger and the cover was designed by Pat Sustendal.

L.C. Cat. Card No.: 75-11277
ISBN 0-87872-089-8

PRINTED IN THE UNITED STATES OF AMERICA

1 2 3 4 5 6 7 8 9 10 -- 79 78 77 76 75

Dedicated to:

Marya D. Grambs   Walter B. Waetjen, Jr.

Sarah S. Grambs   Kristi Jenkins (nee Waetjen)

Peter H. Grambs   Daniel G. Waetjen

Contents

Preface

About a dozen years ago when we were both members of the faculty at the University of Maryland, and had adjoining offices, we suddenly discovered that our professional interests converged. Those interests focused on the way in which sex roles in our society impinged on the academic performance of students. As we discussed this and searched the research literature, our investigation broadened to the extent of examining sex roles as they have a limiting or facilitating effect in societal institutions other than schools or colleges. It was in this way that the present volume came about. Like many scholars in many universities we did not initially intend that a book would be the product of our discussions.

There is an old bromide among statisticians that a difference to be a difference must make a difference. Does sex make a difference? Of course, but maybe gender makes more of a difference. If there is an overarching theme in this book, it speaks to the point that societies must make the fullest use of the human resources and talent in that society. So it is with sex roles. We have tried to set forth research evidence that would suggest ways in which these human resources and talents are or are not being used constructively in our society. Certainly we have not tried to set forth an all-inclusive theory of human existence—as tempting as that may be!

As with all other endeavors, there are many people who have made vital contributions to the preparation of this book. We acknowledge great indebtedness to our spouses; to Judy Goldman, Gail Walters, and Phyllis Cosner for their assistance in working on materials; and to Meg Montoro for her editorial help.

Jean D. Grambs
Walter B. Waetjen

ix

1

A Pink or Blue Blanket?

The First Question

"Is it a boy or a girl?" This is the first question a mother or father asks when a baby is born. The second question: "Is he/she all right?"

It is no accident that the first question regarding a new baby relates to its sex and that this issue has priority over concern for the baby's health. An infant's sex is one of its most significant characteristics. The fact that our world is made up of boys and girls, men and women, is not news to anyone. It is a matter considered so obvious that it appears often to be ignored; mentioning this fact is like pointing out that the sun rises in the east and sets in the west. Yet neither of these obvious facts is really as simple as it seems. The more one studies each phenomenon, the more complex it becomes, and what seems so simple becomes a maze of contradictions, unknowns, theories, and unorganized data.

In this book, we present some findings from a vast array of research on the significance of sex differences as these differences affect all of life's span, and most of life's activities. It is our contention that the very obviousness of sex differences has caused us to overlook the ways in which these differences operate, and that by overlooking or failing to understand these differences, parents, teachers, and others have made grievous mistakes. Boys and girls suffer, men and women suffer, and much human potential remains unrealized. Such waste of human talent and such loss of human happiness would not occur if those working in our institutions and rearing our children were more aware of the role that our attitudes toward sex differences play in everyday decisions.

From the moment of birth, decisions—even minor ones—are made on the basis of a child's sex. Friends of new parents would not dare decide on a blue or pink gift for the child until knowing its sex: a blue blanket for a boy, a pink one for a girl. If they don't know the sex, they play it safe by sending a yellow or white blanket, for new parents would be highly offended if a gift of the wrong color were sent. From the very beginning, everyone dealing with a newborn child deals with it in terms of its sex.

What's in a Name?

The sex identity of a newborn having been established, the parents must name the infant. At one time this was relatively simple; children were named after appropriate saints, or relatives. Today, movie stars or presidents or astronauts or television celebrities are likely to be the source for names.[1]

Analysis of the names given to boys and girls in New York City over the past seventy-five years shows that girls are apt to have more original names than boys, and that boys' names continue to be derived almost wholly from those of saints or relatives. Why is this so? We believe it is because the assigned name suggests a model for the child to emulate: "Remember you were named after your grandfather!" or "Perhaps you will be a famous actress too, like your namesake." Boys get formal, traditional names while girls get fanciful, made-up names; perhaps this is a reflection of "that pervasive division of labor that on the whole assigns 'instrumental' roles to men and 'socio-emotional' roles to women . . ."[2]

There are some who fear that names are being desexed. Charles Winick reports finding sex-distinct names in the birth records of 1948, but in the 1963 records he counted many "sex-neutral" names, a finding he views with alarm.[3] Two psychologists stressing the importance of names note that boys with "peculiar" first names are more likely than boys with ordinary first names to suffer neurotic disturbances.[4] Certainly, girls named Billie and boys named Shirley are bound to have a rough time at some moments in their lives. And one does wonder why parents chose these sex-inappropriate names to begin with.

Just as they quite deliberately dress a baby boy in blue and a baby girl in pink, parents indicate their awareness of their infant's sex by the name they give it.

And Which Kind Do You Prefer?

Whatever the sex of a child, the most important factor for later life is whether its parents want him—or her. There are some parents for whom any child is an unwanted burden, and there are some for whom any child is a blessing. The couple which has waited years for a child couldn't care less whether it is a boy or girl: it is their off-spring, and this is all that matters. For other couples, having a child seems to be the thing to do: after all, why did they get married?

Why individuals have children is a complex and not clearly ana-lyzed matter. The motivations, fantasies, and hopes that surround childbearing are seldom discussed objectively. Not all people are de-signed to be parents, and some people and their children would probably be better off if no family had been produced. It is ironic that adoption agencies take such special care to place children with the "right" parents. It is unfortunate that similar care is not taken when people marry, presumably with the intention of having chil-dren. The state takes a very remote interest in this decision, yet the fact remains that many people have children who neither want to have them nor are able to care for them properly.

Although most couples await the birth of their baby with joy, many have strong feelings about the desired sex of their child. In some cases, the much awaited infant is rejected because it is the "wrong" sex. The typical American couple, responding to ancient roots in Western civilization, desire their firstborn to be a son. If the firstborn is a girl, there is usually a desire to have a second child in hopes that it will be a boy. Thus, the sex of the children affects the size of the family. If a couple has one boy and one girl they are much more likely to stop at two than if both children are of the same sex: then they will try for a child of the other sex. One study showed that significantly more families stopped having children after they had had a boy than after the birth of a girl.[5] A sample of young adults re-ported a 65 percent greater preference for boys than girls.[6]

Despite the almost universal preference that the firstborn—or at least one child—be a boy, most mothers want at least one daugh-ter, and they don't mind more than one, either. But they do build up some resistance to a large family of boys. With each succeeding boy, the mother is less enthusiastic about the child.[7] Similarly, both parents may have such a stake in producing a boy that, after a succession of girls, they may become quite negative if not downright hostile. One couple expecting their fourth child, after three girls, did not even have a girl's name picked out, and they left the baby at the hospital for a few days while the mother went home to recuperate from the shock of having produced another girl. After a few days of adjustment, the couple claimed the infant, and resolved to overcome their initial and brutal disappointment.

It is not only parents who have feelings about the sex of the offspring—their relatives are also interested. The birth of the first grandson is usually a joyous event, for the grandparents know that "the name" will continue; the line will not be lost. When a girl marries, she adopts her husband's last name. Thus both father and grandfather see in the newborn son the continuation of the family name; the birth of a daughter, while it may be welcome and bring delight to new grandparents, does not carry the same connotation of family continuity. If no females have been born in several generations the birth of the first granddaughter would probably cause general elation, and the new mother and grandmother will feel satisfaction in seeing a small female reproduction of themselves. But in the final analysis, given our means of identifying families through "the name," the birth of a son has an extra and special significance. Sex of a child as it relates to family name and personal immortality is consciously or unconsciously included in the parental appraisal of each child.

The Firstborn Is Special

Whether a child is a boy or girl, the very fact of being first born will have a lasting effect on its life. Most parents look toward the birth of their first child with anxiety, and after its birth they invest many of their hopes and dreams in the child. Giving the child a great deal of anxious attention, and encouraging each new movement, each new word, and every step that the first child takes, parents instill in the firstborn a pride in achievement, a desire to reach new goals and win parental praise.

If parents have a preference, it is usually that the firstborn be a son. First born sons are usually high achievers; in fact, statistical evidence indicates that first born males have the best chance of:

. . . becoming president of the United States. Fifty-two percent of our presidents were firstborns.[8]

. . . becoming an astronaut.[9]

. . . being selected for *Who's Who*.[10]

. . . entering such selective colleges as Yale and Reed.[11]

. . . continuing to graduate school.[12]

Psychological studies of first born sons lead to some contradictory conclusions: one study showed them to be more fearful, more conforming, and more dependent than later born children;[13] another study found them to have higher self-esteem than later children.[14]

Harris did a study of eminent men and related their achievements to their birth order.[15] Although the study is not rigorously scientific, he reaches some provocative conclusions regarding the ways in which birth order influences such things as military success and artistic endeavor.

A first born girl is not quite as favored as a first born boy. In fact, she may start out with a distinct handicap since most parents want their firstborn to be a boy.[16] Although they have high needs to achieve, first born girls are apt to be quite conforming and dependent. If parents expect high achievement, then the conforming tendencies of first born girls make them seek to live up to their parents' expectations and seek achievement. A first born girl is also apt to be given more responsibility as other children come along. She may be required to care for later offspring, which thrusts her into a precocious maturity as "mother's little helper." She is more apt to experience the independence that accompanies responsibility; the bossy older sister turns into the school leader. First born boys are not expected to be independent as early as first born girls. In later life first born males accede more easily to social pressure than do later born males.[17] Perhaps the first born sons who became president were leaders who hurried to keep up with their followers.

Why does the firstborn seem to have such a special future? Exposed to two completely inexperienced parents, the first born child might be expected to be more mixed up, but instead this child turns out to have advantages over later born brothers or sisters. He or she gets the undivided attention of the parents, amateurs though they may be. He or she is the first "outsider" to intrude on the marriage, so that both parents are more acutely aware of their feelings for each other as these are highlighted by an insistent and demanding new member. The father is more apt to be an interested and active participant in all the activities of the firstborn.[18]

The fact that the first born son is traditionally heir to the family's fortunes may contribute to the extra solicitude, as well as extra demands, made upon the first born male. One has only to read the speculations regarding the potential of a crown prince to carry on his father's kingly role—or do him one better—to realize how deeply our attitude toward the first born son is molded by history. No wonder they achieve!

More Males Than Females?

Given the intense feelings about the sex of a child, particularly a first born child, would people have more boys if they were able to choose the sex of their child? Would the ratio between the sexes become unequal?

What happens when the ratio of males to females is not 1:1? In all frontier societies there are more men than women.[19] At the turn of the century in the United States there were 153 males for every one hundred females. This imbalance of the sexes had a profound impact on the American view of women. Since women were scarce they appeared more precious and were more highly valued than they might be in areas with a surplus of women or where the sexes were more nearly balanced. Out of the romanticism of the American west came a mythology about women that is now perceived as a burden and a barrier to adequate and objective understanding between the sexes.

New scientific discoveries have led to speculation regarding possible changes in the sex ratio when parents can choose the sex of children. A study of unmarried women indicated that a significant number (36 percent) would prefer to select the sex of their children.[20] Because of the preference for boys as firstborns, population experts have looked at the possibility that an imbalance in the sex ratio might occur, particularly in light of the reduced numbers of children which young people intend to produce. After a careful weighing of known facts regarding such preference with data on population growth, they concluded it is unlikely that the imbalance will become so great that there will be too few females. As sociologists see it, even if there is a temporary oversupply of males because of parental preference, the resulting scarcity of females will swing the scale and parents will place their orders with the obstetrician for a female infant.[21]

The preplanning and self-control involved in selecting the sex of one's offspring probably will be enough in itself to limit the numbers seeking such decision-making. Experience with contraceptives indicates that even individuals who should be most desirous of avoiding pregnancy, the poor and unmarried, often fail to take the simplest precautions. One can therefore predict that only individuals with very strong, even obsessive, feelings about a child's sex would try to best nature's lottery. If this is in fact so, then it would be well to encourage these individuals to plan for the sex of their offspring, since few children suffer more desperately and deeply than children who are emotionally twisted or rejected because they emerged the "wrong" sex.

Is Different Treatment Unfair Treatment?

At a very early age a child learns whether he or she is wanted or unwanted, and whether its sex had anything to do with parental preference or rejection. Sometimes, tragically, children learn late in life that they were treated as though they were not the sex they were born with—and the offices of psychiatrists are recipients of these tragedies. The mother who keeps her son in long curls and dresses long after he is in the run-about stage or the father who treats his daughter like another man about the house often creates great confusion in the child's mind as to just what sex he or she is, and this confusion may be resolved in adult life in ways abhorrent to the parents.[22]

We have assumed up to this point that parents do feel differently about their male and female children. Yet such differences of feeling are passionately denied by many parents. As one research team reported:

We had . . . difficulties in securing information about sex-role differentiation. Many of the mothers disliked the notion of "doing things differently." They interpreted any comparison of the sexes as somehow invidious. It represented an implied derogation of one or the other. . . . Some said it would be "unfair" to treat boys and girls differently, apparently viewing such possible differences mainly in the light of privileges offered to one sex but not the other. This idea troubled many mothers.[23]

It was extremely important for these parents to believe that they treated their boys and girls alike. Yet, one need only ask oneself—or one's brothers or sisters, or friends—if fewer or greater privileges were given because of one's sex. There are many who report painful scars: "Just because she was a girl she could get what she wanted; all she had to do was cry," or "I know they favored Bud because he was the only boy and Dad, well, he just never had time for us girls."

Parental feelings about sex, whether admitted or not, do enter into valuations and treatment of children. What we think we are doing—that is, acting impartially and fairly, treating boys and girls the same—may not, in fact, be what we do at all. It is our contention that sex differences are extremely important in determining how we treat others, and that we treat the sexes differently even in those situations—such as family and school—where we most firmly believe in equal treatment for all. The facts indicate that sex makes a tremendous difference in how a child is treated in the family or in the school. And in the family, it makes a difference whether a child is a first or last born boy, one of five sisters, or the first or last born of a family of boys or girls. Birth order, too, is important.

It is nice to want to treat people equally, but it is far better to recognize the ways in which we do, in fact, treat people differently.

Worth emphasizing is that *treating people—boys and girls—differently, does not mean treating them unfairly*. It was probably a fear of being considered unfair that led the mothers in the interview quoted above to react as they did. But treating boys and girls differently does not have to mean treating them unfairly. Only when different treatment results from different valuations does the unfairness emerge. Children tell us about unfair treatment at home and school many, many times, and many times it is attributed to their sex, and the preferences of mother or father, or of male or female teacher.

The First Question Is the Last Question

As soon as new parents ask about the sex of their child, that child receives a sexual identity. The child is labeled boy or girl, and all who deal with it repeat this verbal labeling by sex. Newborn babies, bundled up in their white hospital blankets, do not reveal by their heads or posture or movements whether they are boys or girls; but they are already *labeled* boy or girl. The hospital puts an appropriately colored bracelet on the baby's wrist, saying "baby boy Grambs" or "baby girl Waetjen," and the child is so labeled from then on.

"You see, children, I hate you both in quite different ways."

Drawing by Chas. Addams; © 1968 The New Yorker Magazine, Inc.

The child learns it is a boy or girl long before it understands what that means in anatomical terms.[24] Ideas of being manly or masculine, or of being feminine come somewhat later, but in the very first year of life the child learns its sex label. The mother will say: "You are a good boy for eating all your cereal" or "You were a nice girl when you brought me the empty glass." Mothers and fathers alike use the term boy or girl as well as the child's name when talking with their children, in chiding or praising them, and they are almost unaware of what they are saying. "That's a good boy," or "that's a good girl" are such common terms of approval that we forget the term boy or girl is included in the phrase of commendation. It is this repetition of boy or girl which lets the child in on the significant information about itself: he is a boy; she is a girl.[25]

There have been cases of children whose sexual anatomy is ambiguous, or with some physiological attributes which deviate from those of a "true" female or male. Through surgery, doctors can eliminate the sex characteristics which seem the least strong, and leave the anatomical features which appear to be the child's more dominant sex. The child is then labeled a boy or girl, though in physiological terms he or she might have been the other sex. The parents and all others respond to what is now the "real" sex of the child, and it is this gender identity which is "imprinted" upon him. This labeling, for both normal and physiologically abnormal children, is practically unchangeable. As one psychologist notes: "Such labeling is perhaps irreversible because basic cognitive categorizations are irreversible. After a certain point, social reinforcements cannot readily reverse or change basic categorizations of constancies in the child's physical world. . . ."[26]

In other words, by labeling a child boy or girl one sets up in the child's mind the abstraction that he is, indeed, what his parents and others say he is. And he cannot change this notion about himself, no matter what. A child learns to distinguish between cat and dog. It is impossible to make him change these labels once he has learned them; he just won't do it because it would not make sense. Labels about oneself are much more significant. I am what you call me, what you perceive me to be: a girl, a woman—or a boy, a man. This acquisition of a sexual self-image is called gender identification.

The "first question" then, has great and enduring significance. The answer to the first question—Is it a boy or a girl?—determines a whole range of social responses. The chromosomal structure which determines a child's sex is reinforced by the way society greets the knowledge that this new member of the world is a boy or a girl. This is true in America, and it is true for all cultures, all over the world.

Sex—Does It Make a Difference?

Even before birth the sex of an individual has an influence, and this influence persists throughout life. One's sex is perhaps one's most important physical attribute. Other physical attributes may be altered: we can become fat, and then thin down again; we can grow our hair long, or shave it off, or dye it purple. Skin color is difficult to change, but having enough money or status wondrously alters the impact of skin color on the perceptions of others. Nose the wrong shape? It can be made beautiful with a little surgery. Ears stick out? A few neat tucks can take care of that. Too short or too tall? Some very powerful and rich men have married women a foot taller than themselves; and platform shoes do wonders for the undersized. But one's sex can hardly be changed. Despite the publicity attending a few sex change operations, the nature of such change is so drastic that very very few venture down that path. Sex is indeed one physical attribute that is not amenable to change or adjustment.

We will find, as we explore the data presented later in the book, that status, money, and power do not accrue equally to the two sexes. Thus the burden of our inquiry is not just what difference it makes to be male or female, but whether the way these differences are socially defined is helpful or hurtful for the development of adequate, fulfilled human beings.

References

1. Alice S. Rossi, "Naming Children in Middle Class Families," *American Sociological Review* 30 (1965).499-513.
2. Elaine Cumming, "The Name Is the Message," *Trans-Action* 4 (July-August 1967):51.
3. Charles S. Winick, *The New People* (New York: Pegasus Books, 1968), pp. 198-206.
4. Albert Ellis and R. M. Beechly, "Emotional Disturbances in Children with Peculiar First Names," *Journal of Genetic Psychology* 85 (1954):337-339; James Bruning and William Albott, "Funny, You Don't Look Cecil . . . ," *Human Behavior* 3 (March 1974):56-57; "Names and Grades," *American Teacher* 58 (September 1973):6.
5. Amitai Etzioni, "Sex Control and Its Consequences," *Current* 101 (November 1968):23-27; see also G. E. Markle and C. Nam, "Sex Predetermination: Its Impact on Fertility," *Social Problems* 18 (March 1971):73-83.
6. Etzioni, *op. cit.*
7. Robert R. Sears, Eleanor E. Maccoby, and Harry Levin, *Patterns of Child Rearing* (Evanston, Illinois: Row, Peterson and Company, 1959), p. 57-58.
8. Kenneth Goodall, "Big Brother and the Presidency," *Psychology Today*, April 1972, p. 24.
9. *Washington Post*, March 2, 1969, p. A-29.
10. Vance Packard, "First, Last, or Middle Child—The Surprising Difference," *Reader's Digest*, December 1959, pp. 25-27.

11. William D. Altus, "Birth Order and Its Sequelae," *Science* 151 (1966): 44–49.
12. Barbara Rothenberg, Research Paper, University of Maryland, 1972.
13. *Science News,* November 13, 1971, p. 327.
14. Morris Rosenberg, *Society and the Adolescent Self-Image* (Princeton: Princeton University Press, 1965), pp. 107–127.
15. Irving C. Harris, *The Promised Seed* (New York: Macmillan, 1964).
16. S. Dinitz, R. R. Dynes, and A. C. Clarke, "Preference for Male or Female Children: Traditional or Affectional," *Journal of Marriage and Family Living* 16 (1954):121–130.
17. William N. Dember, "Birth Order and Need Affiliation," *Journal of Abnormal and Social Psychology* 68 (1964):554–557; see also Edward E. Sampson, "Birth Order, Need Achievement, and Conformity," *Journal of Abnormal and Social Psychology* 64 (1962):155–159.
18. Sears, Maccoby, and Levin, *op. cit.,* pp. 413–414.
19. T. Lynn Smith, "The Population Problems of the Tropics" (Paper presented at the Fourth International Congress on Tropical Medicine and Malaria, Washington, D.C., May 1948).
20. Warren B. Miller, "Letters: Reproduction, Technology, and the Behavioral Sciences," *Science* 183 (January 1974):149.
21. Gale Largey, "Sex Control and Society: A Critical Assessment of Sociological Speculations," *Social Problems* 20 (Winter 1973):310–318; Lawrence Galton, "Decisions, Decisions, Decisions: Choosing the Sex of a Child," *New York Times Magazine,* June 30, 1974, pp. 17–21; Charles F. Estoff and Ronald R. Rindfuss, "Sex Preselection in the United States: Some Implications," *Science* 184 (May 1974):633–636; "Babymaking: Dress Them in Blue," *Science News,* January 12, 1974.
22. Largey, *op. cit.*
23. Sears, Maccoby, and Levin, *op. cit.* p. 400.
24. Robert J. Stoller, *Sex and Gender* (New York: Science House, 1963), p. 39.
25. *Ibid.*; see also John Money and Anke A. Ehrhardt, *Man and Woman Boy and Girl* (Baltimore: Johns Hopkins University Press, 1973).
26. Stoller, *op. cit.*

2

It's the Same

The Whole World Over

An old English ballad has the refrain:

> It's the same
> The whole world over:
> It's the rich what gets the gravy
> And the poor what gets the blame.

And its the same the whole world over: men get the status; women get the work. Men's work is accorded prestige and recognition: women's work is necessary, but who'd want to do it?

In most cultures, men's work and men's social roles have greater status than women's work and women's roles. The status problem is interesting and complex; and it arises from the fact that most cultures sharply define and separate those things that men can and ought to do from those things women can and ought to do. Tasks are divided by sex, as are personality traits and behavioral patterns. Since in every society the male is accorded the higher status, so the activities and tasks undertaken by men are given a higher value.

◆ **Man's Work: Woman's Work**

Of course men do the heavy work; for they are stronger, bigger, and they should do such things. They are also the great poets, musicians, and sculptors, because they are more sensitive, artistic, and have greater creative talents. Only the strong, rugged, objective masculine mind can run a government or head a bank. And of course, because of their greater wisdom and intellect, men are the religious leaders. Women are more delicate, more emotional, and less creative because they are concerned with everyday events. They do not have the shrewdness or intellect to handle the affairs of state.

The above sex-role stereotypes are accepted in most Western societies. But there are other cultures in which these expectations and beliefs are rejected. In an anthropological study of over two hundred cultures, G. P. Murdock identified those tasks that could be done only by men, those that could be done only by women, and those that could be done by persons of either sex.[1] The findings are fascinating: the only jobs done exclusively by men in *all* cultures were hunting of animals and pursuit of sea mammals (Table 2-1). All other tasks could be done in one culture or another by men, by women, or by both. Although most cultures seem to cluster male and female activities with little overlap, this is not wholly true of any activity (with the above two exceptions). For instance, although burdens are carried exclusively by men in twelve cultures; only women do this in fifty-seven. Only men do the fishing in ninety-eight cultures, but in four cultures this is a task exclusively for women. Although women always cook, carry water, and grind grain in most cultures, there are exceptions. In some cultures, these tasks are assigned exclusively to men!

Table 2-2 reveals Murdock's data on division of labor by manufacture of objects. Women are excluded from metalworking and weaponmaking in these pre-industrial cultures. In industrialized societies, women may work on the assembly line of armament industries, although they do not tend steel forges or do other heavy metalworking tasks. It is of interest that men always make the pottery, do the weaving, and make and repair clothing in several cultures, although most cultures assign these tasks exclusively to women.

Despite our strong feeling that certain work is just more suitable for men than women, or vice versa, if we search long enough we will find a culture that believes just the opposite. Thus it is not the *nature* of the task, but rather *the cultural assignment of the task to one sex or the other* that determines who will undertake it.

What are the reasons for sex differentiated work assignments in any given culture? Why does one culture forbid men to cook, and another forbid this task to women? Why are both men and women allowed to make baskets in some cultures, while in others this is

TABLE 2-1. Cross-Cultural Data from 224 Societies on Subsistence Activities and Division of Labor by Sex

ACTIVITY	NUMBER OF SOCIETIES IN WHICH ACTIVITY IS PERFORMED BY:				
	Men always	Men usually	Either sex	Women usually	Women always
Pursuit of sea mammals	34	1	0	0	0
Hunting	166	13	0	0	0
Trapping small animals	128	13	4	1	2
Herding	38	8	4	0	5
Fishing	98	34	19	3	4
Clearing land for agriculture	73	22	17	5	13
Dairy operations	17	4	3	1	13
Preparing and planting soil	31	23	33	20	37
Erecting and dismantling shelter	14	2	5	6	22
Tending fowl and small animals	21	4	8	1	39
Tending and harvesting crops	10	15	35	39	44
Gathering shellfish	9	4	8	7	25
Making and tending fires	18	6	25	22	62
Bearing burdens	12	6	35	20	57
Preparing drinks and narcotics	20	1	13	8	57
Gathering fruits, berries, nuts	12	3	15	13	63
Gathering fuel	22	1	10	19	89
Preservation of meat and fish	8	2	10	14	74
Gathering herbs, roots, seeds	8	1	11	7	74
Cooking	5	1	9	28	158
Carrying water	7	0	5	7	119
Grinding grain	2	4	5	13	114

Source: Roy G. D'Andrade, "Sex Differences and Cultural Institutions," in *The Development of Sex Differences*, ed. Eleanor E. Maccoby (Stanford: Stanford University Press, 1966), p. 177.

restricted sharply to one sex or the other? Anthropologists cannot explain the reasons for sex differentiation in assignment of tasks. However, some clues have been provided by observations of cultures in transition. For example, the !Kung, a society of hunters and gatherers living in the Kalahari Desert of South Africa for the past eleven thousand years, recently underwent their first massive change in lifestyle. They have abandoned hunting and gathering, which meant almost continuous moving from place to place, and are now settling in farming villages near the Bantu. As a hunting and gathering society, the !Kung were noteworthy for the equality accorded to women, the

TABLE 2-2.   Cross-Cultural Data on the Manufacture of Objects and Division of Labor by Sex

ACTIVITY	NUMBER OF SOCIETIES IN WHICH ACTIVITY IS PERFORMED BY:				
	Men always	Men usually	Either sex	Women usually	Women always
Metalworking	78	0	0	0	0
Weaponmaking	121	1	0	0	0
Boat building	91	4	4	0	1
Manufacture of musical instruments	45	2	0	0	1
Work in wood and bark	113	9	5	1	1
Work in stone	68	3	2	0	2
Work in bone, horn, shell	67	4	3	0	3
Manufacture of ceremonial objects	37	1	13	0	1
House building	86	32	25	3	14
Net making	44	6	4	2	11
Manufacture of ornaments	24	3	40	6	18
Manufacture of leather products	29	3	9	3	32
Hide preparation	31	2	4	4	49
Manufacture of nontextile fabrics	14	0	9	2	32
Manufacture of thread and cordage	23	2	11	10	73
Basket making	25	3	10	6	82
Mat making	16	2	6	4	61
Weaving	19	2	2	6	67
Pottery making	13	2	6	8	77
Manufacture and repair of clothing	12	3	8	9	95

Source: Roy G. D'Andrade, "Sex Differences and Cultural Institutions," in *The Development of Sex Differences*, ed. Eleanor E. Maccoby (Stanford: Stanford University Press, 1966), p. 178.

lack of aggression in the children, and the very stable and low birth rate, almost exactly geared to the food supply. Since the !Kung have settled in villages the women's status has dropped, for they must stay home and care for the children. The men, who work with the Bantus, learn the Bantu language. The women, lacking such contacts, do not learn the language. The !Kung men see the Bantu model of male dominance and bring it home with them. The net result of the change is that !Kung women are being reduced to a subservient role.[2] The change from nomadic to settled living has made a significant difference in the work that men and women do and the status accorded to that work.

It's Men's Work That Counts

It could be asserted that the consistency with which various cultures accord men greater power and status is the result of a realistic assessment of their superiority to women. Certainly if one added up the cultural experiences over the eons, that is the safest hypothesis one could expound, since there is overwhelming evidence that societies do concede superiority to men and their activities, and generally consider women inferior. The tasks women do are considered useful, indeed essential, but they are what inferior beings deserve to do. And yet physiology does not appear to be the most important factor in determining who does what task. Work that is considered too hard for women in some cultures is work that *only* women can do in others. These data should make one cautious about asserting that physiological differences determine who does what, because either men or women can, in fact, perform any task that the opposite sex can do.

Sex differentiation in the division of labor cannot account for the higher status of the male, for whatever men do—whether it be basketweaving or waging war—is considered more important than what women do. We seem confronted by a vicious circle: women have little status, their work is perceived to be unimportant; and because their status is low, any job they undertake is demeaned. The opposite pattern holds true for men.

The different valuation accorded the work of the two sexes is directly related to the status and roles prescribed for them. As the noted anthropologist Ralph Linton noted, "The division and ascription of status with relation to sex seems to be basic in all social systems. All societies prescribe different attitudes and activities to men and to women."[3] In those few societies where the female has the higher status and plays the dominant role, the work done by women is highly valued. But in most societies women have the lesser status, and the sex role prescribed for them demeans their work as much as it demeans them.

◆   **Sex Roles: What Is Their Function?**

Sex Roles: Expectations and Preparation

We do not know why males have been so universally favored. The superiority of males in terms of muscle power and strength could be one source of their higher valuation. In societies dependent on hunting and/or fighting, such strength is essential. However, more settled cultures dependent on the harvesting of carefully tended crops are quite as likely to derogate the female role, although both men and women perform the same food producing tasks.[4] As in more primitive cultures, male strength is valued.

Even in technologically advanced societies males are expected to demonstrate physical strength from puberty onward. Puberty rites serve to measure a boy's strength and endurance; they are a symbolic introduction to adult life. The role of puberty rites in the formation of male character is important to consider. In many of these rituals the emphasis is on endurance, with boys confronting various tortures, facing frightening objects, being isolated for terrifying periods of time, suffering cruelty and scarring.[5] The resultant "warrior" personality is no accident. In those cultures not dependent on warring, puberty rites are less tests of manhood than inductions into the male religious mysteries. The rigorous training in the United States armed services during the first months after induction is a sort of puberty rite. The training given Marines in boot camp has long been called necessary to "make men" as well as Marines out of these raw youths. The initiation rites of fraternities appear to be lineal descendents of the tribal initiations common in preliterate societies. Each year one or more youths suffer irreparable physical damage and even death from cruel or stupid initiation rites. The initiation rites of sororities are marked by semireligious rituals, with candles, songs, long gowns, solemn pledging to the sisterhood, and then celebration. Such ceremonies bear some resemblance to the female initiation rites of other cultures where future roles as mothers and subservient family members were stressed.[6] We can see in these modern-day rituals a vestige of the emphasis on sex differences so apparent in primitive cultures.

Although not all the ceremonies used to induct boys into manhood are brutal or brutalizing, such ceremonies do raise doubts about the degree of security with which men regard their masculinity.[7] Puberty rites appear to be tests of a boy's ability to emulate the traditional masculine model—to prove that he can take on any challenge. Beyond this, puberty rites indicate that a boy will be expected to achieve, to bear heavy burdens, and that he will be rewarded for doing so. "The ceremonies emphasize a social fact: the adult prerogatives of men are more far-reaching in every culture than woman's, and consequently . . . it is more common for societies to take note of . . . [puberty] in boys than in girls."[8]

Societies have devised additional ways to ensure that males are in fact stronger and more able to survive the stress of battle; thus it is the boys and young men who participate in sport and games. The Greek games of antiquity were reserved for males—as was war. The relation between games and war is not too hard to find; and in the words of modern psychologists, perhaps in some more rational time games can become the psychological equivalent of war.

The current dispute about equalizing athletic opportunities for boys and girls in schools and colleges has aroused some of the old arguments about women's greater delicacy and their inability to undertake rigorous sport. One female commentator, who has a black belt in goju karate commented, "Women's physical helplessness is not their natural state: it requires a lifetime of careful deprivation to achieve."[9] Few technologically advanced societies allow women to attain anything like the physical strength of men.

While boys and men are tested for their physical and psychological endurance, females are nurtured into softness and dependence. In our culture they are discouraged from acquiring muscle power or achieving success in the larger world, and are told they must be a man's partner, his helper. But females too are expected to fulfill a difficult role, and that role is motherhood. Much of the modern woman's rage arises from the fact that the strength, the patience, the endurance necessary to good mothering are ignored. While male activities are overvalued, this primary female activity is undervalued.

No male can bear a child, and no woman can induce conception. The length of the infancy of the human child appears to be the critical variable in the way human society has organized family relations. If, as with many other animal infants, the human infant could forage for food and move about on its own soon after birth, sex roles would undoubtedly be quite different. But a human infant, unless carefully nursed and tended for many years, will not grow up into a self-sufficient adult. Who is to do the twenty-four-hour baby-tending job so crucial in earliest infancy? Why, the mother, of course. Thus she cannot do the other jobs that are essential to the child's existence and her own: providing food, shelter, clothing, safety. These tasks must be carried out by someone, and if there is a man around—as there usually is—he does the chores of family maintenance.

Cultures weigh these two ranges of activities on a value scale: is it better to be the bearer and first teacher of children? Or is it more valuable to be the one who keeps peace and order (government and fighting), "brings back the bacon" (or the antelope), and builds the hut? In most societies, and throughout Western history, the activities undertaken by men are valued, and those identified with women are demeaned. Motherhood may be prized, but it carries less status than almost any male activity.

If this is so, why then is there the idealization of female virtue, the Catholic veneration of the Virgin Mary, the lavish gifts provided for mother on Mother's Day? Other societies, not just Western civilization, have likewise venerated female goddesses, endowed women with special virtues and surrounded them with a veil of mystery.

The Mythology of the Female Role: Witch or Seductress?

The female role has been shaped by cultural expectations and societal needs; it is supposed to complement the male role. The roles prescribed for men and women have evolved through the ages, and are based as much on irrational beliefs as on objective or rational needs for differential behavior. The origins of the female role are buried under a body of myths, fears, and fancies. These myths appear to be exaggerations of the behavior expected of women and can give us some clue as to why the female role has been fashioned as it has. In some cultures woman is the temptress, in some she is evil and dangerous, while others see her as the embodiment and protectress of all the virtues.[10]

Before we examine the various myths about women, we need to ask why such myths seemed necessary. The myths appear to derive from a need to rationalize or explain the discriminatory treatment accorded women in almost all cultures. If women are not educated, it is because they will misuse knowledge, or are too weak-brained to be educable. If women are not accorded equal justice, it is because they must be kept strictly in place, for given free rein they would be wicked and destructive. Women must be locked up and never allowed outside the house without watchful escorts, for they are so attractive and their nature so seductive that they will turn the heads of any passing man; their bodies must be covered so completely that they have no recognizable shape.

Parallel myths have not been produced about men, except for the myth of divinity, which is often restricted to a male image. The myths about women are worth some attention, not only because they are pervasive, but because they have served to trap women, culturally speaking, in roles that are restrictive and distorting.

Women are the source of evil: Pandora opened the forbidden box and let forth all the evils hidden there upon the world. Eve listened to the serpent and ate the forbidden fruit; subsequently Adam was ensnared and sin was loosed upon the earth. All humanity suffers from Eve's transgression.

Women are weak as well as evil. Many passages in both the Old and New Testaments assert the "lower" nature of woman, her weakness, her inability to resist sin. She is seen as seducing men away from virtuous living. Daughters are difficult to raise because they will cause trouble; says Ecclesiasticus "A daughter is to a father a treasure of sleeplessness." The harsher discipline which even today is administered to girls is foreshadowed by advice Ecclesiasticus gives to the father: "Over thy daughter keep a strict watch, lest she make thee a name of evil odour—a byword in the city and accursed of the people —and shame thee in the assembly of the gate."[11]

The teachings of the early Christian church were quite specific about the way women should be treated. Females were to be subordinate to males in all things, and woman was in fact created for man.[12]

St. Paul's advice was:

Let the woman learn in silence with all subjection.
But I suffer not a woman to teach, nor to usurp authority
      over the man, but to be in silence.
For Adam was first formed, then Eve.
And Adam was not deceived, but the woman being deceived
      was in the transgression.
Notwithstanding, she shall be saved in childbearing, if
      they continue in faith and charity and holiness with sobriety.[13]

The Old Testament gives some indication of the higher value accorded males in Hebrew culture. A woman who gives birth to a male child is unclean for thirty-three days, but after the birth of a female a woman is unclean for sixty-six days.[14]

As in ancient times, today's orthodox Jew begins his day with thanks to God that he was not created a woman.[15] Although Jewish teachings abound with admonitions to honor both father and mother, Jewish scripture everywhere speaks of the father before the mother, because the teachings of the sages is that both a man and his mother are bound to honor the father.[16] To this day among orthodox Jews women are segregated to a separate portion of the temple when at worship and must be hidden from the view of the men behind a sheer curtain.

There is no doubt that the biblical view of the roles and status of the sexes exerted an enormous influence upon Western civilization. Priests, preachers, and writers were primarily and foremost students of the bible long before secular literature developed. Secular literature was for centuries influenced by religious indoctrination, since the only education available was under religious auspices. It is quite apparent as one reads of the struggle for women's legal equality in Western history[17] that much of the resistance to change has rested upon biblical arguments.[18]

The Muslim religion, once strong in Mediterranean Europe, and

now the major religion in most Arab, North African, and Middle East-
ern countries, also views women as inferior to men, relatively powerless, and having few rights. The koran states that men are superior to
women, and the birth of a daughter is not a matter for rejoicing, although there are specific injunctions against burying infant females
alive.[19]

Cultures influenced by Judeo-Christian and Islamic beliefs
clearly show the significance of such doctrines in the continued
myths of women's lower nature. But these cultures are not alone; the
view of women as the evil sex seems to permeate many cultures.
Among the Arunta, women are believed to have the power to lure a
man to his doom; therefore, he must beware of them. In one East
African tribe, after the necessities of procreation a man and woman
may not sleep together; it is believed that she could steal his breath
and weaken him. Because women may have this power to weaken
men, they must be kept subjugated: in one area of India they may
not eat the flesh of the tiger, lest they gain in strength; in one African
tribe they are kept ignorant of the source of fire. Early California
Indians had special ceremonies to frighten women so as to insure
their submission to men.[20]

There is a general assumption that women are more religious
than men; statistics of attendance at church bear this out. But women
are barred from becoming priests in most religions. A few Protestant
sects permit the ordination of women, and a few women have been
allowed to serve as rabbis in reformed Jewish congregations. The
reaction against the ordination of eleven women to the Episcopal
ministry in September 1974, was evidence that religious practices are
extremely difficult to modify. Exclusion of women from religious
leadership is true in most cultures. In some primitive tribes women
could practice "medicine" but were rarely permitted to take an equal
role with men in the religious mysteries of the group. Women are expected to play supportive, not decisive, religious roles.[21]

Cassandra, Salome, Lot's wife, Circe, Madame DuFarge, Cleo-
patra, Helen of Troy, Hedda Gabler, Lady Macbeth—our mythology,
our history, and our literature are filled with the names of women
associated with seduction, temptation, or the downfall and destruction of men or nations. The Penelopes are few and far between. The
temptress, the evil genius, or the earth mother and goddess of fertility
—these are the dichotomous roles invented for women. No wonder
women are confused. By contrast, the mythology about men is nei-

ther as wildly divergent nor as monolithic. Contemporary youth must carve out roles for men and women free of the myths of the past.

Marriage Practices and Valuation of the Sexes

Like other animals, the human is inextricably bound up in the problems of succession and continuity. In the grand design, whether of God or nature, people invest their tremendous energy and intellect on two major activities: self-preservation, and preservation of the group—family, tribe, nation. The family is vital to the survival of the species, but the definition of "family" varies widely from culture to culture.

Anthropological research is replete with analysis and discussion of the family systems of different societies. Basic to these reports are the ways in which every society deals with the problem of family continuity. The valuation accorded to boys and girls depends to a great extent upon the system used by the cultural group to preserve the identity of kin or clan.

Families continue through marriage, and thus the choice of marital partner is a matter of great concern to family members. Will the new marriage create alliances with another strong family group who can be called upon in times of crisis for economic assistance or mutual protection? Or is the other family poor in money or power so that any alliance is weakening? The various cultures have devised many means of assuring selection of the proper marital partner. In traditional Japan, the mother typically contacted a marriage broker who established the range of possible marriage partners, depending on family wealth, connections, age of child, and so on.[22] The role of the marriage broker in traditional Jewish life has been described in many stories.

Traditionally, the Irish rural family evaluated a prospective bride in terms of the extent of her dowry. The bride's parents assessed the amount of land to be "settled" on the prospective bridegroom to see if it equaled the dowry the bride had to bring. The bride's family had to have sufficient dowry money to get rid of their daughters; likewise a young man needed some land and farm animals provided by his father to acquire a well-dowered wife.[23] It is quite possible that the dowry practice contributed to the lower status of the female child. "Where the father has to pay large sums of money in connection with the loss of his daughter, there may often be a tendency for women to lose status and for the birth of a daughter to be regarded as a trag-edy."[24] In the average household, the dowry practice often delayed the age of marriage and thus the childbearing years of the daughter.

Remnants of the dowry tradition can be seen in the American marriage norm, in which the bride's father, immortalized in Streeter's *Father of the Bride*, spends the equivalent of a dowry on a wedding extravaganza. The bride's parents expect the new husband to provide adequately for their daughter. In the United States, male pride has traditionally rested upon a man's ability to support his wife.

A bride-price system, in which a young man must gather enough worldly goods to purchase a wife, is an inversion of the dowry prac-tice. Like the dowry system, it puts restraints upon who will or can marry whom. After all, a major exchange of economic goods is not undertaken lightly. Kinfolk, who may have to help in gathering to-gether enough cattle or other medium of exchange for a suitable bride-price, would have a large say in deciding who the bride (and the bride's family) would be.

Perpetuation of the family, and the protection of family mem-bers, is a complex problem, and every culture has carefully elaborated ways of identifying who can marry whom, and how property is trans-ferred from person to person, from family to family, and from par-ents to heirs. In Western cultures lineage is through the male.

Most societies identify lineage through the family of the father (patrilineal descent) and only a few through that of the mother (mat-rilineal descent). The male brings in a new bride, and her children be-long to the kin group of marriage. Family identity is reinforced through the woman's change of name at marriage. This is a visible if vestigial reminder of who "belongs" to whom. Since it is the male who is responsible for the continuity of the family line, a male child is the more valued; for centuries a valid reason for the annulment of a marriage, or the taking of a second wife or a concubine, was the failure of a wife to produce a son. This custom still prevails in many cultures.

Like adoption of the father's name, there are other customs re-lating to the fact that although one can know with 100 percent cer-tainty who the mother is, there *can* be doubt regarding the father's identity. As man discovered this basic fact, he began to devise means of ensuring the fidelity of his woman or women: in purdah, as prac-ticed in the Middle East; in the chastity belt of medieval times; or in the threat of heavy punishment, including death, for a woman caught in adultery. In some more permissive tribes, as long as the woman was the wife in the household, all children were considered children of the man of the house even though there might be good reason to doubt this. In Israel in 1972 a father asked the courts to declare his children Jews and entitle them to Israeli citizenship. However, although his wife had converted to Judaism, she was not a Jew through descent. The court adhered to the principle that the mother must be Jewish through descent to entitle children to citizenship.

Changing Times: New Roles

For most of the world, the relationships between men and women and the ways in which boys and girls are reared to fulfill their sex roles have remained relatively unchanged for generations. The patriarchal household is the norm in most Western countries; women are primarily housewives and childrearers. If women work, they do so at clerical tasks or in semiskilled jobs in factories. Legal and religious restrictions and beliefs relegate women to unequal status.

However, there are distinct changes occurring which, although they now may affect very few, have potential for an unprecedented revolution in social and personal relationships during the next several generations.

As technology advances, and as populations shift from subsistence agriculture to industrial production, different kinds of jobs become available requiring different talents and training. As we pointed out in the study of the !Kung tribe, women lost status when the tribe became settled and the men participated in the trade and commercial life of villages. In a different fashion, the revolution in modern China has produced a shift toward greater equality for women in agricultural areas, for the government has downgraded the importance of the extended family, ancestor worship, and the significance of sons as the bearers of family traditions.[25]

Technology is undoubtedly a basic ingredient in determining the allocation of behaviors appropriate to the two sexes. Where technology reduces the emphasis on physical strength, then access to money, power, and status are the means of male domination.[26] The best way to keep women from having power, money, and status is to deny them education. Data from the underdeveloped countries, and those undergoing technological modernization in recent years, show the acceptance of education for males but not for females. Female illiteracy is cited over and over again as one of the main deterrents to the improved health, and thus improved chances for surviving, of infants and children.[27] Of the estimated 800 million illiterates in the world, over 60 percent are women. They participate far less than men in the economic life of their countries, they are inferior in civil law, and "in no country in the world do women participate in the activities of the governing or policymaking bodies on the local, national or regional level to an equal degree with men, and in most countries their participation is minimal."[28]

As reports from all over the world indicate, some women in every country are becoming aware of these inequities. They also are aware of the consequences of their lack of education, the lack of opportunities to work and achieve, and their legal and political powerlessness. There is no doubt that in the next few generations women will challenge the power men have held to restrict them to household and childrearing tasks, or to inferior legal and social status in every country in the world. The personal tensions which result from any revolution are hard to assess; and it is sadly true that no provision is made to think ahead and help men and women move into new relationships easily. Instead, we can predict painful years of reassessment and readjustment, taking their toll in the lives of boys and girls and men and women as they struggle to see each other beyond old forms and old sex-role stereotypes.

◆ **Summary**

Every society has labeled appropriate sex roles and appropriate sex behaviors, has normalized a system of kinship and lineal descent, and has extended social valuations accordingly.[29]

The question, "What is normal?" in terms of sex-role behavior is irrelevant. From a world view there is no "normal" or "right" pattern. Each culture and each social group has devised patterns that fit its own circumstances and its own social and cultural history. As times change, as populations ebb and flow, as new technologies are devised, new roles for men and women, boys and girls emerge.[30]

"Maleness and femaleness are institutionalized as statuses in all cultures. Such statuses have physiological identities for most individuals. Usually individuals learn to want to occupy the sex status they are assigned . . . ."[31] It is when such status assignment begins to be questioned, when men and women become uncomfortable with their roles; and when such concepts as woman's innate wickedness and inferiority or man's innate aggressiveness and superiority are seen to be more myth than fact, that radical change can occur. Verities which appeared to be eternal may not last under the questioning gaze of scientists and young people. What, then, will take their place? Can there be, and will there be, a new equality between the sexes? Or what?

In discussing the ways that Western culture deals with sex differences, we can note two prominent—and divergent—themes: one is the derivation of attitudes from Judeo-Christian concepts fixed in biblical statements and interpretations, and the other is the influence of changing social and economic conditions. These two major forces —one conserving an ancient and revered system of beliefs, and the other impelling shifts and reappraisals of traditional forms of social arrangements—are on a collision course. One cannot want to stay the same and also want to change without feeling unbalanced, confused, and uneasy.

As we view attitudes toward sex differences in the latter part of the twentieth century, it is clear that there is a sense of uncertainty and distress. Time and again we hear the agonizing plea from young people: "But what am I *supposed* to do?" followed almost immediately by, "I want to make up my own mind about what is best for *me*." No wonder the older generation thinks today's young people are a very difficult group indeed; the young people themselves are often in hearty agreement. It was all right for young men of past generations to sow their wild oats, but there is real uneasiness when young women claim the same privilege. It just doesn't seem right— traditional sex-role behaviors are being challenged. This challenge goes to the core of human society, whether in the microcosm of the home or the macrocosm of national affairs.

References

1. G. P. Murdock, "Comparative Data on the Division of Labor by Sex," *Social Forces* 15 (1935):551–553.
2. Gina Bari Kolata, "!Kung Hunter-Gatherers: Feminism, Diet, and Birth Control," *Science* 185 (September 1974):936.
3. Ralph Linton, *The Study of Man* (New York: Appleton-Century-Crofts, 1936), p. 113.
4. Mellville Jacobs, *Patterns in Cultural Anthropology* (Homewood, Ill.:Dorsey Press, 1964), p. 199.

5. Robert Lowie, *Primitive Religion* (New York: Liveright Publishing Co., 1948), pp. 205–220.

6. Frank W. Young, *Initiation Ceremonies* (Indianapolis: Bobbs-Merrill, 1965), p. 20.

7. Karen Horney, *Feminine Psychology* (New York: W. W. Norton, 1967).

8. Ruth Benedict, *Patterns of Culture* (Boston: Houghton Mifflin, 1934), p. 26.

9. Susan Murdock, "Rape and Women's Self-Defense," *New York Times*, September 8, 1974.

10. Dena Justin, "From Mother Goddess to Dishwasher," *Natural History* 82 (February 1973):41–44.

11. Quoted in Katherine M. Rogers, *The Troublesome Helpmate: A History of Misogyny in Literature* (Seattle: University of Washington Press, 1966), p. 12.

12. 1 Cor. 11:3, 7–9.

13. 1 Tim. 2:11–15.

14. Lev. 12:6.

15. Horney, *op. cit.*, p. 99.

16. Arthur Hertzberg, *Judaism* (New York: Braziller, 1962), p. 99.

17. William L. O'Neill, *The Woman Movement: Feminism in the United States and England* (New York: Barnes and Noble, 1069); see also Leo Kanowitz, *Women and the Law: The Unfinished Revolution* (Albuquerque: University of New Mexico Press, 1969).

18. Mary Beard, *Women as Force in History* (New York: Macmillan-Collier Books, 1946).

19. Julia O'Faolain and Lauro Martinex, eds., *Not in God's Image* (New York: Harper and Row, 1973), pp. 106–115.

20. Lowie, *op. cit.*

21. *Ibid.*; Horney, *op. cit.*, p. 112–113; Benedict, *op. cit.*, p. 68.

22. Ezta Vogel, "The Go-Between in a Developing Society: The Case of the Japanese Marriage Arranger," *Human Organization* 20 (Fall 1961):112–120.

23. Conrad M. Arensberg, *The Irish Countryman* (New York: Macmillan, 1937), pp. 72–79.

24. Alan R. Beals, *Culture in Process* (New York: Holt, Rhinehart and Winston, 1967), p. 114.

25. William Brugger, "The Male (and Female) in Chinese Society," *Impact of Science on Society* 21 (January–March 1971):5–20.

26. E. G. LeMasters, "The Passing of the Dominant Husband-Father," *Impact of Science on Society* 21 (January–March 1971):21–30.

27. "Children in a Crowded World," *UNICEF News*, December 1973–January 1974, pp. 1–44.

28. Helvi L. Sipila, "Equal Rights for the World's Women," Report Number 18,

The Victor-Bostrom Fund for the International Planned Parenthood Federation (Washington, D.C.:1974), p.3.

29.   G. Rattray Taylor, *Sex in History* (New York: Harper Torchbooks, 1970).

30.   Joe David Brown, *Sex in the 60's: A Candid Look at the Age of Mini-Morals* (New York: Time-Life Books, 1968).

31.   Roy G. D'Andrade, "Sex Differences and Cultural Institutions," in *The Development of Sex Differences*, ed. Eleanor E. Maccoby (Stanford: Stanford University Press, 1966), p. 177.

3

Anatomy Is Destiny?

Long before Sigmund Freud made his oft quoted statement "anatomy is destiny," the peoples of the world acted as though this were so. Physiology seems to have destined men and women to fill very different and well defined social roles. Few people disagree with the comforting folksaying "you can't change human nature." We are what we were born with; it is all programmed inside those magical genes and chromosomes. Just look at boys and girls, men and women: don't they look different? Don't they have very distinctive and essential roles to play in procreation, the most important natural activity of any living thing? The vast difference between male and female is just too obvious to debate. Or is it? Must those physiological differences relating to the sex act also determine other major differences in character, personality, ability, and aptitude between the sexes?

Our knowledge of human physiology, although extensive, is still far from complete. Many physical activities and attributes can be described, but how or why they function as they do is open to speculation. Human physiological sex differences are not as definitive as many would wish. As in any apparently simple situation, the more closely one studies, and the more one learns, the less certain one becomes. Although man is an animal, he is a thinking animal, with language and the capacity to make tools. No other animal has all of these capacities. It is therefore with caution that one can extrapolate from knowledge gained in experiments with rats or studies of baboons, and apply it to human behavior. Only human beings can be ir-

Acknowledgment is made to Dr. John Chapin for assistance in preliminary drafts of this chapter.

31

rational, since only human beings can be self-consciously rational. Therefore we proceed with due caution to assess what is known about the physiology of human sex differences, and attempt to answer the question of the links between anatomy and destiny.

◆ Sex Determination

The ancient Greeks believed that the male delivered into the female womb a miniature boy or girl. Many nonliterate and prescientific cultures have accepted the notion that procreation is primarily a male activity, with women serving merely as available vessels. When Leeuwenhoek observed the wriggling spermatazoa in 1677 he immediately asserted that he had discovered the babies carried by the male, and even thought he could identify the sex of these "animalcules." The mammalian ovum was not discovered until 1827, but again it was relegated to an ancillary role in procreation. In 1861 the ovum was identified not just as the source of nourishment for the fetus, but as the female sex cell. Mendel asserted that male and female sex cells contributed equally to the genetic makeup of the child, but popular belief assigned the more significant role to the male. Even today a man refers to his wife as "the mother of my children," and a woman will report, "I bore his children," while children are educated to believe that babies are started when "daddy plants the seed in mommy."[1]

It is relatively common knowledge today that one's sex is established by the kind of chromosomes one has. In 1891 a German scientist discovered sex chromosomes in a species of obscure insects. By 1902 human sex chromosomes had been discovered. Later research revealed the complex process whereby males and females are formed at conception.

From the moment of fertilization an embryo's sex is genetically determined, but until the fifth or sixth week of fetal life all embryos are sexually undifferentiated; the influence of the sex chromosomes does not occur until after the fifth or sixth week of pregnancy. If the embryo is to become male, the beginning of differentiation continues through the twelfth week of life when the reproductive tract is established.[2] "The sex of an embryo is determined at conception, but the structural differentiation of the sexes does not become apparent until the seventh week of embryonic life. It seems likely that in the beginning the sex glands have the potentialities of both sexes. At some critical stage the presence or absence of a normal Y chromosome is probably all-important. If a Y chromosome is present, the sex glands develop into testes; if there is no Y chromosome, ovaries form."[3]

The cause of the higher rate of prenatal deaths and sexual anomalies among males is still a matter of conjecture. The feminists interpret the delicacy of the male fetus as suggesting that, rather than Eve being produced of Adam, it was really the other way around.[4]

Every normal human ovum contains twenty-two chromosomes, plus one X chromosome. Every normal sperm cell carries twenty-two "ordinary" chromosomes plus one X or one Y chromosome. This X chromosome has been named the female chromosome, while the Y is called the male chromosome; it is this X or Y chromosome which determines sex. If a sperm with a Y chromosome fertilizes the ovum, then the baby has forty-four chromosomes, plus one X and one Y, and it develops into a normal male. If the sperm has an X chromosome, then the baby has forty-four chromosomes plus two X chromosomes and develops into a female. This is the normal pattern of sexual differentiation.

Although the female has two X chromosomes in any one cell, only one remains functional. The other X chromosome curls up in the corner of the nucleus and is called a Barr body. Not until 1956 was it found that some individuals who are regarded as normal do not have such regularly assigned chromosomes. Some females might have three X chromosomes, and some might have only one. Boys might be born with one extra X chromosome (XXY), or an extra Y chromosome (XYY). There have been cases with XXXXY chromosomes, and XXYY, plus other variations. There are even individuals who have some cells in the body bearing an XY chromosome count while other cells may be XXXY. Infants with one X and no Y chromosome (XO) are said to have Turner's syndrome and are biologically female. With males, an extra X chromosome (XXY combination) is termed Klinefelter's syndrome; this may predispose such persons toward difficulty in sexual adjustment.[5] Most people go through life without ever having a chromosome count. Not very much is known about the impact of chromosomal variations, since many of these have only recently been identified.[6]

Of interest to us, however, is the fact that, although no sophisticated knowledge is obtained about an infant's chromosomes, a sex is assigned to it at birth on the basis of obvious genital differences, and the child adopts the gender identity assigned to it. Sometimes the "obvious" genital differences are misleading, as the elaborate and extensive investigations by John Money at Johns Hopkins have shown.[7] Some infants are born with ambiguous sets of reproductive organs, or only partially developed organs. Surgery can provide the infant with one identifiable set of organs, although these may not be suitable for the purpose of reproduction. When parents are told the child is a girl or boy they treat it accordingly, and the child assumes the gender that is assigned to it, despite any chromosomal abnormalities or genital anomalies.

The difference between sex and gender is the difference between what is biologically inherited and what is socially assigned. Are we to conclude therefore that biological sex is less significant than socially defined sex? The new discoveries about the action of hormones upon physical and psychological development may in time help us unravel the contributions of nature and of nurture to human sexual differences.[8]

Genetic Inheritance and Sex Differences[9]

A defective gene which is recessive will not affect an individual in the presence of a normal gene for the same trait. Most sex-linked defects are carried by the X chromosome. Since females have two X chromosomes, the defective gene recedes and the normal gene on the other X chromosome is dominant. Thus, color blindness, for example, is found almost exclusively among males; it is inherited from their mothers who themselves are not color blind. A boy has only one X chromosome and if this chromosome is defective for color vision, he will be color blind.

Montague has collected an impressive list of sixty-two physical defects, almost all of which can be attributed to heredity and most of which affect males only.[10] Montague attributes the superior physiological defenses of women to the fact that they have two X chromosomes, to the male's single one. An infant can survive with one X chromosome, or two, or XY, but never with one or even two Y chromosomes only. The X chromosome is absolutely essential to survival; the Y is not.[11]

Only very recently have researchers been able to photograph the difference between sperm which carries a Y chromosome (androsperm) and that which carries an X chromosome (gynosperm).

What is of interest is that the androsperm is speedier, having a longer tail, but the gynosperm is hardier. If the egg is ready for fertilization, the Y sperm is more likely to reach the egg first and a male would be conceived. If there must be a wait until the egg is ready for fertilization, the X sperm, taking a longer time to reach the site of fertilization, will be more likely to fertilize the ovum. Alkaline secretions have been detected in females following orgasm; these secretions are less favorable to the X chromosome.[12]

It has been speculated, on the basis of what is now known, that the timing of intercourse in relation to ovulation may well be a factor in determining the embryo's sex, since the life of a sperm with an X or a Y burden is of different duration.

The male fetus appears to be more prone to miscarriage or spontaneous abortion than the female.[13] One study of the numbers of male and female children born showed that there is a nonrandom occurrence of families which produce male children early in the birth order and only female children later. It is suggested that the mother has become sensitized to some substances produced by and under control of the Y chromosome, and that this causes rejection of the male fetus. This may account for the higher rate of spontaneously aborted male fetuses.[14]

Chances of having a son decrease as parents age. Fewer males are born to older women; the cause of this appears to be the father's increased age rather than the age of the mother.[15]

◆ Sexual Dimorphism: Physical Differences and Sex Differences

The esoteric sounding term, sexual dimorphism means simply that two sexes are needed for reproduction and that each sex has distinctive physical characteristics. The two sexes are distinguished on the basis of genital differences that are present from birth. With growth, members of each sex develop further characteristic physical differences. Between the sexes there are consistent differences in size, weight, and other physical attributes. This is true for most, but not all, animal species.[16]

Sexual dimorphism among humans has caused us to expect that most boys will grow larger and heavier than their sisters. Anthropologists' field reports as well as historical records suggest that not in all cultures nor in all eras have men been larger and stronger than women.[17] In the United States the average height of adult males ranges from 5 feet, 7 inches to 5 feet, 9 inches, and the average height of adult females is between 5 feet, 2 inches and 5 feet, 4 inches—but there is a wide range for each sex. Some women are taller than the average man; some men are shorter than the average woman. The social implications of these variations are painfully obvious to tall women and short men, from adolescence to death.

Another typical physiological distinction between men and women is their different centers of gravity. Women, on the average, have relatively heavier hips and thighs while men have relatively heavier chests and shoulders. There are two tricks that will demonstrate this sex difference:

Kneel on the floor. Put your elbow against your knee and extend your forearm and hand. Place a pack of cigarettes on the floor at the tip of your index finger. Then, fold both hands behind your back and try to knock over the pack of cigarettes with your nose. Very few men can do this without falling on their faces but most women can do it easily.

Place a chair with its back to a wall. Stand just beyond this chair and lean over so your forehead rests against the wall. Now, without jerking it, pick up the chair and step away from the wall with it. Most women can do it. Most men cannot.

Theoretically it should be possible to identify the sex of skeletons, but many skeletons cannot be sexed correctly since there are many broad-hipped men and narrow-hipped women. Skeleton sexing by rib-counting does not work: men have as many ribs as women.

There is a distinction between men and women in the distribution of fat. It is estimated that if a man saturates his adipose tissue (tissue capable of holding fat), then 19 percent of his body weight will be fat. If a woman saturates her adipose tissue, she will be 26 percent fat.

Most young men in our culture do not saturate their adipose tissue, but young women do. Some studies indicate that young men carry only 11 to 11.5 percent of their body weight as fat, while young women carry 28 to 28.5 percent of body weight as fat. There are sex differences in the pattern of fat distribution. Women accumulate fat all over the body beneath the skin. This subcutaneous fat provides a measure of insulation against heat loss but it also smoothes bodily contours and makes their skin "soft to the touch." Women, much to their chagrin, also accumulate fat on the outer curve of their calves, on their thighs and hips, and beneath the upper arm. Men accumulate fat around the waist. There are differences in fat distribu tion along ethnic, sexual, and family lines. African bushmen, when they gain weight, tend to lay down fat on the rear end.

Sexual distinctions do not extend to all aspects of physiology, however. Muscle tissue is muscle tissue whether it is attached to a male or female leg or arm. There is evidence that male muscle is stronger than female muscle when corrected for size, but females in our culture are rarely encouraged to undertake activities that would strengthen their muscles. Male muscles are to be built, female muscles are to be toned. It is difficult to assess the effect of this cultural bias upon female form or physical capacity in the United States; the famous female pearl divers of Japan have developed physiological attributes that few American males could equal. These include very large lungs capable of holding breath underwater for long periods as well as very strong muscles used for diving and swimming.

We find significant differences between the sexes when metabolic rate is measured. Males consume more oxygen than females from the earliest years; this continues throughout life.[18] This difference in metabolism, in the body's ability to utilize fuel, is an important difference which is apt to be overlooked or misunderstood. The greater metabolic rate of boys means that their "inner engines" are going around at a faster pace than those of girls. Thus in the primary grades boys are much more restless and active than young girls. If boys, and any girls who wanted to, were allowed to run around at high energy levels more frequently in the early grades there would probably be far fewer requests for parent conferences because of the disturbing behavior of boys.

Body Types

Relationships between skeletal frame and fat and weight distribution have been studied to determine if there are some constant elements. W. H. Sheldon, a noted physiologist, devoted a lifetime to the study of body types which he called "somatotypes." He identified three basic body types: endomorphs, mesomorphs, and ectomorphs. Endomorphs are fatter and larger. Ectomorphs are tall and lean, with shallow chests, thin arms, and long and narrow muscles. Mesomorphs are large boned with big faces, thick necks, deep chests, large wrists and hands. Each of these extreme types constitute only a small percentage of the population; most people are mixtures. According to Sheldon's complicated classification system, 343 possible somatotypes were identified, but of this number only seventy-six actually exist, and both men and women can fall into every one of these seventy-six classifications. Women, however, are less apt to be meso-morphic—big muscled and large boned—and more apt to be endo-morphic, fatter, and more lethargic.[19]

To what extent these somatotypes are related to personality is open to considerable debate. Many would say that body type has no bearing on personality development. But after studying thousands of juvenile delinquents the Gluecks have asserted that mesomorphic boys are more likely to become delinquent (given other predisposing factors) than their brothers who do not share this body build, be-cause our culture equates masculinity and mesomorphy.[20]

In assessing Sheldon's theory of body type and personality de-velopment, we may agree with Krech that "a kernel of truth is lurk-ing here. If and when the existence of a physique-temperament relationship is firmly established, the next challenge will be to deter-mine the roles of genetic and cultural factors in such a link."[21] What is of significance is that each of us, male or female, responds to what others think about our appearance, and our body build is of course an important factor in their assessment of us. If our culture values skinny, tall persons, then these individuals will have a relatively higher self-esteem than lesser valued short, fat people. Does physique determine temperament? Or does temperament and personality re-sult from social valuations of physique? Sheldon made a pioneering effort to find out, and his findings, while generally ignored today, may be worth another look as we study how boys and girls grow, and how they view themselves, given different body packages.

Sheldon reported that girls who mature early are high in both mesomorphy and endomorphy but low in ectomorphy. They are the girls who are the tallest in their fifth and sixth grade classes. The fact that these girls do not always become the tallest adults is little consolation for nine to fourteen-year-old boys who are shorter than many of these girls. The situation is only slightly better for the girls, for while they know they are not supposed to be taller than their male peers, at least they have a newfound maturity. But what of the very late maturing boy who is smaller than almost all the other boys and girls until he is sixteen or seventeen years of age?

Sex Differences and Hormones

Folklore, literature, and music are replete with references to women being more emotional, more unpredictable—more "hormonal." The monthly cycle of ovulation in women occurs in response to a series of interrelated hormonal events. The female sex hormones, estrogen and progesterone, are the "releasing" hormones in ovulation,[22] and thus are the main ingredients in birth control pills.[23]

Males produce androgens, the most powerful of which is testosterone. These hormones stimulate the production of sperm.[24] Although androgens are essential to sperm production, women as well as men produce androgens in their adrenal cortices. Likewise, men produce estrogen, but in far smaller amounts than women. Thus, although androgens are called male hormones and estrogens are female hormones, each sex produces both, but in different proportions.[25]

Androgens, which males produce in greater quantity than females, is strongly involved in tissue growth. Some athletes may take the androgen, testosterone, to increase muscle mass, but this has the unwelcome side effect of decreasing the normal production of the gonadal androgens responsible for fertile sperm production. The lack of androgens in women with Addison's disease has been shown to eliminate the sex drive.[26]

Up to the age of eight boys and girls have essentially no sex hormones. It is tempting to assume that any behavioral differences between boys and girls is caused by culture rather than by nature. Yet there are important differences which are the result of hormone effects. Girls reach maturity before boys. Girls develop certain skills earlier, and they seem more mature even at birth.[27] If it is androgen that causes boys to mature more slowly, this effect must be produced *in utero* since young boys have no more *circulating* androgen than young girls.[28] The androgens produced during late childhood are thought to be of adrenal rather than gonadal origin; this androgen production is not sufficient to cause the appearance of male secondary sex characteristics.[29] Under the influence of adrenal androgen, children of both sexes grow stronger at about age eight. Growth occurs through the influence of growth hormone, thyroxine, insulin, vitamin A, and good nutrition. The higher the growth hormone level, the faster the rate of growth. Some individuals may have high levels of growth hormone while others have low levels. Sex hormones influence the rate of bone growth. Sexual maturity halts long bone growth. The long bones of children who reach sexual maturity early stop growing under the influence of sex hormones. Children who grow slowly and reach sexual maturity later may catch up with and grow taller than their peers because they have a longer time to grow.[30] If height increases after sex hormones become active, it is not through increase in leg length, but rather through increase in trunk length.

The influence of hormones can be seen when one plots height or weight as a function of age. Among young children, size differentiation according to sex is negligible. Variations in size among boys or among girls is far greater than size differences between the sexes. The average boy and girl are neck and neck until they are nine or ten years old when the girl surges ahead in her preadolescent growth spurt. By the time they are twelve she is both taller and heavier. In the sixth and seventh grades boys look up at girls with whom they once saw eye to eye and note with dismay that the girls' hands are larger, sometimes disproportionately large, like the paws of puppies. This is a period when girls should, or could, be stronger than boys if society approved. By ninth grade most boys are well into their own growth spurts. They catch up to the girls and surge beyond them before androgens bring long bone growth to a halt.

There is a trend toward earlier and earlier sexual maturity. In seventeenth century Austria, girls reached menarche between seventeen and twenty years of age, while in the early nineteenth century, English girls were 15.7 years at menarche. In 1934, American girls showed an average age of 13.5 years at menarche; at present the average age is 12.5 years.[31]

Puberty plunges both boys and girls into new psychological states in response to a changing body, but, as we indicated, these changes occur at different times for boys and girls. One negative impact of our rigid age-graded school is that girls, who generally reach puberty one to two years ahead of boys, will be experiencing new emotional states that are not comprehensible to their male classmates. A girl who was perfectly "normal" may, within a short space of time, show different moods, feelings, and behaviors.

The thirteen-year-old boy whose voice breaks in the middle of singing practice has always been the butt of jokes and teasing, but it is no fun for the boy. Teachers who complain of the lack of cooperation from boys in music classes in junior high should know the possible cause. Boys' resistance to gang showers in physical education during these years is not because boys are more attached to dirt or allergic to soap and water than girls, but is due rather to fear of having their immature genitals on display, or the first signs of pubic hair greeted with public acclaim. Although the bodily changes in adolescent boys are less dramatically apparent than in girls, there is ample evidence that it is a period of uncertainty, psychological and physiological disorganization, and readjustment for both sexes. All boys and girls experience drastic shifts in body image and self-image, but at different times. Not all boys or girls mature at the same time,[32] and their maturation has different meanings for them in the context of our culture and our schools.

The confusion for both boys and girls who lack information about the full impact of puberty on their sense of self as well as their physiological status is not relieved by current school practices. Menstruation is still treated by school personnel as something too "dirty" to discuss publicly. Girls may be given some scant information, but rarely are boys initiated into the mysteries of female ovulation and menstruation. Many if not most sex education programs are planned for the junior or senior high school years; in fact the major physiological changes of puberty now occur in sixth grade in many girls. School programs reach only a few students, and parents are not very helpful. Most adolescents still get their sex education from their peers.[33] It is certainly appropriate to inquire if parents and the school could not more adequately explain how bodies grow and develop; as it is, our children know less than many preliterate peoples.

Adolescent girls who are told that the blood of menstruation is evil and that this is a time of month to be dreaded and hated will have one response; girls whose first menstruation is greeted with celebration and welcome, who are informed that this event is valued evidence of maturity and future fulfillment, will have quite a different response.

Sex Differences and the Brain

For centuries, there have been notions of male intellectual superiority based upon the observation that the male brain was larger and heavier than the female. The average difference between the male and female brains is about 4 ounces, but when brain weight is related to body weight the difference shifts in favor of women; it has been calculated that the brain accounts for about 2.5 percent of female body weight and about 2 percent of male body weight.[34] We now know that size of brain is not really related to intelligence, but the myth of brain size as an indicator of intellectual ability dies hard.

Are there any differences between the male and female brain?

We now know that there are "fetal hormones on that part of the brain, the hypothalamus, which will subsequently relate the cycles of sexual functioning in the female or their absence in the male."[35] It would appear that "nature's basic premise is to make a female. To make a male, something must be added. . . . When radioactive-labeled male hormone is administered to the fetus either through the mother or, directly, in the case of the rat which is immature, its uptake can be traced to various organs, including cells in the hypothalamus [brain]."[36]

There may be critical stages at or before birth when areas of the brain are sensitive to androgens. These sensitized areas may influence sexual behavior later in life.[37] Thus, male hormones present before birth may organize the brain into a male pattern of sexual response, while the absence of these hormones may create a female sexual response pattern. In one very interesting study, the phenomenon of penis erection during sleep was shown to occur among average males most commonly during dreaming sleep (Rapid Eye Movement, or REM sleep). This kind of sleep has its precursor in brain "pulsing" identified during prenatal life. Sexuality in men seems to be one aspect of a complex neurophysiological process "built into certain primitive parts of the human brain."[38]

The impact of hormones on intellectual functioning has not been clearly established. The discussion between those who claim that hormones do influence cognitive functioning and those who deny it can be found in the scholarly literature.[39] Different researchers come up with findings that appear to support their own predilections and, as one commentator stated, any one of these studies "represents another in a series of purportedly objective, scientifically empty statements on the topic of sex differences."[40]

◆   The Weaker Sex?

"Some peoples think of women as too weak to work out of doors, others regard women as the appropriate bearers of heavy burdens, 'because their heads are stronger than men's.' "[41] Persons reared in Western culture are quite sure that woman is the weaker sex. Women are spoken of as frail, emotional, sensitive, easily shocked, to be treated with tender loving care. Why this view of women came to dominate Western mores in the nineteenth and through the mid-twentieth century is a problem for social historians. The data prove that before the advent of protective legislation women were worked as hard and as long, and were treated as harshly as were any men.

The low esteem in which women were held was a carryover from the low value placed on female babies. Women were more prone to illness and early death partly because they were less valued, and also because they bore children. Until very recent times childbirth was a hazardous undertaking. In a society lacking knowledge of antiseptics or nutrition, the physical stress of childbirth was not easily withstood.[42] Although accurate vital statistics were not kept until very recent decades,[43] there is considerable evidence that it was not unusual for a family to produce fifteen to twenty infants, although relatively few of these lived to adulthood. Because childbirth took such a toll on women, it was common for men to remarry in order to have a mother for the surviving children and to produce more children who could contribute their labor to the support of the family.

Medical advances finally tipped the scale in favor of women; by 1900 the life expectancy for white men in the United States was 46.3 years; for women it was 48.3. By 1930 women could expect to live for 61.6 years, while the life expectancy of men was only 58.1 years. The gap increased with each decade: by 1960 women's life expectancy had increased to 73.1 years, while men were given 66.6 years. In 1970, women were expected to live to an average age of 74.6 years, males to 67.1.[44]

Although these developments may be reassuring to women, they may be due to the restrictions on women's participation in life. Women do not fight in the front lines in battle; women do not bear the stress of decision-making at top executive levels; women are not exposed to the dangers and diseases of coal mining; women do not drive heavy trucks, dig tunnels, or work on the high beams of one hundred-story buildings. Society protects woman from these perils—no wonder she lives longer than man. But even in societies where women do not have the full benefit of "protection" from war and hard labor, a woman's life expectancy is typically two or three years greater than a man's.

Longevity may be a mixed blessing for women. A widow's existence is lonely, and widows are far less likely to remarry than widowers. Senility is another hazard of old age. Our nursing homes are filled with older women who are no longer able to manage their own bodies and whose minds have deteriorated with age. Many women fear they will be a senile burden on their families, and in fact this unlovely prospect does confront the children of older women. One psychiatrist reported an alarming rate of suicides—3.5 times the average—among older women in affluent areas of Washington, D.C. These suicides are probably among the lonely and desperate widows of the many retired military and congressional personnel in Washington.[45]

Women have greater resistance to illness and disease than men. Montague listed the differential incidence of diseases for men and women, and he reported that there are fifty-nine ailments which occur more frequently among men than women and only twenty-nine that occur more frequently in women than men.[46] "We may postulate that certain factors located on the X-chromosome tend to protect against specific degenerative diseases or to increase resistance to a variety of infectious and toxic agents through hormonal or other biochemical actions."[47]

Our culture encourages adventurous exploratory behavior among young boys, and as a result the rate of accidents for boys is much higher than for girls.[48] Interestingly, this continues into adulthood. The accident rate for male drivers is so high that insurance rates for young men are astronomical in comparison to those for young women. Because boys engage in contact sports they are more apt to break bones and suffer other hazards of aggressive exertion. As women engage in more activities on a par with men, their longevity advantage will probably decline. With the increase in the number of heavy smokers among them, there is already a growing incidence of lung cancer among women.

Women have benefited from some medical advances much more than men, for the greatest killer of women was childbirth, and the incidence of death from childbirth is now very low. With the legalization of abortion, fewer women will die as a result of illegal operations.

Sex differences in physique and temperament are so complicated that it is misleading to assert that one sex is stronger or weaker than the other. As old myths and stereotypes fade away, as boys and girls have more equal access to vigorous play, to adventure and excitement, to achievement and prestige, it is likely that there will be an equalizing of the score, with men and women having approximately the same life expectancy.

Physiology, Emotionality, and Sex Differences

In 1970 a minor explosion occurred in the mass media when Dr. Edgar E. Berman, a surgeon, a friend and adviser to Hubert Humphrey, and one-time consultant on Latin American health problems to the State Department, asserted in a press conference that "raging hormonal" imbalances each month made women irrational and unfit for positions of high responsibility. Dr. Berman asked what might have been the consequences had women been in charge of decision-making at the Bay of Pigs debacle, when an ill-advised American group attempted to challenge Fidel Castro. The reply was immediate and scathing. Dr. Estelle Ramey, an eminent female geneticist, responded: ". . . what *did* happen? And who *was* in control?"[49] As the rhetorical question suggests, the men in charge made some unfortunate errors of judgment which have dogged American foreign relations ever since, and presumably no hormones were at work.

What about women's "raging hormones?" Studies of time lost from work because of monthly distress do not support the impression that this is a period when most women are "sick." Most women feel little if any discomfort, particularly when there are necessary or interesting activities awaiting them. Bans against bathing, swimming, vigorous games, and horseback riding during menstruation have gone the way of other prescientific myths, even though some women may still invoke such notions to gain attention or to escape.[50]

The relationship between increased sexual interest and premenstrual tension was recognized by Karen Horney in 1931. According to her findings, women with adequate sexual (marital) relationships are far less troubled by premenstrual tension.[51] Current data indicate that hormonal changes during the menstrual cycle may precipitate a "raging sexual appetite" in the ten to fourteen days prior to menstruation. Analysis of the physiology of the female orgasm, Sherfey concludes, shows that the engorgement of the female organs prior to the menstrual flow is sexually exciting; when there is no release available there will be feelings of discomfort, depression, and related psychological disturbances.[52]

Data on the menstruating woman are contradictory and controversial. Whether the menstrual cycle affects her work and her mood has not really been determined. In Europe studies of behavioral change associated with women's monthly cycle showed that crimes, suicides, and accidents, as well as decline in tested intelligence, in quality of school work, in visual acuity, and speed of response were related to phases of the menstrual cycle.[53] Although few studies have been made with American subjects, one recent report showed a monthly variation in perception of flashing lights, in anxiety, aggressiveness, and depression.[54] A pilot study of American girls compared them with Lebanese, Apache, Japanese, Nigerian, and Greek subjects. Similar patterns were found in all of these cultures: there was premenstrual tension accompanied by feelings of irritability, nervousness, depression, fatigue, backache, and moodiness.[55]

In many cultures the menstruating woman has been regarded as unclean and evil, or else endowed with special gifts from the gods. The anthropological literature reports numerous instances of segregation of menstruating females on the basis that they are unclean. A different hypothesis might be suggested: perhaps women enjoy having a four-or five-day "vacation" every month in which to gossip at leisure with other women! How else could women in pretechnological cultures find any excuse to cease their labors in the home or on the land? The women who take to bed in our culture may also find the pains and inconvenience of menstruation an excuse to get rest, to be waited on, to relinquish responsibility for home, family, and job.[56]

Interestingly, the anthropological literature contains little about the procedures women use to collect and dispose of the menstrual flow. The sanitary napkin (itself a euphemism) is a relatively recent invention. The term "wearing the rag" literally referred to menstrual rags which were washed and reused. Tampax, an internal absorbent tube, was at first greeted as dangerous and sinful. Experiments by avant garde women with menstrual extraction have created a furor in female and medical circles. A simple suction procedure extracts the menstrual tissue, and for those choosing menstrual extraction "the period" is a thing of the past. The centuries of silence and ignorance regarding women's physiology have been harmful for both men and women. A recognition of what is now known about the hormonal cycle could probably aid marital adjustment.

It is clear from the previous discussion that menstruation has baffled societies from prescientific times into our own era. The eons of myth and taboo surrounding the event of menstruation still influence our research and thinking. With more objective analysis, it is possible that future generations of women will have some clear guidance regarding that which is psychological and that which is physiological in their response to the menstrual cycle.

Similar to the aversion to menstruation is the negative reaction to menopause. In earlier times, most women died during their childbearing years, and the phenomenon of the menopause may not have been commonly recognized. Even today, few men and women understand what is involved in menopause, despite the fact that most Western women live long enough to experience this "change of life." The average woman views menopause as a time when she will be physically uncomfortable, prone to depression and feelings of loss, and she believes that when the process is complete she will immediately look older.

In the past the "change of life" was just that. It was thought that postmenopausal women had no interest in sex, nor were they considered sexually desirable. With menopause, life had indeed changed—and for the worse. Through hormone therapy today's women can be helped to adapt to the different hormonal patterns that follow menopause. The estrogens that women produce prior to menopause protect them from heart attacks, and are responsible for their feminine appearance. Can these estrogens be continued indefinitely when nature no longer supplies them? Some doctors feel this may induce cancer or otherwise adversely affect the body, which *should* age. Other doctors disagree. It is evident, however, that moderate hormonal therapy during the period of adjustment to the gradual cessation of menstruation averts any acute physical and emotional response.[57]

Men seem to have a physiological cycle, although it is much less obvious and has not been studied extensively. "Emotional rhythms usually pass unremarked in the normal person," states one summary of the data, with the note that observations of cyclic patterns in males come almost exclusively from nineteenth and early twentieth century studies.[58] But a German physiologist recently reported that sperm cells mature in about twenty-seven days, beard-hair follicles in sixteen to twenty days, and he believes there may be a correlation between these cycles and male emotional and behavioral responses.[59]

Is interest in sex different for male and female? Although sexuality has been an obsession of post-Victorian society it remains true that there are "no experts in this field of human behavior. The lack of experts is a product of the prudish taboos of our cultural heritage.

Until Masters and Johnson publicly declared their breaking of the taboo, for medical and scientific purposes, of watching people copulate, it was as morally illicit to be a sexual observer as it had been, in the sixteenth century, for Vesalius to dissect a human cadaver and establish the science of anatomy."[60] The data available today indicate that sexual interest and satisfaction is as active, pervasive, and important to females as to males. With this knowledge in hand, we should make every effort to promote healthful social and personal goals in the years ahead.

Both men and women can and do remain sexually active into their eighth decade. Men of seventy and eighty years have fathered children. The apparent male decline may be due to the shift away from achievement and ambition and toward the prospect of retirement, with a consequent loss of self-confidence and psychic energy.

In a graceful summary, Money and Ehrhardt point out what is now known about the physiology of sexual aging in humans:

In normal aging, there is a gradual quantitative tapering off of male hormone production, but no dramatic change, as in the cessation of hormonal cycling that heralds the finish of menstrual periods in the female. The older male is likely to find that his penis obliges with an erection less often than his libidinal desire would dictate, for he undergoes a slow diminution, in this respect, from the typical pneumatic-hammer insistence of the penis in early adolescence to its quietude in the eighth and ninth decades. The female may undergo a corresponding progressive libidinal quiescence, but her copulatory role is such that she possesses, mechanistically speaking, an orifice and a cavity that will awaken to their own feelings while they are in copulatory use, instead of as a prerequisite to their being put to such use which is the way of the penis.[61]

Sex Differences and Mental Health

More women than men are admitted to psychiatric institutions, and more women than men seek and receive care for emotional or mental stress. Do these facts indicate a differential incidence of mental illness or do they reflect differential treatment by society? Recently it has been asked whether the data reflect the true rate of mental illness among women.

It is possible that psychiatric personnel have a rigid view of normal female behavior and consequently find a higher rate of abnormality than actually exists. In the last fifty years there have been very few studies of the extent to which the sex of a psychologist or psychiatrist influences his/her judgments.[62] There are twice as many male than female clinical psychologists, and 90 percent of all psychiatrists are male. Chesler believes that male psychiatrists define female mental illness, and female nurses and social workers accept these definitions as consistent with their own sex-role attitudes and behaviors.[63] In one study, clinicians were asked to describe the mentally healthy person and mentally healthy man were almost identical; in contrast, a mentally healthy woman was depicted as being more submissive than a mentally healthy person, as well as more dependent, more easily influenced, more excitable, more conceited, and less interested in math and science.[64] Male and female clinicians agreed on these ratings. A woman who is close to the clinical view of the mentally healthy *person* would be judged abnormal by these clinicians. No wonder women professionals, who are assertive, independent, objective, and unexcitable, are considered not quite normal by men, other women, and sometimes even by themselves. In 1973 male and female clinicians rated personality self-studies of a group of normal male and female subjects. The results showed that male clinicians were more critical of both men and women subjects for any deviation from a sex-role stereotype—they criticized dependence or passivity in men and assertiveness or "bitchiness" in women. Female clinicians reacted negatively to condescension and overconcern with power and control in men, and to "overfemininity" in any subject. As the researchers noted, "It is as though men keep a sharper eye out for defections from the male stereotype (as they may define it) while women are more alert to the excesses of males in the service of that stereotype."[65]

The source of the greater rate of mental illness among women may be male bias in institutionalizing them. Or there may be factors in the lives of women that precipitate them toward a "career" in mental illness, as Chesler terms it. She believes it may be easier for some women to go mad than to face the irreconcilable problems of being a woman in modern society.

On the other hand, men are more reluctant than women to seek help; it is just not masculine to admit anxiety or worry or fear. When the world is too much to bear, men find release in alcohol, drugs, or suicide. When angered, men commit more lethal acts and thus end up in prison rather than a mental hospital. A woman who is angered may become uncontrollably hysterical, but she does not shoot; she is sent to a hospital for the mentally ill.

'I am too listening: Your life seems meaningless. By the way, what's for dinner?'

© Chronicle Features, 1973

Men convicted of sex crimes such as indecent exposure, homosexuality, or rape are put in jail. That these may be psychiatric problems rather than criminal problems is only rarely considered.

Among the young, there is a higher incidence of mental illness and defects in males. Up to age thirty, there are more males seen in out-patient clinics and admitted to institutions.[66] Studies of childhood psychosis indicate a considerably higher incidence among boys. However, there may be a bias in the identification of pathological behavior in young males. Are young males with behavior disorders detected more often because there is a greater social loss with a male deviant than with girls who are "different?"

Far more boys than girls are referred to clinics because of mental retardation. There is "more concern likely to be shown toward the possible academic failure of a boy than a girl, and he will therefore probably be referred for attention—and tested—more consistently than in the case of girls."[67] The true incidence of mental retardation—and by analogy, of mental superiority—cannot be known by current testing or referral procedures.

It is difficult to know which sex is more prone to emotional pathology or mental deficiency. However, it does seem clear that current sex roles must be discarded insofar as they interfere with our psychological well-being.

◆ Summary

We know that there are certain physiological differences between male and female, but we do not know the relative importance of physiology and culture in determining character, ability, and temperament. Both biology and society, in complex interaction, guide boys and girls into their adult roles. Differences in physique as well as differences in cultural background reveal a tremendous spectrum of possibilities for both sexes.

The argument that women are more emotional, dependent, fickle, or weak because of physiological characteristics is just not true.[68] Nor is it true that their physiology makes men more aggressive, violent, or creative. It is society that rewards those attributes that are valued in males and those valued in females. We are so accustomed to sex-appropriate behaviors for men and women that we have come to believe in them as universals, although nothing could be further from the truth.

Though male or female we will always be, we should develop more fully the idea of the person. To some this raises the dreadful spectre of uni-sex. One can only respond: nonsense. A male or a female who views himself or herself as a fully functioning person is sexually fulfilled and is far less sexually disturbed than many who follow our current ambivalent practices.

References

1. Una Stannard, "Adam's Rib, or the Woman Within," *Trans-Action* 8 (November-December 1970):24–35.
2. Frank Faulkner, ed., *Human Development*, (Philadelphia: W. B. Saunders, 1966), pp. 45–61.

3. Ursula Mittwoch, "Sex Differences in Cells," *Scientific American* 209 (July 1963) pp. 54–62.

4. Mary Jane Sherfey, *The Nature and Evolution of Female Sexuality* (New York: Random House, 1972), p. 39.

5. Edward M. Brecher, *The Sex Researchers* (Boston: Little, Brown, 1969), pp. 189–199; John Money, "Sexual Dimorphism and Homosexual Gender Identity," *Psychological Bulletin* 74 (1970):425–440.

6. Ernest B. Hook, "Behavioral Implications of the Human XYY Genotype," *Science* 179 (January 1973):139–150; see also the extensive review by David R. Owen, "The 47, XYY Male: A Review," *Psychological Bulletin* 78 (September 1972):209–233; Barbara J. Culliton, "Patients' Rights: Harvard is Site of Battle Over X and Y Chromosomes," *Science* 186 (November 1974):715–717.

7. John Money and Anke A. Ehrhardt, *Man and Woman/Boy and Girl* (Baltimore: Johns Hopkins University Press, 1972), p. 235.

8. David A. Hamburg and Donald T. Lunde, "Sex Hormones in the Development of Sex Differences in Human Behavior," in *The Development of Sex Differences*, ed. Eleanor Maccoby (Stanford: Stanford University Press, 1966) pp. 1–24; see also Money and Ehrhardt, *op. cit.*; Christopher Ounsted and D. C. Taylor, eds., *Gender Differences* (Edinburgh: Churchill Livingstone, Pub., 1972).

9. For an excellent, although technical, review of the research see Bernard Campbell, ed., *Sexual Selection and the Descent of Man: 1871–1971* (Chicago: Aldine, 1972). See also Christopher Ounsted and D. C. Taylor, eds., *Gender Differences* (Edinburgh: Churchill Livingstone, Pub., 1972).

10. Ashley Montague, *The Natural Superiority of Women*, rev. ed. (New York: Collier-Macmillan, 1970), pp. 77–78.

11. *Ibid.*, pp. 73–74.

12. Albert Rosenfeld, "If Oedipus' Parents Had Only Known," *Saturday Review/World*, September 1974, pp. 49–52.

13. Richard L. Masland, Seymour S. Sarason, and Thomas Gladwin, *Mental Subnormality* (New York: Basic Books, 1958).

14. Judith E. Singer, Milton Westphal, and Kenneth R. Niswander, "Sex Differences in the Incidence of Neonatal Abnormalities and Abnormal Performance in Early Childhood," *Child Development* 39 (1968):103–122.

15. Masland, Sarason, and Gladwin, *op. cit.*, p. 70.

16. Minda Borun *et al.*, *Women's Liberation: An Anthropological View* (Pittsburg: KNOW, Inc., 1971).

17. Nancy Reeves, *Womankind: Beyond the Stereotypes* (Chicago: Aldine-Atherton, 1971), pp. 85–97.

18. S. Carn and L. C. Clark, Jr., "The Sex Difference in the Basal Metabolic Rate," *Child Development* 24 (nos. 3–4):215–224.

19. W. H. Sheldon and S. S. Stevens, *The Varieties of Temperament* (New York: Harper and Row, 1943).

20. Sheldon Glueck and Eleanor Glueck, *Unraveling Juvenile Delinquency* (Cambridge: Harvard University Press, 1966).
21. David S. Krech *et al.*, *Elements of Psychology* (New York: Alfred A. Knopf, 1970), p. 425.
22. E. C. Reifenstein, *Pathologic Physiology*, 3rd ed. (Philadelphia: W. B. Saunders, 1961).
23. *Ibid.*, see also F. E. Yates et al., *Annual Review of Physiology* 33 (1971): 393–444.
24. Yates, *op. cit.*
25. Reifenstein, *op. cit.*
26. Money and Ehrhardt, *op. cit.*
27. Hunt, *op. cit.*
28. Reifenstein, *op. cit.*
29. *Ibid.*
30. Sheldon and Stevens, *op. cit.*
31. Walter Sullivan, "Boys and Girls Are Now Maturing Earlier" *New York Times*, January 24, 1971.
32. J. M. Tanner, "Sequence, Tempo and Individual Variation in the Growth and Development of Boys and Girls Aged Twelve to Sixteen," *Daedalus* 100 (Fall 1971):907–930.
33. H. D. Thornburg, "A Comparative Study of Sex Information Sources," *Journal of School Health* 42 (1972):88–91; see also: Mary Breasted, *Oh!* *Sex Education* (New York: Praeger Publishers, 1970).
34. Montague, *op. cit.*
35. Money and Ehrhardt, *op. cit.*; see also Seymour Levine, "Sex Differences and the Brain," *Scientific American* 214 (April 1966), pp. 84–90.
36. Money and Ehrhardt, *op. cit.*
37. Seymour and Gay Luce, "Hormones in the Development of Behavior," *Journal of Comparative Physiological Psychology* 60:37–57.
38. Robert J. Stoller, *Sex and Gender* (New York: Science House, 1968), pp. 15–16.
39. D. M. Broverman *et al.*, "Roles of Activation and Inhibition in Sex Differences in Cognitive Abilities," *Psychological Review* 75 (1968):23–50; Mary B. Parlee, "Comments on 'Roles of Activation and Inhibition in Sex Differences in Cognitive Abilities' by D. M. Broverman, E. L. Klaiber, Y. Kobayashi, and W. Vogel," *Psychological Review* 79 (1972):180–184.
40. Parlee, *op. cit.*
41. Margaret Mead, *Male and Female* (New York: Wm. Morrow, 1949), p. 7.
42. Reeves, *op. cit.*, pp. 90–91.
43. "Historical Population Studies," *Daedalus* 97 (Spring 1968): entire issue.
44. Population Reference Bureau, *Population Information for 127 Countries* (Washington, D.C.: Population Reference Bureau, 1963).
45. "Washington Widows," *Behavior Today*, December 4, 1972.
46. Montague, *op. cit.*, pp. 82–83.

47.   Lissy F. Jarrick, "Sex Differences in Longevity," in *Advances in Sex Research*, ed. Hugo G. Beigel (New York: Harper and Row, 1963), p. 156.

48.   D. Dickson *et al.*, "Accidents in Childhood," *American Journal of Diseases of Children* 45 (1964):101–104.

49.   Estelle Ramey, "Well, Fellows, What Did Happen at the Bay of Pigs? And Who Was in Control?" *McCalls*, January 1971, pp. 81+.

50.   Edmund W. Overstreet, "The Biological Make-up of Woman," in *The Potential of Woman*, ed. P. M. Farber and R. H. L. Wilson (New York: McGraw-Hill, 1963), pp. 13–23.

51.   Karen Horney, *Feminine Psychology* (New York: W. W. Norton, 1967), pp. 99–106.

52.   Sherfey, *op. cit.*

53.   Katherine Dalton, *The Premenstrual Syndrome* (Springfield, Ill.: Charles C. Thomas, 1964).

54.   Gay Gaer Luce, *Biological Rhythms in Psychiatry and Medicine* (Chevy Chase, Md.: National Institute of Mental Health, 1970), p. 110.

55.   *Ibid.*

56.   Nancy Scheper-Hughes, "Woman as Witch," *Popular Psychology*, January 1973, pp. 57–64.

57.   Ellen Switzer, "Can You Sail Through Menopause Without Synthetic Estrogen? No? Yes!," *New Woman*, June 1971, pp. 68–69+.

58.   Luce, *op. cit.*, pp. 110–111.

59.   *Science News*, November 20, 1971, p. 343.

60.   Money and Ehrhardt, *op. cit.*, p. 193.

61.   *Ibid.*, p. 220.

62.   Norma Haan and Norman Livson, "Sex Differences in the Eyes of Expert Personality Assessors: Blind Spots," *Journal of Personality Assessment* 38 (1974): 145–151.

63.   Phyllis Chesler, *Woman and Madness* (Garden City, N.Y.: Doubleday, 1972).

64.   Inge K. Broverman *et al.*, "Sex-Role Stereotypes and Clinical Judgments of Mental Health," *Journal of Consulting and Clinical Psychology* 34 (1970): 1–7.

65.   Haan and Livson, *op. cit.*

66.   Richard H. Williams, Clark Tibbitts, and Wilma Donahue, eds., *Processes of Aging* (New York: Atherton Press, 1963), 2:176–191.

67.   Masland, Sarason, and Gladwin, *op. cit.*, p. 263.

68.   For an extensive review of the research on the psychology of sex differences see: Eleanor E. Maccoby and Carol N. Jacklin, *The Psychology of Sex Differences* (Stanford: Stanford University Press, 1974).

4

The Family:

A Changing Institution

It is within the family that we learn our sex roles during childhood and it is within a family that most of us fulfill our sex roles—as husbands and wives, fathers and mothers. In fact, it was undoubtedly due to the need for the family, for the sharing of procreation and responsibility for the young, that mankind derived different and often complementary roles for men and women. But now these roles are being questioned, and implicitly the family itself is perhaps being challenged. Traditional patterns of family life are changing, and the resultant strains are reflected in the rising divorce rate.

Is there a typical American family? If so, what new challenges must it face? What are the strengths and weaknesses of American family life? And what are the prospects for family life in America? In this chapter we will try to answer these questions and derive some insights into the relationship between traditional sex roles and family life.

◆ The Family—A Venerable Tradition

Throughout history, societies have created certain groups to assure generational continuity, to protect the very young and old, and to solidify the bonds of blood. The family, the clan, the tribe, the nation—all such groups derive from the need to preserve the species and protect the weak.

In preindustrial societies the extended family, which included grandparents, aunts, uncles, and cousins as well as immediate family, served as a protective and supportive unit for all members. But twentieth century industrial society has produced unprecedented occupational, social, and geographic mobility, and anyone wishing to participate in this mobility must break away from the family and plunge into the "atomized society" where each individual is on his own. In America, atomization has been so complete that few extended families remain. Instead, individuals establish nuclear families composed of husband, wife, and children, and ties with grandparents, aunts, uncles, or cousins are loose, at best. The nuclear family must absorb the strains of daily life—illness, financial difficulties, career problems, emotional stress—without the support of close family ties.

The nuclear family is standard in America, and in this chapter we will examine it in some detail. But first, we would like to inquire into an alternative to the nuclear family—we will look at the single lifestyle.

One Is a Lonely Number

Throughout history, marriage and procreation have been the norm. Few individuals could survive without the assistance of spouse and children. Rural life required the efforts of an entire family group. Modern technological society is probably the first society in which marriage and family ties are not necessary for survival. Nevertheless, those opting for the single life are still regarded with curiosity. We continue to have difficulty admitting the desirability of the single life. It seems we remain bound by the folk view that to be unmarried is to be outcast: the unmarried have no home, no hearth, no descendants.

Although both men and women suffer discrimination for their single status, the problems facing them are not identical. Perhaps the greatest problem facing the single woman over age thirty is social rejection. Toward this woman, friends and relatives alike show discrimination. The single woman is rarely a welcome guest at a social occasion, for she may present married friends with too much "competition." She has little in common with old friends who are caught up with marriage and family, and she is constantly urged to get married and settle down. If she doesn't marry, it will be said that no one wanted her.[1] Perhaps because of this, most American women do marry; in fact, 93 percent of American women in their thirties have married at least once.[2] Undoubtedly, many men and women are not suited for marriage, but women are trained from childhood to seek marriage and family as their life goals. The female sex role demands that a woman marry to give proof of her desirability and that she remain married to give evidence of her skill in the wifely arts. If an unmarried woman protests that she prefers a career to marriage, she is thought to have a case of "sour grapes."

In most instances, the difficulties facing the single man relate to his career rather than his social life. A bachelor is usually a desired guest at social functions, and few bachelors have trouble finding women to date. But since it is widely believed that "any man can marry if he wants to," a bachelor who is more than thirty years old is regarded with suspicion in professional circles. Why doesn't he marry? Does he have a sex problem? Is he a homosexual? Is he unstable? Is he a swinger? Few confirmed bachelors have risen to high positions in the military, in large corporations, government, or labor unions. A single man may have a successful career in the academic world or in the arts, but even there his single state is suspect. It may be said, in general, marriage and the appearance of normalcy will aid a man's career prospects.

Discrimination against the unmarried has reached the point of absurdity—for example, there is legal discrimination against a single person making his/her own wine! Federal law permits the head of a household to produce up to 200 gallons of wine annually without taxation. But how many singles can qualify as head of a household?

The fact is that we expect all men and women to marry, and if they refuse to do so we punish them with social, legal, and professional discrimination. The suspect status of the unmarried may be related to our fear of and distaste for homosexuality. Although any homosexual is viewed with alarm, Americans reserve their strongest condemnation for those male homosexuals who make it obvious that they are "gay." These men appear to have rejected the traditional male role, they demonstrate "unmasculine" traits and temperament, and they refuse traditional heterosexual relationships. This is too much for most Americans to take, and they feel revulsion toward the obvious homosexual for his refusal to assume the traditional male role. Gay Power groups have been formed to fight social and job discrimination, and to educate the public to the acceptance of homosexuality.

Our distaste for the unmarried, whether they be single, homosexual, divorced, or widowed, demonstrates the strength of our belief in marriage as an integral part of the American dream. Although being challenged on many fronts, marriage and family are still seen as the most desirable lifestyle. Despite the new challenges facing family life, the family is in no danger of disappearing in America! Let us look at American patterns of family life and see what the "typical" American family is like.[3]

Is There an American Family?

Describe one style of family living and we can produce ten others that are quite different. A close look at those communities that appear to be thoroughly homogeneous will reveal great variations in patterns of family living. Who is defined as a member of the family; how relatives are included or ignored; how authority is exercised and children rewarded or punished; how meals are served and eaten: each of these facts tells us something about the family's lifestyle. Children growing up in these communities can find many different models of family life.[4] But how does a child know which is the "right" one? Is it better to have new clothes for Easter or a season ticket to the symphony? Is Christmas an agony or an ecstasy? Are those whose mother works to be pitied or envied? Is Mother's Day holy and Father's Day sacred, or are neither noticed, rejected as crassly materialistic?

This very diversity of American family life has often been camouflaged in our attempt to create and sustain a "typical" American family. We want our idealized family so much that we make it almost impossible to be realized. The growing child is apt to be caught between Textbook Town[5] and the reality at home. Yet the diversity may be our greatest blessing. If life at home is somewhat less than ideal, a child may find a better model in the house down the street. At least there are several kinds of families to study and observe. So, despite us, our children will learn that not all families are good—or bad. They are different, and with time we may come to prize these differences.

Perhaps part of our uneasiness with differences in family lifestyle is due to the fact that so many family styles derive from a cast-off model: the lifestyle brought over from the old country. As Kazan notes in his autobiography, to become American was the passionate hope the immigrant had for his child; and as Margaret Mead points out, the second generation intergenerational conflict is woven into much of our history and traditions.⁶ As she says, we are in one way or another all second generation.

Each ethnic group coming to the United States has brought its own distinctive family style. The English family style dominated New England and the south long into the nineteenth century. Although later immigrant groups brought family styles peculiar to their own culture, all shared an acceptance of the patriarchal family and subordination of the female.

Some ethnic subgroups remain attached to a family model that most Americans have discarded. The Mexican-American, Chinese-American, Japanese, Italian, and Jewish groups often adhere to the extended family model. In these ethnic groups young married couples often remain in the parents' home or live nearby. There is continuous visiting back and forth which is typically restricted to relatives, and there may be as many as one hundred relatives in the visiting cycle.⁷ The support provided by such a family system is obvious; new immigrants are helped to find their way, and they are fed and housed while they gain skills and learn English.⁸ The lower the economic level of these families, the greater the pressure on children to leave school and go to work to provide income for family maintenance. With marriage, girls stay home, and in turn produce sons to help with family support. Studies of these ethnic groups have shown that this system has made for strong families but has allowed few individuals to advance professionally or economically.⁹

Ambitious Jewish families likewise insist on close family bonds, but they perceive success to be a product of higher education. Severe constraints against interreligious marriage have kept Jewish groups relatively intact. Even at upper financial levels marriage within the same few families has been encouraged.¹⁰

If a second generation American from these groups throws off family norms, he is adrift and confused. How should children be raised? The wisdom of non-English-speaking parents or grandparents is suspect. But meanwhile the children are learning that many families are more egalitarian, that the mother has rights, that the father's word is not law, that a daughter is not expected to ask permission to go out on a date, nor be cross-examined on her behavior when she returns. Second generation parents who leave the ethnic community must deal with children who are thoroughly integrated into American culture and with grandparents who adhere to old norms.

Many second generation Americans are moving away from their

ethnic communities and into the suburbs, and the ethnic pockets of many large cities are dwindling in size. The migration of blacks and the Spanish speaking into the cities has served to disperse other ethnic groups into scattered neighborhoods, and many of the customs and cultural traditions associated with foreign born ethnics have disappeared. Despite the current resurgence of interest in cultural differences,[11] ethnic pluralism is more apt to be a darling of sociologists than a behavioral guide for upwardly mobile youth.

Due to our immigrant tradition, diversity of family styles has long been part of the American landscape. Yet we live uneasily with this diversity, and become nervous when seeing somewhat different models on television or when hearing about exploration in nontraditional family styles.

And the Laws Came Tumbling Down . . . .

Lacking a folk system that defines proper behavior and imposes strong community sanctions for deviation, Americans are prone to make laws about everything, and they have been doing so since the founding of the colonies. Most laws regarding the rights of men and women, fathers, mothers, and children, as well as the legal concept of the family are derived from English common law. This body of common law matured during the Elizabethan era and was transported by English gentlemen to the new world.

In 1766 the great English jurist, Blackstone, issued his *Commentaries* on English common law; these *Commentaries* were, in effect, a codification of existing practices and precedents. Following the Revolution, legal education in America was basically the study of Blackstone. And according to Blackstone: "As the marriage creates a unity, and the husband is religiously the head of the family, the law declares, that the external powers of this family, in respect to property and government, shall vest in the husband."[12] He further enunciated the legal death of a woman upon marriage: "The very being or legal existence of the woman is suspended during marriage, or at least incorporated and consolidated into that of the husband: under whose wing, protection, and *cover*, she performs everything."[13]

Laws relating to marriage have not undergone substantial change. Upon entering marriage, a woman must relinquish her maiden name. This action is symbolic of the woman's changed status, for she is no longer regarded as an independent, self-supporting individual. In fact, the law requires the husband to support his wife, and only the husband bears full accountability for payment of debts. Although she is no longer viewed as her husband's property, the married woman is still regarded as her husband's responsibility. Marriage laws should be reformed so that both parties are regarded as independent, fully responsible individuals, each contributing something to the union and mutually responsible for its successes and failures.[14]

While marriage laws remain stifling, divorce laws have been liberalized. Until the twentieth century, it was almost impossible for an American woman to obtain a divorce.[15] A man might be an adulterer, charlatan, murderer, or madman, but his wife could not divorce him. If a woman transgressed, however, the law was merciless. Her husband could obtain a divorce with ease, and he had absolute rights to the children.

Even now, divorce laws are chaotically different from state to state. Although the rights of women—regarding child custody, right to sue, and alimony—are now protected, many inequities remain. It is difficult to determine whether men or women are the chief victims of these inequities, and both sexes are organizing to challenge current divorce laws. For instance, a group entitled "Fathers United for Equal Rights" sued in a class action in Baltimore County, Maryland, claiming that judges had been applying divorce, nonsupport, custody, and alimony statutes with bias against males. Interestingly, a woman joined in this suit because she felt it demeaning to be "regarded anachronistically as being helpless, feckless, in need of a surrogate, and incapable of handling her own and her family's affairs without the unequal assistance of the court as to her former husband." She wanted the court to relieve her former husband of the obligation to support her.[16] The National Organization for Women, after studying the serious problems that women face when divorce occurs, has prepared a model divorce reform bill.[17]

Although a woman's legal position in a divorce suit has changed in some respects, in other ways previous attitudes toward women still hold. Since women are not considered responsible wage earners, the husband may be liable for support of his ex-spouse even if she is earning more than he is, and this support may continue throughout her life under court order. On the other hand a wife suing for divorce may find that she is not considered a producer of "real" income, and thus she may lose her fair share of jointly purchased property as a result of a divorce settlement.[18] Sex-role stereotyping and the legal precedents accumulating over several hundred years of litigation are not easily overcome. Family and divorce laws are prime examples of the way tradition beclouds the legal rights of *persons*, irrespective of sex. We still have a long way to go![19]

The marital laws that denied women any personhood were later extended into the field of employment to "protect" her and to keep her in her place—often a lowly and ill-paid one.[20] But just as divorce laws were successfully challenged, so are unfair employment practices being challenged. The Equal Rights Amendment, which may well be law soon after this book is published, is a big step forward in securing equal employment status for women. Like reforms in marriage and divorce laws, it is hoped that the Equal Rights Amendment will produce a society that distributes opportunities and responsibilities equally between men and women.[21]

Perhaps the most significant legal advance relating to family life is the Supreme Court ruling striking down state statutes against abortion. The legalization of abortion and invention of the contraceptive pill are undoubtedly the most important and far-reaching events in what may be the greatest revolution of our time—the revolution in the relationships between the sexes and within the family. The full impact of this revolution will be examined in greater detail in the last chapter.

Finding that legal and medical advances gave her new rights to her own body,[22] the American woman has begun demanding other rights. Property rights, for instance. Who owns the family car? Usually the husband. Why? Married women can rarely obtain credit unless their applications are cosigned by their husbands.[23] And insurance rights: "Insurance for women is decidedly discriminatory. Policies for disability insurance for women provide substantially less coverage than for men with greatly lowered benefits from the same accidents. Health coverage for women discriminates against female-related disorders, including pregnancy, so that companies that employ women and provide some coverage for them are running the risk of higher claims."[24] Other discriminatory practices are being discovered by incredulous women—and they are marching to the nearest courtroom to demand rectification of injustices.[25]

What will all this do to family life? A great deal!

"We're collecting for Amy. She's not going to have a baby."

◆ The All-American Family

What is this American family that we predict will soon be shaken to its roots? Despite considerable diversity in family lifestyles, there are some typical American ways of living. We will briefly examine some attitudes and practices common to family life in America.

In-laws Are Outlawed

The popularity of in-law jokes is not an accident; a great deal of marital discord arises from problems with in-laws, particularly parents-in-law. The commonest clash is between wife and husband's mother.[26] Consequently, many couples try to limit contacts with parents. For this and many other reasons, the nuclear family—father, mother, and children—has become the standard pattern in America. Typically, such a family is pitied if an aged parent moves in.

With so many couples refusing or unable to provide a home for parents, the only alternatives for many is a nursing home or remarriage. In fact, the current increase in the rate of remarriage of the widowed is attributed to the need for companionship and a home.[27] Rejected by their children, many older persons seek a new mate to care for them and provide some security. Ironically, our Social Security laws encourage these older couples to live together illegally, for with marriage their Social Security benefits are cut.[28] Social Security provides significantly greater benefits for widowed or single than for married individuals.

The irony of these Social Security policies is compounded by the fact that it is the unmarried older person who is most likely to become a social burden through inability to exist without institutional care. If they were free to remarry, these slightly disabled persons could live comfortably together caring for each other in their own homes.

Upon entering a custodial institution, the older person usually must surrender Social Security payments in return for room and board. Although food and medical care may be guaranteed, personal wishes and feelings are rigidly controlled. The possibility of sexual attraction between two older persons is considered indecent if not obscene. The staff of one nursing home was always alerted to "clear out the chapel" before opening the institution to visitors. The chapel served as a refuge—it was the only place the old people could share any kind of physical intimacy! Stereotyped thinking regarding sex-appropriate behavior (and in this instance age-appropriate behavior) puts limits on our freedom of choice and restricts human happiness.

The problems of the elderly are now receiving broad attention, and we can hope that legislation will be passed to ensure adequate financial resources for all older people, regardless of status or level of previous earnings. With some modification of our attitudes and laws, those older people displaced by the nuclear family could enjoy satisfying and fulfilling lives.

Who Rules the Roost?

Who runs the family? Where does the power lie? Various studies reveal significant differences in perception of power relationships within the family. One study showed husbands crediting the wife with more power than she gave herself. Did wives who were more influential downgrade their roles because they felt it was not "right" for the woman to be dominant in the family?[29] Male supremacy within the family has a fairly strong hold on American mores. In a "good" family, child discipline will be shared by husband and wife, with the father expected to be stricter and do the punishing. (But, since he controls the purse strings, he may also be the source of indulgences.)

Women's liberation groups have rejected the idea that the husband is head of the household, and by definition the source of authority and control. Women accepted male dominance in the family when the husband was the sole or primary source of income, for a woman was very obviously dependent upon her husband for her own welfare and that of their children. Today there are rumblings as women find that, whether they work or not, they are not necessarily subservient and powerless. Most women have worked and lived on their own income before marriage, and many do not take kindly to having their freedom curtailed. Power relationships in the family are being examined, and men are voicing concern and even fear. In this particular power struggle, we can predict more not less trouble.

Housework: Woman's Work

When asked what his mother did, one youngster replied, "She doesn't do any work; she stays home."[30]

In the small American family the division of work puts daily care of the home in the hands of the mother. In the words of one commentator, "Women are still household servants in conventional marriages because their economic disadvantage makes this part of the standard sexual contract."[31] As housekeeper, the wife depends on her husband for daily expenses and any luxuries.

If tastes and priorities match, the wife's purchases and her housekeeping and childrearing practices can reinforce marital stability. Unfortunately, in many instances marriage is contracted by love-dazed youth who know little if anything about each other's intimate preferences and habits. Due to America's regional and cultural diversity, many a husband and wife were raised to have different and even conflicting views of the proper way to eat, dress, furnish a house, and discipline children. Marital uneasiness is inevitable, and divorce may not be far behind.

The wife entertains her husband's friends and work associates. Her husband's interests, since they are perceived to contribute most to the family's economic welfare, come first. The husband might undertake certain household tasks, but typically they are "male" chores: gardening, do-it-yourself improvements for the house or car. Child care and children's medical and school needs are left to the wife.[32]

Most family clothing and food purchases are in the hands of women; however, the amount is determined not only by the husband's income, but by his decision as to how much she will be allowed to spend. The heavy barrage of advertising directed at women indicates their important role as consumers. Because a woman's self-concept is closely related to the amount and quality of the things she can display in her house, she is susceptible to advertising for new gadgets and replacements for household equipment. A good white refrigerator is not as self-enhancing as a new colored refrigerator.

The husband's obligation to care for his family and provide education for his children places a special burden on the male. He is the one who is blamed when investments fail or the crop is lost. He is the bargainer in the marketplace; if he is shrewd, the family will prosper. If he is not, the family suffers. There is public and continuous pressure on the male to provide as well as possible for his family. Since the quality of her life and that of the children depends upon the success or failure of her husband, a wife watches him with an eagle eye. That men find this burden difficult and sometimes excessive is indicated by the high rates of "poor man's divorce," separations, and escapes into alcoholism, gambling, overwork, and suicide.

Rightfully, men are beginning to question whether this is the best way to run a family enterprise. They may feel exploited (although many won't admit it) by a selfish, ambitious, or careless wife and arrogant youngsters. Many young people, who have seen their parents' marriage collapse under such pressures and resentments, are trying to work out more relaxed ways of living.

How Good Is Family Life?

Divorce

Divorce statistics are often cited as evidence of family decay. The data show certain patterns in divorce: men who married at age twenty-one or under and women who married at age nineteen or under are likely to end an unhappy marriage with divorce. Divorce rates are also high among couples at upper income levels, with higher than average levels of education, where there is a working wife or less than average religious commitment.[33]

In a followup study of a group of married couples, it was noted that husbands become disenchanted with marriage and their spouse sooner than wives.[34] But all longitudinal studies of marriage indicate that dissatisfaction increases over time, particularly for wives.[35] The source of dissatisfaction is related to socioeconomic status. Lower class wives are more likely to complain about financial problems, physical abuse, and drinking. Lower class husbands complain about the infidelity of wives. Among the middle classes, both husbands and wives find a loss of love in the marriage.[36]

A major source of marital problems can be found in the very different expectations of their marital roles that many husbands and wives bring to the marriage. The following study shows a sharp disparity between men's and women's expectations of the woman's role in marriage (Table 4-1). It is troubling that while only 5 percent of this sample of college women had realistic expectations that they would be housewives after marriage, 25 percent of the men expected this to be true. Although one-fifth of these women wanted to combine family and career, only 12 percent had realistic expectations of doing so—and only 6 percent of the men expected this of their wives. While only 1 percent of the women preferred a career to marriage, a fearful 5 percent thought this might be their doom. The collision between women's expectations of marriage and men's expectations of the wife's role is apparent from these data. The rising divorce rate reflects more than disappointed expectations; it indicates parents' increased awareness of the damage done to children by a home atmosphere of conflict and tension.[37]

Although divorce is now common, Americans continue to view it as a tragic ending rather than a solution to marital problems. Our ambivalence regarding divorce is reflected in the retention of Mrs. and the married name by divorced women even though most states permit reversion to the maiden name. It is as though women want it known that they were good enough to have been married at one time. Even if a woman wishes to keep a former marriage from public knowledge, school and college records carry the name change. A man is not dogged by such problems; he is Mr. no matter what his marital status.

Although many divorced persons remarry, fewer women than

TABLE 4–1. Career Preferences for Women: Male and Female College Seniors, 1964 (percent)

LIFE CAREER	FEMALE		MALE
	First Preference for life career	Realistic expectations	Preference for wife's role
Housewife only	8	5	25
Work only before children are born	20	24	34
Work after children are grown	35	34	25
Occasional work throughout	12	17	6
Combine family and career	20	12	8
Combine family and steady job	1	2	1
Marriage and career: no children	2	1	1
No marriage: career only	2	5	—
Total	100	100	100
	(10,031)	(9,835)	(11,607)

Based on a National Opinion Research Center sample of college seniors outside the South. (From Valerie K. Oppenheimer, *Population* (New York: Foreign Policy Association, Headline Series, No. 206, 1971), p. 64.

men do so. Statistics indicate that out of every thousand divorced persons aged twenty-five to forty-four, 306.6 men remarry, while only 179 women remarry. In the next age bracket, forty-five to sixty-four, only 45.2 women out of a thousand remarry, while 89.5 men do so. After age sixty-five, 26.5 men out of a thousand remarry after divorce, but only 9.7 women per thousand do so at this age level.[38] Despite the apparent ease with which Americans divorce each other, there is probably a large group of unhappily married people who refrain from divorce out of fear of loneliness. Is the high rate of dissatisfaction with marriage in America due to the fact that we have been raised to expect too much of marriage? The fairy tale always ended: ". . . and they were married and lived happily ever after." The women's movement sees this as pernicious mythology: a short tale for children was published to end with exactly the opposite conclusion: "so they did not marry and lived happily ever after."[39]

Emotional Problems

The increase in numbers of the emotionally disturbed is usually viewed as another symptom of the breakdown of American family life. However, we should be cautious about reaching such conclusions, for these figures may reflect greater sensitivity to unhappiness and greater willingness to admit to emotional distress. In addition, the increase in medical facilities and the widespread use of psychologically trained personnel in industry, business, and in government may increase the statistical incidence of emotional illness without indicating that there is more distress now than in earlier times.

Evidence is accumulating, however, that the small nuclear family is not the best place to raise children or to live out one's mature years in peace and productivity. The very privacy that Americans so value is in itself a hazard. The anxious mother who wonders if her infant is starting to talk too late, or walking too early, or not eating enough, or eating too much, has no one but the doctor to ask for advice.[40] If she is lucky she may have an accessible, sympathetic, and experienced neighbor. Pity the newcomer to an established neighborhood who is of a different color, or is a member of a minority religious group, or who has exotic interests in ballet or chamber music or meditation. Then the small family may be excluded from even neighborhood channels of support.

In the small nuclear family husband and wife are thrown into close communication with each other, with no other adult translators at hand. Middle and upper class men and women may have shared relatively similar worlds. Typically they met while in college, or through family friends or relatives of the same social class and occupational strata. The blue-collar marriage is more apt to be marked by the strain of poor communication and the inability to build a bridge between different worlds:

Men and women live in different psychological worlds. . . . The gulf between the sexes may be wider in the working class than among the educated middle classes. A number of our couples found the gulf so wide that neither could serve as a satisfying audience to the other. They repeatedly missed the cues and, when they did understand the other's concerns, found them trivial and boring.[41]

The coeducational high school provides some aid in bridging the gap between the sexes, though only accidentally. The typical classroom restricts interchange among students, and classroom socializing is furtive and sporadic. Junior and senior high school students develop distinctive cliques along social class lines. Thus blue-collar youth are effectively insulated from middle or upper class students. If the blue-collar youngster goes on to college, he or she finds a world whose values conflict with his/her own. This can produce great confusion and lasting self-doubts. Marital happiness may be one of the victims.

The intense pressures of today's complex world beat upon men and women, and many succumb. It is predicted that one out of every three adults will have an emotional crisis necessitating medical care or institutionalization. Most adults will have a severe illness or a critical automobile accident. Coping with chronic illness or death are experiences most families are not prepared for. The nuclear family is extremely vulnerable to these and other social pressures.[42]

What's Ahead?

For decades prophets of doom have predicted that the family, and all the virtues and verities associated with it, is on its way out. Nothing seems farther from the truth. Youth are getting married at the same high rate as in former years, and with the same exuberance and expectation of fulfillment.

However, new forms of family life are a popular topic of discussion. Communes of various kinds are described in the popular press. Utopian communities, in which family life and sex roles would be controlled according to an ideal, have been a concern of "futurologists" for centuries. Edward Bellamy, Anatole France, and Thomas More have described what relations between the sexes might be like in utopian communities.[43] American utopian communities, such as Brook Farm, Amana, and The Harmony Society, were our earliest planned communities. Sex roles were clearly defined, and in most instances the traditional division of labor between male and female was strictly adhered to.[44]

The modern commune is usually an earnest effort to permit equality in family life and satisfaction in productive enterprise. Many communes have lasted a few years, but economic problems plus previous socialization in traditional male and female roles create almost insuperable barriers to success. Extreme dedication and commitment are necessary in anyone opting for communal life.[45] The experiences with communal day care programs in the Soviet Union and the

People's Republic of China, and the kibbutz of Israel indicate the difficulties as well as the potential of shared childrearing.[46]

The traditional marital contract is being scrutinized with some disillusionment by both men and women. For decades, men have been using money, and women using sex to manipulate each other toward marriage.

. . . the . . . marriage market is organized around male trades of economic and status resources for possession of women. . . . The ideology arising from this situation is that of romantic love. . . . [A woman] maximizes her bargaining power by appearing both as attractive and inaccessible as possible, [and] an element of sexual repression is thus built into the situation in which men and women bargain with unequal goods.[47]

Today, some women are advocating a written marriage contract that specifies roles and responsibilities.[48] There seems little doubt that more and more contemporary marriages will be preceded by candid discussion of marital roles.[49] The widespread practice of living together has made it possible for young people to try each other out in the intimacy of shared quarters without the irrevocability of marriage.

Though experiments with new forms of family life and the changed lifestyles implicit in new moral codes may seem to portend a major revolution in the American family,[50] one must be cautious about predictions. Some conscientious scholars believe that the old fashioned family, supported by paternal authority, provides the most stable and rewarding setting for childrearing and for adult relationships. "To flee from family is to abandon humanness."[51]

While doubting that traditional patterns of male dominance and female dependency within the family will survive the challenges of the 1970s, we believe that marriage and family will endure. The individual need for love, intimacy, and privacy, and our age-old experience with the family as the means of fulfilling these needs, will not be swept aside. We may fashion somewhat different forms of marriage, we may move in and out of marital relationships with greater ease, but the basic family unit within which children are produced and nurtured will remain. Power relationships between husbands and wives will become more equal and complementary, and the disappearance of the rigid, patriarchal, authoritarian, suffocating nuclear family should not be regretted. The moral and ethical assumptions behind this family style had been distorted by personal and economic concerns that we have outgrown. However, identical ethical concerns seem to be motivating today's young people. They seek fulfillment and commitment, and they desire to raise healthy and happy children. The family style through which they seek their goals may seem quite different from traditional family styles; the goals, however, remain very much the same.

◆   Summary

The family has been the social unit for eons. In response to the social and technological developments of the twentieth century, the nuclear family has emerged as the norm. Faced by many challenges and pressures, the nuclear family has not responded as well as many would like. But young people are seriously addressing themselves to the problems of marriage and childrearing, and are devising creative new responses to contemporary challenges. Marriage and the family will survive, strengthened by new forms and by new patterns of family interaction.

References

1.   For fictional representation see: Theodore I. Rubin, *The Twenty-Ninth Summer* (New York: Pocket Books, 1963); Gail Parent, *Sheila Levine Is Dead and Living in New York* (New York: Putnam's Sons, 1972).
2.   Marion K. Sanders, "Case of the Vanishing Spinster," *New York Times Magazine*, September 22, 1963.
3.   A good general overview of the changing family can be found in Daniel A. Schulz, *The Changing Family* (Englewood Cliffs, N.J.: Prentice Hall, 1972).
4.   Louis H. Masotti and Jeffrey K. Hadden, eds., *The Urbanization of the Suburbs* (Beverly Hills, Calif.: Sage Publications, 1973).
5.   Abraham Tannenbaum, "Family Living in Textbook Town," *Progressive Education* 31 (1954):133-141. See also Chapter 7 of this volume.
6.   Alfred Kazan, *A Walker in the City* (New York: Harcourt, Brace, 1951); Margaret Mead, *And Keep Your Powder Dry* (New York: Wm. Morrow, 1942).
7.   Jack Balswick, "Are American Jewish Families Closely Knit?," in *The Jewish Family*, ed. Benjamin Schlesinger (Toronto: University of Toronto Press, 1971), pp. 15-24; C. C. Harris, ed., *Readings in Kinship in Urban Society* (New York: Pergamon Press, 1970).
8.   Nathan Glazer and Daniel P. Moynihan, *Beyond the Melting Pot: The*

Negroes, Puerto Ricans, Jews, Italians and Irish of New York, 2nd ed. (Cambridge, Mass.: The MIT Press, 1970).

9. H. J. Gans, *Urban Villages* (New York: Free Press, 1962).

10. Stephen Birmingham, *The Grandees: America's Sephardic Elite* (New York: Harper and Bros., 1971); idem, *"Our Crowd" the Great Jewish Families of New York* (New York: Harper and Row, 1967).

11. See publications of National Project on Ethnic Americans, Institute of Human Relations, 165 E. 56th Street, New York, N.Y.

12. Mary Beard, *Woman as Force in History* (New York: Macmillan-Collier, 1946), p. 123.

13. *Ibid.*, p. 126.

14. John S. Bradway, ed., "Progress in Family Law," *Annals of the American Academy of Political and Social Sciences* 383 (1969):1-144.

15. "Domestic Relations: Reed V. Reed: Women and the 14th Amendment," *Women's Rights Law Reporter* No. 2 (1972): 7-40; see also Robert R. Lavercombe, "No Fault Divorce?," *Educational Leadership* 31 (November 1973):134-136; Mel Krantzler, *Creative Divorce* (New York: M. Evans and Co., 1974).

16. "Divorce and Separation," *Women's Rights Law Reporter* No. 2 (1972): 16-24.

17. *Ibid.*, p. 17.

18. "Case Summaries: Divorce," *Women's Rights Law Reporter* No. 1 (1974): 26-33.

19. Krantzler, *op. cit.*

20. "Sex Discrimination in Employment," *Women's Rights Law Reporter* No. 1 (1973):1-17.

21. "Washington Blue Sheet," *Do It NOW*, January-February 1974.

22. Genevieve Stuttford, *Our Bodies, Ourselves* (New York: Simon and Schuster, 1973).

23. *The Spokeswoman*, July 1, 1972, p. 7.

24. Suzanne Stoiber, "Insured in Case of War, Suicide, and Organs Peculiar to Females," *Ms*, June 1973, pp. 114-119.

25. See all issues of *Women's Rights Law Reporter*, 1973-1974.

26. Bert N. Adams, "Isolation, Function, and Beyond: American Kinships in the 1960s," *Journal of Marriage and the Family* 32 (November 1970): 575-597.

27. George S. Rosenberg, *The Worker Grows Older* (San Francisco: Jossey-Blass, 1970), pp. 108-154.

28. Robert C. Alberts, "Catch 65," *New York Times Magazine*, August 4, 1974; "Letters," *New York Times Magazine*, September 8, 1974, pp. 52, 74.

29. David M. Heer, "Husband and Wife Perceptions of Family Power Structure," *Journal of Marriage and the Family* 24 (February 1962):65-67;

see also Norman M. Lobsenz, "Who Makes the Decisions in Your Home?," *Woman's Day*, January 1974, p. 26.

30.   Helena Z. Lopata, *Occupation: Housewife* (New York: Oxford University Press, 1971).

31.   Randall Collins, "A Conflict Theory of Sexual Stratification," *Social Problems* 19 (Summer 1971): 3-21; Clarice S. Stoll, "Comments," *Social Problems* 20 (Winter 1973):390-395; Randall Collins, "Rejoinder," *Social Problems* 20 (Winter 1973):395-397.

32.   Constantina Safilios-Rothschild, "The Study of Family Power Structure," *Journal of Marriage and the Family* 32 (November 1970): 539-574.

33.   Judson T. Landis, "Social Correlates of Divorce or Non-Divorce Among the Unhappily Married," *Journal of Marriage and Family Living* 25 (May 1963): 178-180; Larry Bumpass and James A. Sweet, "Differentials in Marital Instability:1970," *American Sociological Review* 37 (1972): 754-766.

34.   Peter C. Pineo, "Disenchantment in the Later Years of Marriage," *Journal of Marriage and Family Living* 23 (February 1961):3-11.

35.   Bethel L. Paris and Eleanor B. Paris, "A Longitudinal Study in Marital Satisfaction," *Sociological and Social Research* 50 (January 1966):212-222.

36.   George Levinger, "Sources of Marital Dissatisfaction Among Applicants for Divorce," *American Journal of Orthopsychiatry* 36 (1966): 803-807.

37.   Yet, in a group of unhappily married couples, the children were considered the only source of satisfaction sufficient to keep the marriage going; see Eleanor B. Luckey and Joyce K. Bain, "Children: A Factor in Marital Satisfaction," *Journal of Marriage and the Family* 32 (January 1970): 43-44.

38.   Inge Powell Bell, "The Double Standard," *Trans-Action* 8 (1970):75-80.

39.   Betty Miles, "Atalanta and the Race," *Ms*, March 1973, pp. 75-78.

40.   H. Reed Geersten and Robert M. Gray, "Familistic Orientation and Inclination Toward Adopting the Sick Role," *Journal of Marriage and the Family* 32 (November 1970): 638-646. See also: Suzanne K. Steinmetz and Murray A. Straus, "The Family as Cradle of Violence," *Society* 10 (September-October 1973): 50-56.

41.   Mirra Komarovsky, "Learning Conjugal Roles," in *Life Styles: Diversity in American Society*, ed. Saul D. Feldman and Gerald W. Thielbar (Boston: Little, Brown, 1972), pp. 163-164.

42.   "A Middle American Marriage," *Harper's*, February 1973, pp. 56-68.

43.   "Wraparound," *Harper's*, March 1973, p. 10.

44.   Rosabeth Moss Kanter, *Commitment and Community: Communes and Utopias in Sociological Perspective* (Cambridge: Harvard University Press, 1972).

45.   Marty Jezer, "Psychic Farming," *Saturday Review of the Society*, February 1973, pp. 43-47.

46. Ruth Sidel, *Women and Child Care in China* (New York: Hill and Wang, 1972); Robert D. Barendson, "Mao's Educational Revolution," *American Education* 8 (1972):4-13; Bruno Bettelheim, *The Children of the Dream* (New York: Macmillan, 1969); Kitty D. Weaver, *Lenin's Grandchildren* (New York: Simon and Schuster, 1971).

47. Randall Collins, "A Conflict Theory of Sexual Stratification," *Social Problems* 19 (Summer 1971): 3-21.

48. Susan Edmiston, "To Love, Honor and Negotiate," *Woman's Day*, July 1971, p. 144; John S. Kafka and Robert C. Ryder, "Notes on Marriages in the Counterculture," *Journal of Applied Behavioral Science* 9:321-330.

49. An example of a new marriage contract can be found in "To Love, Honor, and Share: Marriage Contract of Harriet Mary Cody and Harvey Joseph Sadis," *Ms*, June 1973, pp. 62ff.; Amy Vanderbilt, "Those New-Style Weddings," *Ladies Home Journal*, May 1973, pp. 30-35; Marcia Seligson, *The Eternal Bliss Machine* (New York: Wm. Morrow Co., 1973).

50. James R. Smith and Lynn G. Smith, "Co-Marital Sex and the Sexual Freedom Movement," *Journal of Sex Research* 6 (1970):131-142; Mary L. Walschok, "The Emergence of Middle-Class Deviant Subcultures: The Case of Swingers," *Social Problems* 18 (1971):488-495; Caroline Gordon, *The Beginner's Guide to Group Sex* (New York: Drake Publishing Co., 1973).

51. Lawrence H. Fuchs, *Family Matters* (New York: Random House, 1972), p. 229.

5

Mothers and Fathers = People

In all the parlor discussions of families and the innumerable books and articles diagnosing ills and prescribing remedies, there is relatively little literature about parental roles as such. There are the "how to rear your baby" books, of which Dr. Spock's is the most famous, but the stress is as much on the physical care of the child as on other aspects of childrearing. The feelings of the father or mother are touched on briefly and superficially, if at all. Adaptation to parenthood is taken for granted: now proceed to take care of the child.

In this chapter we will look more closely at the meaning of parenthood for men and women. In the previous chapter we looked at sex roles and their implications for family life, and we attempted to provide some perspective on the contemporary family situation. Now we will look inside the family to assess how mothers and fathers see themselves as parents and how they rear boys and girls on the way to manhood, womanhood, and personhood.

◆ Motherhood

Becoming a Mother: Pregnancy

Becoming a parent is an irrevocable act: "We can have ex-spouses and ex-jobs, but no ex-children."[1]

Parental roles are learned easily in nomadic or agrarian folk societies. Many models exist. Learning what mothers do and what fathers do is a continuous experience for children in such cultures. Not so in modern America. Few new mothers have had intimate contact with newborn babies before having their own.

Mothers pass on psychological handicaps to children, and they also pass on physical deficiencies. One of the most obvious and yet one of the most neglected is malnutrition. A mother who is severely undernourished will pass on to her child physical defects which may take as many as three generations to overcome.[2] A mother who is addicted to hard drugs may produce a child addicted at birth, or pass on her addiction if the child is breast-fed.

It is not possible to deny the significance of a mother for the well-being of a child. One critic of the women's liberation movement observed that much of their literature "is distinguished by its lack of reference to children, except as cause for monotony and drudgery," and "There is an astonishing and depressing devaluation of the intricacies and pleasures of child-bearing and rearing, and it appears to be tied to a corollary glorification of paid work of almost any kind."[3]

Perhaps the women's groups are taking a hard line against the sugary sentimentality surrounding motherhood in the soap operas and women's magazines. The myth of motherhood, they are saying, may be one big fraud; these feelings are evidenced in such book titles as *The Baby Trap* and *The Love Fraud*.[4] Yet, as shown in numerous articles in *Ms* magazine, which brightly presents the new woman's point of view, there is a full recognition of the fact that most women are, or will be, mothers. A more balanced view is needed to show that motherhood is not all it is touted to be, thus freeing from guilt many women who do not really want to be mothers, or do not like this role even if they accept it for whatever reason. The rosy clouds of rhetoric that surround motherhood must be dispersed before we can come to a realization of what being a mother and raising a child is all about.[5]

Having a baby is an important, unprecedented experience for a woman. Nothing like this has ever before happened to her body. She faces physiological changes paralleled by emotional states that no textbook can prepare her for. How much do we know about what happens? Actually, very little.

Pregnancy has been surrounded by myths and taboos. Depending on the culture, pregnancy may be valued or punished.[6] Until very recently in our culture a pregnant woman was kept at home, an object of shame as well as pride. Only in the last few decades have pregnant women become a commonplace phenomenon in public places. Many pregnant women are fearful—of their own death, or of bearing a dead or deformed child.[7] For others, pregnancy brings a sense of social approval for a completely "female" act. The nine months can induce a sense of personal well-being and satisfaction. It has been claimed that the high illegitimacy rates among the ghettoized poor may be due to the fact that, by becoming pregnant, a girl is able to assert in the most visible way possible that she is female and therefore worthwhile. Another explanation is that such girls are often themselves without love, discarded by distraught parents, and having a child provides them with something of their very own.[8]

According to one authority, husbands' feelings about pregnancy, and the effect of their reactions on the future mother's adjustment have never been studied.[9] When it comes to childbearing and child-rearing, women are the almost exclusive focus of attention.[10] Neglect of the feelings as well as the rights of fathers is poignantly brought out in the case of the unmarried father. In one study the fathers were found to be bitter and angry because no one seemed to care about them or how they felt. It is generally believed that unmarried fathers do not care about any pregnancy resulting from their sexual exploits but instead consider it just another demonstration of their prowess. Data, which are scarce indeed, suggest that many of the young men are pushed aside by authorities who assume, in many cases wrongly, that the unmarried father has no interest in his impending parenthood.[11]

Traditionally, society has taken the attitude that pregnant women should remain at home, protected by their husbands. This attitude was vividly reflected in employment practices. Employed women who became pregnant were not covered by the usual sick leave benefits until March 24, 1972, when the Federal government directed that pregnant women might receive these benefits. Prior to this, most pregnant employees were required to stay off the job, and in some cases were forced to resign. Many firms still do not permit a woman to return to work before a specified time, nor will she get sick pay or time accumulated for seniority benefits. Recently, a teacher successfully sued the Chicago school board over its policies regarding pregnant teachers. These policies required a teacher to leave after four months of pregnancy; then her position was declared vacant and she was not allowed even to apply for a new position until six months after delivery.[12] Professional women are now requesting that colleges and universities provide sick leave and maternity benefits, and employ mothers of young children on a regular basis, even if only half-time, so that seniority toward promotion can be accrued.

School policies toward pregnant and married students vary. In a few school systems a girl is forced to drop out as soon as she gets married;[13] most school systems allow a girl to continue until she gets pregnant. As soon as this occurs she is required to drop out. Some recent court decisions have upheld the rights of pregnant, unmarried girls to attend classes on a regular basis, and have held that unwed mothers cannot be excluded from school on that basis alone. Recently, a school district was told to permit married students to participate in extracurricular activities.[14] In most schools, no special provision for instruction in infant care, diet, or other fundamentals of home and family are provided for the married or pregnant girl. Medical school treatment of women medical students has been no model. Not only have pregnant medical students been denied sick leave when giving birth, in some instances they have been required to forfeit a whole semester's credit unless they were back on duty or in class within three days.[15]

Social policies of this sort convey a very clear message: it is fine to get pregnant and bear children, but this must take place within a traditional family lifestyle. The pregnant woman is supposed to stay home, and remain at home after the child is born while her husband provides for her. Pregnant women are barred from work as though they had a contagious disease. Such policies, though the object of female protest for many years, are just now coming to public notice, and are now the object of legal attack.

The First Child

In a very interesting and careful study of eight families, Senn and Hartford describe in detail how parents responded to the birth and management of their first child. All eight couples showed uncertainty and anxiety about doing the "right thing" for the child.[16] Parenthood presents men and women with new burdens as well as a new source of happiness and fulfillment. A couple's reaction to their first child is usually a mixture of joy and anxiety, and both sentiments are reflected in the attentiveness which they direct toward the child.

Owing to the enormous amount of parental attention they receive in their formative years, first born children are likely to be high achievers. A firstborn's high level of achievement is usually obtained at some price, however, for early in life they learn that parental approval and praise are won primarily through achievement. Parents anxiously await the first child's earliest accomplishments, ranging from the first smile when the child is five weeks old to the first coherent sentences when it is about three years old.

Although parents lavish praise on the first child for even the simplest achievements, they often use love-control techniques—psychological rather than physical discipline—to force the child into desired behavioral patterns. Alternating with praise for accomplishments, this use of psychological discipline can create a highly dependent child. Psychological discipline is used especially with girls, and its use may well account for the greater adult orientation of first born girls. But although first born girls are more open with their parents and are more sensitive to parental expectations, they do not necessarily hold to parental values more than later born siblings. Traditionally, first born girls were expected to put aside their own ambitions in order to help younger brothers go to college. But no one would ask this of the oldest girl today, and thus we should see more first born girls surging ahead toward the achievement levels promised by their earliest years.

Although the father takes a great deal of interest in the activities of the first born child, it is the mother's constant and undivided attention that motivates the first child to say that one extra word, take that one extra step. The mother is a particularly strong source of achievement motivation for boys, and the disproportionate amount of attention that a first born boy receives from his mother provides him from birth with a spur to achievement.

What about later born children? Do parents lose their enthusiasm for and interest in the individual children as a family enlarges? Some data would indicate that, in a large family, the last born child is apt to feel unwanted.[17] Last born boys, if there are several boys already in the family, are particularly apt to be treated by their mothers with coldness and rejection. Yet mothers do not respond coldly to the last born girl, even if she is preceded by several children of the same sex.[18]

Do later born children have the self-confidence and high achievement orientation of the firstborn? Studies indicate that having older—and more competent—siblings has an adverse effect on the development of a child's self-concept and self-esteem. And this in turn influences ambitions and desire for achievement. However, in many lower class families the youngest child is urged on to reach goals that older brothers and sisters had to forgo in order to go to work.

All of these data demonstrate one thing: that parents create a different climate for each succeeding child. They react differently toward each child. A child's sex, its sequence in the birth order, the number of other children in the family—each of these factors will influence the parents' feelings and behavior toward a child. Too frequently—we suspect in most cases—parents are quite unaware of these influences and they earnestly believe that they treat all of their children in an identical manner. Perhaps if they studied their own actions, parents could see the differing attitudes and behavior they display toward each child.

"The Hand That Rocks the Cradle. . . ."[19]

To read standard American textbooks on psychology and/or child development is to gain quickly an impression that only mothers are engaged in childrearing.[20]

Most studies of childrearing practices depend on observations of mothers, or on reports by mothers of what they have done. One oft cited volume on childrearing practices is the result of a research project to learn of children's home experiences with *parents*, yet as one critic noted, "not a single father was interviewed in this elaborate research effort."[21]

The exclusion of fathers from research has given us a one-sided picture of childrearing. "The compelling legend of maternal influences in child behavior . . . does not have its roots in solid data, and its . . . verification remains in many respects a subject for future research."[22] Mothers are held responsible for the development of aggressive behavior in boys and for repressing the initiative and independence of girls. The researchers cited above report that "many of the hypotheses that have been advanced relating the child's aggression to frustrations and punishments and rewards in the rearing practices of the mother have not been substantially supported" by their own data, nor by the data of other researchers.[23]

Both fathers and mothers play important roles in childrearing, and both sexes should be prepared for parenthood through education. But formal educational institutions have failed to recognize that teaching children to become parents is as much an educational task as teaching the rules of grammar. The schools have been bound by traditional assumptions about what are fit subjects of instruction. These assumptions were valid when education was a privilege for men, the affluent, and the clergy, and when folk societies provided ample education in childrearing. Since girls did not go to school, they were available twenty-four hours a day for instruction in caring for a regular succession of infants. That today's society is far removed from such a folk system is obvious, and there have been recent changes in school curricula in some areas indicating an awareness of the need to educate youth for their parental roles. Child development courses have been introduced, sometimes as an offering in social studies, other times through the home economics department. An experimental program developed by Educational Development Corporation focuses on providing an understanding of how human beings grow as social beings, with an emphasis on parental roles.[24]

Formal training in parental roles may give boys and girls the knowledge necessary to be more adequate parents. Yet education alone will not restrain the neurotic parent from imposing his or her neurotic attitudes and behavior on a child.

In the case histories of a significant number of homosexual men, there are reports that their mothers dressed them and treated them as girls during their early years.[25] As we know from studies of the sex-role identification of pseudohermaphrodites—individuals with the gonads of one sex and genitalia that are ambiguous—a child identifies with the sex or gender that is assigned to it. It is understandable that a boy will feel acute confusion if he has perceived himself to be more a girl than a boy for several years, and then is switched to a stereotypic male role. The early behavior forced on such a child by a neurotic parent will cause lasting damage.

The way a mother views her own sex identity will have a significant impact on her children. The low self-esteem which many women experience because of the still pervasive prejudices against them, particularly toward expressions of strength, assertiveness, or superiority, is not necessarily removed by becoming a mother. The many ways in which women are ambivalent about their own worth are apt to be projected onto their daughters. About one-third of all women have said they would prefer to be men. Daughters of such women may grow up to reject the female sex role and may identify with their fathers. "A kind of man-girl develops who remains highly attractive to many men who feel themselves understood on account of the male identifications and the projection which such a female can make more easily than a woman exclusively identified with her own sex."[26] As these women become mothers themselves, the cycle of ambivalence is renewed.

Cases of child abuse shock authorities. One of the few studies of abused children showed that "Across all groups, girls were consistently punished earlier: by the age of nine months, 31 percent of the girls, but only 5 percent of the boys were being punished; by eighteen months, the figures rose to 70 percent and 50 percent for the boys and girls, respectively."[27] The abused infant was apt to be second born and born soon after the first child; most of the infants were female.[28] The fact that even more mothers than fathers were responsible for such extreme abuse is hard for us to understand.

The mother is expected to be the primary source of food and care for the new infant. Without such care, the infant may just not grow. Studies of dwarfism have shown that, where no physiological reason could be identified, lack of mothering was the key factor. One study of twins, a boy and a girl, showed that the mother had provided consistently less care for the boy because of anger at the father; as a result, the boy was noticeably smaller than his sister. After hospital treatment and the return of the father, the boy started to grow again and eventually caught up with his sister.[29]

In addition to physical care, the mother provides the child with the greatest source of psychological support. A child's educational and occupational aspirations are directly linked to support from the mother. If a boy wants to go to college, and is strongly supported by his mother, he will get there. If his mother is only lukewarm, or opposed, his chances are diminished. His father's view on the subject is less influential. A daughter's education is very closely tied to that of her mother; the more education the mother has, the more likely will she be to encourage her daughter.[30] Lower class mothers (who are more likely to be away from home working) exert a more powerful influence on their children's aspirations and careers than do middle class mothers, although the latter are more likely to be at home, particularly in the early years.[31] Many studies of occupational mobility, level of aspiration, and sources of attitudes among boys report *father's* education and occupation on the assumption that the role of the father is critical. Yet mother's education, mother's views (and mother's occupation?) may be more directly influential.

The Maternal Role

The concept of "maternal instinct" probably needs more objective analysis than many other social myths which cloud our view of reality. Studies of rat mothers who were taken away from their own mothers right after weaning typically show deficiencies in "mothering." Animal mothers in zoos who have not had the opportunity to "learn mothering" from others of their species are very often poor mothers. Does this also apply to humans?

Human history is full of tales of maternal destructiveness. The figures on infant mortality in the eighteenth and nineteenth centuries present an appalling picture of infanticide.[32] Inability to control the birth of unwanted children forced parents to resort to infant destruction. Among the Bushmen, who foraged for food, a child was not wanted until the previous infant could walk; infanticide was practiced to achieve adequate spacing.[33] Instead of portraying a picture of maternal protection, history can show that fathers were often more protective (more "maternal") than women.[34] There is some reason to think that our ideas of the sacredness of human life and our glorification of motherhood are the luxuries of a world with abundant material resources.

It has long been accepted that a woman's major satisfactions in life come from the successes of her children. With one, two, or at most three children to invest in, both mother and children may be the losers when such views prevail. Since much of the mother's self-esteem is tied up with her children, she may, and often does, smother them with attention and concern. Every little bit of behavior is put in the ledger: credit or debit. The mother is the one who tells everyone about "my son, the doctor," and whose overriding concern about her daughter is not only who she will marry but that she *will* marry.

Middle class mothers are a particularly vulnerable group. They usually believe fervently in the importance of rearing their children well, but since most of them realize how little they know about child-rearing, they are insecure and anxious. Every child failure is the mother's failure, although success is shared by father and fond relatives. This is particularly true of school failures and successes. As one columnist responded to a question about working mothers and school responsibilities, "I think that children who have working mothers may possibly feel that their mothers' work is more important than they are. . . . It is clear that when the working mother cannot participate in school activities, the situation may lead to a child's underachievement—or the development of other types of disruption in his schoolwork."[35] It is quite clear that a child's success or lack of it in school is something only the mother will be held accountable for. No wonder some mothers who have careers are dogged by guilt.

To guard a fragile ego against devastating guilt when child failure seems possible, some mothers become cold. Or they become so over-anxious that the child is not allowed to develop a separate and firm identity. The struggle of adolescents to become free of their mothers becomes acute and for good reason. As one commentator put it, "the present parental generation dwells on fantasies of intimacy with and autonomy for its children," dreams which rarely materialize.[36] Youth turn to their buddies, their best friends, their social and age peers for the intimacy mothers yearn for; mom must struggle with harsh demands for independence without any of the balm of close-ness and affection. To make up for this lack, it is consoling to note that one study found that mothers who felt they had done a success-ful job rearing children reported significantly less illness than those who felt they had not been successful.[37]

As children grow up and enter the world of professions, business, and marriage, the mother is left with the proverbial empty nest. "Training in the qualities and skills needed for family roles in con temporary society may be inadequate for both sexes, but the lower-ing of self-esteem in middle age occurs only among women because their primary adult roles are within the family system."[38] At a time when her husband may be realizing his mature ambitions and gaining his greatest success in the outside world, mothers are faced with dev-astation at home.

Although it is expected that women who have stayed home throughout the years of the children's growing up will be depressed by their departure, in some families marital discord is reduced after the children leave. Since children are the focus of much parental dis-pute, some mothers and fathers breathe a sigh of relief when they are no longer underfoot.[39]

The fear expressed by some critics of the women's movement, that women will cease to have children, is undoubtedly an overreaction to some of the shriller spokeswomen for the cause. Yet their fear is understandable. It is frightening for the traditionally oriented to look into a future in which women will have children only because they want to. A study of the impact of legal abortion indicates that abortion has prevented the birth of thousands of unwanted infants in a short time span.[40] A woman is now free to decide whether to have a child, and little can be done to compel her to have one if she doesn't want to. One husband sued his spouse, who was filing for divorce, to prevent her from obtaining an abortion. He claimed that he had a right to the unborn child equal to that of the mother. Some men are realizing that a new era has dawned. It would now seem that after marriage a husband may have to do some fast talking and fast work to convince his liberated spouse that children are desirable.

In fact, the decision to have children should be one that is shared; the woman should no more be at the mercy of the roulette wheel of intercourse and ovulation, than a man at the mercy of his wife's whims.[41] Children are too important. Decisions to have them— or not to have them—must be made jointly by father and mother who together look into the future and accept parental responsibilities equally, honestly, and freely.

◆   **Fathers Are Parents, Too**

Children like to brag. And when they brag, they are more likely to brag about their fathers than their mothers.[42] Boys are likely to report that their fathers had more education than they really had. Boys also overestimate the size of their fathers in relation to other adults.[43] Fathers *are* important; one authority states that "In fact, more than ever it seems that the key to real quality in family life is father, not mother."[44]

How does a boy learn about fathering? Many see their fathers for only a few moments a day. As boys grow older, fathers may try to include sons in their hobby activities, or get them to assist in the masculine tasks of repairing toilets, fixing balky cars, mowing lawns, and shoveling snow. We have little information on how fathers act toward children. Very few objective studies of paternal behavior are available.

Since Freud, intense concern has been focused on the boy's relationship with his mother—the famous Oedipal complex. This phenomenon is the boy's identification with, and love for, his mother, growing awareness that he is not like his mother, and his recognition that his father is his chief rival for his mother's affection and attention. How can he admire his father and hope to be like him when, in fact, he hates him for taking his mother away? How can he learn to love another woman when, in fact, he has placed his full load of affection upon his mother? Why, by marrying a girl just like dear old mom! If the Oedipal conflict does in fact influence basic behavior, then the boy faces a long uphill road to become a father himself—because father was the hated rival.

Since Freud's presentation of the Oedipal conflict as one explanation of conflicting behavior, there has been further study of the male developmental process. Few child development authorities today accept Freud's analysis without question. There is sufficient evidence of boys' difficulty in sex role learning, and fathers' insecurity in their role, to suggest that the Oedipal complex might not explain everything.

Boys do not speculate about their future family roles. In fact, so little are boys concerned with their future family role that the dating process itself is necessary to convince a boy that he might just like a girl enough to forego his attachment to his male peers and get married. Benson argues that without the extra push of romantic love, boys might escape marriage much more successfully than they do! He points out that girls are quite clearheaded about assessing mate potential; boys just fall in love.[45] The fantasy life of girls is filled with ideas of home and family; the fantasy life of boys rarely if ever includes a wife and children.[46]

One of the traumas associated with the birth of the first child is the husband's recognition that he has a very active, very vocal, and completely dominating rival. Food, care, attention, even sex, become secondary to the demands of a squalling baby. As more children come, the husband is transformed into a father and is put in his place, which is *after* the children. No wonder the assertion of patriarchal controls becomes louder and louder—how else can the father keep his place in the family? In fact, one explanation for alcoholism among men is that it reflects a need to assert power within the family.[47]

The Absent Father

The mythology about mothers as the only and best childrearers is almost matched by the mythology about the *absent* father.

The earliest years are crucial for the development of sexual identity, and the absence of either parent during the first two to four years is considered particularly critical. As the child grows older it is not the quantity but the quality of the relationship with the father that is most important.[48] The role the father plays at home is supposed to provide a model for both son and daughter. And if the father is not home? What then?

A storm of controversy greeted a report on the Negro family authored by Moynihan.[49] Most of the ills of black youth were attributed to the fact that many come from so-called fatherless homes that are headed by females. The report provoked an immediate response which challenged two of Moynihan's assumptions: 1) that a matriarchal family was necessarily bad and 2) that father absence was a phenomenon peculiar to Negro homes. Research shows that the strong matriarchal family is not necessarily a bad one.

Assessing the impact of poverty and father absence on youngsters is not simple. A careful study of black boys from fatherless homes and those from intact homes revealed no difference in school performance.[50] Research has shown that for both white and black boys father absence diminishes the chances of completing high school. A recent summary of the literature and independent research by Kandel indicates that regardless of race the mother is stronger in intact homes. It was also found that educational aspirations for their children are as high among black as white mothers. These data repudiate the claim that black boys' identification with their mothers lessens their achievement motivation. Again, it is the *quality* of the parental relationship, whether the parent is present or absent, that is now perceived as critical.[51]

Some studies show that boys with a strong father identification had a better chance than others to do well in reading, while boys whose fathers were absent at critical points in their lives did less well mathematically, and in general had lower college aptitude scores.[52] These findings may appear to contradict an earlier statement regarding the lack of definitive evidence indicating the harm produced by father absence. What seems apparent is not that the absence of a father is without effect, but that it may not be as damaging as some would assert. It is one thing to note that in some cases father absence affects boys' mathematical ability as tested in late adolescence, and another to assert that a boy will be likely to grow up a delinquent if there is no father in the home. The latter assertion is one we reject.

Lower class boys of whatever color bother school people and other authorities by an exaggeration of masculine qualities—behavior which is presumed related to father absence. However, these boys learn the male role primarily from their peers on the street, many of whom have already been inducted into the criminal subculture.

One may conclude that the effect of the father's absence varies according to the treatment the child receives from the mother, and access to supportive or deviant male peers or adults.

There is some evidence that sons in fatherless families are handicapped in forming socially appropriate sex identities. That this is necessarily handicapping in educational and occupational achievement, however, is not certain. Furthermore, there is even evidence that if the father is typically authoritarian, his absence from the household frees the son to develop a high achievement motive. Where the absence of the father leads to strong mother-son ties and the son's dependency upon his mother, overindulgence, and low standards, the result is a low achievement motive.[53]

If the father's absence is ascribed to shiftlessness and a boy is told, "Don't you grow up to be a no good S.O.B. like your father," the boy is presented with a negative model. This may occur in lower class families where the absent father has deserted the family and has not helped to maintain it. A positive view is more likely to be presented in middle class homes. In middle class homes the father may be absent for significant time periods, but this is because of career demands,[54] and thus he is perceived as a good father who is helping his family.[55] It is assumed that it is better for a girl to have a good father around so that she can learn how to relate to males, but this is not necessarily the case. In girls, major personality differences due to father absence would appear, if at all, in latency and adolescence. Few studies have been made of the influence of father absence on girls.[56] Perhaps it is assumed that mothers provide all the guidance girls need in understanding men.

It is quite clear that work, occupation, or profession have the first claim on a man's time and attention. A man would find it difficult to refuse a job promotion just because it means moving his family. Big corporations, the military, and government agencies often have rotation policies which require family moves at stated intervals. The more successful a man is in today's corporate world the less able he is to be more than a part-time father. To rise in corporations, or even in military, governmental, or university hierarchies men must be available at any moment (including weekends and holidays), take few vacations, and be able to be absent from home for days or weeks at a time, with wives who can survive this kind of lifestyle.[57] If a major article in *Fortune* is an indicator, it would seem that the significance of family life in the career and personal development of executives may soon be given more consideration in the corporate decision-making that has been bouncing upwardly mobile staff hither and yon. As the *Fortune* article points out, the arbitrary and frequent moves that so many corporations impose on their career personnel may be unnecessary for the corporation, and exceedingly harmful for the innocent victims—executive wives and children.

The confusion about appropriate behavior in children whose fathers are absent from home may cause these children not to conform fully to traditional sex roles. Flacks summarizes the impact of observable trends in family relationships in a very provocative statement:

Boys who have ambivalent fathers or who tend to identify with their mothers and have accepting, nonpunitive parents are likely to define masculinity in ways that are quite untraditional. They are likely to be less physically competitive, and more emotionally expressive and aesthetically inclined. Presumably, many girls raised in these ways are likely to be less submissive, more assertive, and more self-assured and independent. Insofar as parents continue to expect conventional sex role performance on the part of their children—and insofar as such performance is expected by the schools and by peers—confusion and feelings of inadequacy can be the result.[58]

The confusion about appropriate male and parental behavior that boys and girls face in the years ahead is compounded by the models provided in the mass media. The daily doses of television news, dramatic violence, and glamorized aggression present a style of life which excludes or dismisses family relationships. Fathers of the future are going to have a difficult role to play.

New Freedom for Fathers?

One interesting trend, observable among upper middle class college youth in particular, is a rejection of the executive rat race. Both young men and women are beginning to rearrange their priorities, with family considerations coming first. A large percentage of graduates from Ivy League colleges have disavowed competitive occupations, and have opted instead for service jobs or ones which, while having limited upward potential, provide for adequate and secure family living. In this new emphasis on personal values, home and family are seen as the basic source of individual satisfaction. Many of those choosing less competitive, more subdued, more personalized lifestyles are among the most able intellectually, and are from more affluent social groups. Replacing them in the executive race may well be the upwardly mobile sons (and daughters) of the lower middle class, a phenomenon that one author has called "the blue-collar revolution."[59] The competitive, assertive, materialistic goals of this social level may cancel out the humanistic, cultural values of the older monied generations.

What happens to the wife when she has a husband around the home most of the time? Are women ready to share family life and childrearing? For many women with undeveloped interests, child caring, childrearing, and related domestic duties are their *raison d'être.* Now women perceive men asking for a larger share in family activities. Initially, this may be welcomed, but what will happen when the father is not only the chief breadwinner, but also shares authority in childrearing? What role is left for the wife unless she too moves out of the house for personal satisfactions? It is probable that the children of such couples will be more stable, warmer, and less ambitious. The differences in cognitive style, in emotional life between boys and girls will decrease. Boys may be less competitive and girls more assertive. To the degree that the "new father" and "new mother" remain comfortable in their roles, to that extent will boys and girls grow up more assured, and less limited by sex roles.

◆ Nonsexist Childrearing: Is It Possible?

Since the sexual identity of a child is its most salient characteristic, it is hardly possible to talk reasonably about nonsexist childrearing if one means asexual or unisexual. In our definition of the term, nonsexist childrearing means nonpreferential treatment of one sex as against the other.

Parents become disturbed when one points out the subtle and not so subtle ways in which preference for one sex or another may manifest itself. "I treat all my children the same," is what most parents say. The data show differently. Parents do favor one child as against another. And often this preference is related to the child's sex. So a parent's first task is to examine his or her own sex bias: do I prefer boys to girls? Or vice versa? If there is a preference, it would be helpful to analyze it. By understanding such a preference, one can lessen its manifestations in behavior.

Nonsexist childrearing then, does not deny the child's sex, but does respect each child regardless of its sex. In nonsexist childrearing, parents take care to provide language and play and affectional environments which are sex-neutral.

Many parents treat infants according to sex in ways they are not aware of. For instance, studies of mothers and children show that girl babies are talked to more than boy babies. Boy babies, however, are touched more often, and produce more parental reactions, since they tend to be more fretful during the first months of life.[60] In a play situation, mothers will allow toddling girls to stay close to them, while sending the staggering boy infant out toward play objects.[61]

As children grow, parents touch and fondle the girl more than the boy. One study of parental language showed that:

Fathers and mothers did not talk in exactly the same way to the babies, and there seemed to be some sex differences as well in how the babies were addressed. Some of the boy babies were addressed, especially by their fathers, in a sort of Hail-Baby-Well-Met style: while turning them upside down or engaged in similar play the fathers said things like "Come here, you little nut!" or "Hey, fruitcake!" Baby girls were dealt with more gently, both physically and verbally.[62]

Girls learn that touching and holding others of their sex is permissible up to adolescence, but when boys pass beyond the toddler stage mother and father reduce their physical contacts. A boy can touch others, but only in rough and tumble physical play with other boys or adults; they are prohibited from touching girls or women. Fear of strangers is instilled into girls at a very early age, and they are cautioned against roaming any distance from home. Boys are encouraged to explore, with an ever extending range to be discovered.

Such differential treatment of children instills traditional sex-role stereotypes in their minds. If play opportunities were distributed more evenly between the sexes, children could grow beyond these stereotypes.

There is evidence that boys who want to become scientists tend to establish their interests by age ten to fourteen, and that the kind of play they were exposed to in early years has some impact. "With all this in mind," says one authority, "research might be done to test the effects of encouraging changes in the play of girls to foster greater preparation for the vocational and public life of adults, including both broader interests and the objective reciprocity which comes from applying rules in collective games."[63] Instead of giving toy soldiers only

"We'd better have Rodney analyzed. He just turned off
Batman to do his homework."

Cartoon by Joe Buresch, courtesy of *Today's Education.*

to boys, and cuddly baby dolls only to girls, parents should give both
sexes boy and girl dolls, stuffed animals, and fantasy animals or
puppets. Instead of model car games for boys and miniature tea sets
for girls, both boys and girls can play with full size pots and pans, with
boards and hammers, nails and paints, and paper and scissors. Drums
and simple recorders (flutes) and balls both big and small are just
as much fun for girls as for boys. Above all, no play activity or toy
should be labeled "boys only" or "girls only." There should be no
parental caution: "Oh, boys never do that!" or "How nice, Susan is
doing just what little girls should!"

In nonsexist childrearing the assignment of helping roles would
not be sex linked. The boy is not automatically sent off to help father
clean the garage or oil the mower nor is the girl automatically set to
baking cookies or making beds. Home tasks and work activities are
rotated, so that the girl helps with the car and the boy scrubs the
pots.

In the same way, of course, parental models are not caught up in sex-limiting activities. One young mother reported the shock that went round the block when her young daughter trotted from door to door saying: "Come see my momma, she is under the car!" And of course the neighbors trooped out, fearing the worst. All she was doing was draining the oil. One indignant male neighbor exclaimed: "Why didn't you ask me? I would have been happy to do it." Her answer, "But I know how; I can do it," left her neighbor baffled, confused and, she was sure, angry!

Boys and girls need to see fathers happily tending an infant without having the mother fuss and exclaim over how nice it is that he is helping. When it is a matter of course for infants to be fed, washed, loved by mother *and* father, the children will be exposed to nonsexist role models. The future for such children should then be more free, with less struggle and strain induced by inappropriate sex-limiting self-expectations.

◆ Summary

Becoming a parent is an irrevocable act. Most of us are complete amateurs at this task, having had little or no opportunity to observe other adults while they were occupied with infant care or childrearing, and having no help from the institutions, school or church, with which we might have had contact. Yet with few exceptions most young people look forward to establishing their own family unit, and having one or more children.

Social changes are bringing new considerations to the fore. Women are increasingly aware of their own potential as wage earners, and many have career goals. Where is the place for children when women need to work or want to work in ever increasing numbers? And whose choice is child production? Such issues are pressing upon more and more young adults and their anxious, watchful parents.

The parental role, once well defined and stable, with secure power relationships within the family, is in need of redefinition as new options become available for women, and thus for their husbands as well. The sex-role stereotypes of the happy housewife and earnest breadwinner no longer serve man or woman or their children very well. Legal confusion over the basis for marital stability or marital dissolution does not help. A rearrangement of priorities, possibly a prime result of the youth revolution of the 1960s, has caused an increasing number of men and women to think of their own happiness and fulfillment as far more important than the happiness of others or the social good.

Human nature does not change quite so rapidly, however. Though personal satisfaction may push aside traditionally valued social arrangements, it seems obvious that the need to love, to be loved, to produce and rear young, are important and deep drives. Family roles may well shift, but families in some form or another seem here to stay.

References

1. Alice S. Rossi, "Transition to Parenthood," *Journal of Marriage and the Family* 30 (February 1968): 26–30.
2. Francis Kepple, "Food for Thought," in *Malnutrition, Learning and Behavior*, ed. Bevis S. Scrimshaw and John E. Gordon (Cambridge: The MIT Press, 1968), pp. 4-9; see also Margot Higgins, "Woman—The Forgotten Factor," *War on Hunger* 7 (February 1973): 6-8.
3. Lemberg Center for the Study of Violence, Brandeis University, *Confrontation* (April 1971):16; see also Edith de Rham, *The Love Fraud* (New York: Clarkson N. Potter, 1965).
4. de Rham, *op cit.*; Ellen Peck, *The Baby Trap* (New York: Bernard Geis, 1971).
5. "Debunking the Maternal Instinct," *Human Behavior* 3 (March 1974): 63; see also Gary Mitchell *et al.*, "Males Can Raise Babies: Lesson from a Primate," *Psychology Today* 7 (April 1974): 63-68.
6. Elaine R. Grimm, "Women's Attitudes and Reactions to Childbearing," in *Modern Woman: Her Psychology and Sexuality*, ed. George D. Goldman Donald S. Milman (Springfield, Illinois: Charles C. Thomas, 1969), pp. 129-160.
7. *Ibid.*, pp. 129-163.
8. Gisela Konopka, *The Adolescent Girl in Conflict* (Englewood Cliffs, New Jersey: Prentice Hall, 1966); see also Katrina Maxton-Graham, *Pregnant by Mistake* (New York: Liveright, 1973); Alice Shiller, *The Unmarried Mother* (New York Public Affairs Committee, 1969).
9. Grimm, *op. cit.*, p. 161.
10. E. E. LeMasters, *Parents in Modern America* (Homewood, Ill.: Dorsey Press, 1970), p. 139.
11. Robert F. Perkins and Ellis S. Grayson, "The Juvenile Unwed Father," in *Effective Services for Unmarried Parents and Their Children*, ed. National Council on Illegitimacy (New York: National Council on Illegitimacy, 1968).
12. *Washington Post*, May 1, 1972, p. A-18.

13. State Department of Education, "The Legal Status of Married Students in Texas Secondary Schools," mimeographed (Austin, Texas, 1970).

14. Citizens Advisory Council on the Status of Women, "Need for Studies of Sex Discrimination in Public Schools," mimeographed (Washington, D.C., June 1972).

15. Harold I. Kaplan, "Women Physicians: The More Effective Recruitment and Utilization of Their Talents and the Resistance to It—The Final Conclusions of a Seven Year Study," *The Woman Physician* 25 (September 1970): 561–570; see also Sheila K. Johnson, "A Woman Anthropologist Offers a Solution to the Woman Problem," *New York Times Magazine*, August 27, 1972.

16. Milton J. E. Senn and Claire Hartford, *The Firstborn: Experience of Eight American Families* (Cambridge: Harvard University Press, 1968).

17. I. Gregory, "An Analysis of Familial Data on Psychiatric Patients: Parental Age, Family Size, Birth Order, and Ordinal Position," *British Journal of Preventive and Social Medicine* 12 (1958): 42–59. Stanley Schacter, "Birth Order, Eminence, and Higher Education" *American Sociological Review* 28 (1963) 750–757; Eleanor Singer, "Adult Orientation of the First and Later Children" *Sociometry* 34 (Sept. 1971) 320–330; David M. Wark, Edward O. Swanson and Judy Mack, "More on Birth Order: Intelligence and College Plans" *Journal of Individual Psychology* 30 (November, 1974) 221–226. For a contrary view see Carmi Schooler, "Birth Order Effects: Not Here, Not Now" *Psychological Bulletin* 78 (1972) 150–162.

18. Robert R. Sears, Eleanor E. Maccoby, and Harry Levin, *Patterns of Child Rearing* (Evanston, Ill.: Row, Peterson and Company, 1959), p. 57–58.

19. P. J. Greven, Jr., *Child-Rearing Concepts, 1628–1861* (Itasca, Ill.: F. E. Peacock Publishing Company, 1973).

20. For example: Ernest R. Hilgard, Richard C. Atkinson, and Rita L. Atkinson, *Introduction to Psychology* (New York: Harcourt, Brace, Jovanovich, 1972), pp. 67–76.

21. LeMasters, *op. cit.*, p. 139.

22. Marian Radke Yarrow, John D. Campbell, and Roger V. Verton, *Child Rearing: An Inquiry into Research and Methods* (San Francisco: Jossey-Bass Publishing Company, 1968), p. 152.

23. *Ibid.*, p. 92.

24. Educational Development Corporation, Cambridge, Mass.

25. Lional Ovesey, *Homosexuality and Pseudohomosexuality* (New York: Science House, 1969), pp. 72–99.

26. Edrita Fried, "The Fear of Loving," in *Modern Woman: Her Psychology and Sexuality*, ed. George D. Goldman and Donald S. Milman (Springfield, Ill.: Charles C. Thomas, 1969), pp. 129–160.

27. Julius Segal, ed., *Mental Health Program Reports—5* (Rockville, Md.: Department of Health, Education, and Welfare, Public Health Service. Publication Number (HSM) 72-9042, 1971), p. 79.

28.   *Ibid.*, p. 69.

29.   Lytt I. Gardner, "Deprivation Dwarfism," *Scientific American*, July 1972, pp. 76–82.

30.   Denise Kandel and Gerald S. Lesser, "School, Family and Peer Influences on Educational Plans of Adolescents in the U.S. and Denmark," *Sociology of Education* 43 (Summer 1970): 270–286.

31.   William S. Bennett, Jr. and Noel P. Gist, "Class and Family Influences on Student Aspiration," *Social Forces* (December 1964): 167–173.

32.   William L. Langer, "Infanticide: A Historical Survey," *History of Childhood Quarterly* 1 (Winter 1974): 353–366; Richard C. Trexler, "Infanticide in Florence: New Sources and First Results," *History of Childhood Quarterly* 1 (Summer 1973): 98–116. Una Stannard, "Adam's Rib, or the Woman Within," *Trans-Action* 8 (November-December 1970): 24–35.

33.   M. J. Konner, "Newborn Walking: Additional Data," *Science* 179 (January 1972): 307.

34.   Stannard, *op. cit.*

35.   Lee Salk, "You and Your Family," *McCall's*, August 1972, p. 52.

36.   Robert S. Lauffer, "Sources of Generational Consciousness and Conflict," *Annals of American Academy of Political and Social Science* 395 (May 1971): 81–94.

37.   Stephen Cole and Robert Lejeune, "Illness and the Legitimization of Failure," *American Sociological Review* 37 (June 1972): 347–356.

38.   Rossi, *op. cit.*, pp. 26–30.

39.   Norman M. Bradburn and David Caplovits, *Reports on Happiness* (Chicago: Aldine Publishing Company, 1965).

40.   June Skar and Beth Berkov, "Abortion, Illegitimacy, and the American Birth Rate," *Science* 125 (September 1974): 909–915.

41.   J. E. Veevers, "Voluntarily Childless Wives: An Exploratory Study," *Sociology and Social Research* 57 (1973): 356–366.

42.   Nancy St. John, "The Validity of Children's Reports on Their Parents' Educational Level: A Methodological Note," *Sociology of Education* 43 (Summer 1970): 255–269.

43.   E. K. Beller and J. L. B. Turner, "Personality Correlates of Children's Perception of Human Size," *Child Development* 35 (1964): 441–449.

44.   Leonard Benson, *The Family Bond* (New York: Random House, 1971), pp. 126–127.

45.   *Ibid.*, pp. 51–70, 103–123.

46.   Patricia Horn *et al.*, "Newsline: The Little Person Who Wasn't There," *Psychology Today*, July 1973, pp. 13–14.

47.   David G. Winter, "The Need for Power in College Men: Action Correlates and Relationship to Drinking," in *The Drinking Man*, ed. David C. McClelland *et al.* (New York: Free Press, 1972), pp. 99–119.

48.   Clemmont E. Vontress, "The Black Male Personality," *The Black Scholar* 2 (June 1971): 10–16.

49. Lee Rainwater and William L. Yancy, *The Moynihan Report and the Politics of Controversy* (Cambridge: The MIT Press, 1967).

50. Herbert L. Wasserman, "A Comparative Study of School Performance Among Boys from Broken and Intact Black Homes," *The Journal of Negro Education* (Spring 1972): 137–141.

51. Denise B. Kandel, "Race, Maternal Authority, and Adolescent Aspiration," *American Journal of Sociology* (May 1971): 999–1020.

52. Henry B. Biller, *Father, Child and Sex Role* (Lexington, Massachusetts: D. C. Heath and Co., Heath Lexington Books, 1971), pp. 56–58.

53. Louis Kriesberg, *Mothers in Poverty: A Study of Fatherless Families* (Chicago: Aldine Publishing Company, 1970), p. 247; see also Timothy F. Hartnagel, "Father Absence and Self Concept Among Lower Class White and Negro Boys," *Social Problems* 18 (Fall 1970): 152–163.

54. Urie Bronfronbrenner, "The Study of Identifications Through Interpersonal Perception," in *Person Perception and Interpersonal Behavior*, ed. Renato Tagiuri and Luigo Petrollo (Stanford: Stanford University Press, 1958), pp. 110–130.

55. For a comprehensive review of the research literature see: Elizabeth Herzog and Celia E. Sudia, *Boys in Fatherless Families* (Washington, D.C.: Department of Health, Education, and Welfare, Publication number (OCD) 72-33, 1971).

56. E. Mavis Hetherington, "Girls Without Fathers," *Psychology Today*, February 1973, pp. 47–52.

57. Jules Archer, *The Executive "Success"* (New York: Grosset and Dunlap, 1969): see also William H. Whyte, Jr., "The Wife Problem," *Life*, January 1952, pp. 32–48.

58. Richard Flacks, *Youth and Social Change* (Chicago: Markham Publishing Company, 1971), p. 32.

59. Peter and Brigitte Berger, "The Blueing of America," *New York Times Magazine*, February 15, 1971.

60. Michael Lewis, "Parents and Children: Sex-Role Development," *School Review* 80 (February 1972): 229–240.

61. Jerome Kagan, "The Emergence of Sex Differences," *School Review* 80 (February 1972): 217–227.

62. Jean B. Gleason, "Code Switching in Children's Language," Paper presented at the Linguistics Institute, Buffalo, New York, August, 1971.

63. David B. Lynn, "Determinants of Intellectual Growth in Women," *School Review* 80 (February 1972): 241–260.

6

Friends and Foes:

Forces in Sex-Role Learning

Cultural prescriptions regarding sex-appropriate behaviors shape male and female personalities into quite dissimilar patterns. Every society rewards certain critical sex-appropriate behaviors and punishes those considered sex-inappropriate. In each culture there is remarkable consistency across social class lines regarding the approved behavior for each sex. Although individuals may stray away from the prescribed norms, they are always aware of the norms. How are these norms learned? One major source of sex-role training is the family. Other major sources are the peer group, the mass media, and formal social institutions, particularly the school.

In this chapter we will examine the role of peers in molding male and female behavior. What peers communicate to each other about behavior is first learned in the family and then refined by forces outside the home. Although, as we shall see in later chapters, the school has an influence on sex-role learning, it is the nonfamily, nonschool world which may in the long run have the greatest influence. An assessment of boys' and girls' behavior in relation to their peers leads us to inquire about the pathway to maturity—how similar are the maturational experiences of boys and girls? Does one sex face more personal and social hazards than the other in the process of growing up?

99

◆ Group Influence

"The group," said Kurt Lewin, "is the ground on which we stand." Without a group an individual is lonely, rootless, and alienated, unhappy, angry, and destructive. Within a group, an individual feels safe: valued, identifiable, and purposeful. In every society there are functional social groupings to answer this intense need to belong.

After the family, the peer group has the strongest influence over one's ultimate fortunes. In a technological society, with ever more leisure time and lengthened years of schooling, peers tell boys and girls who they are and assess their attributes more effectively than does the family. Between parents and children there is a generation gap that is constantly being widened by new inventions both technological and social which propel youth into a world their parents never knew, and whose ways are known only to other adolescents. In this tangled society of youth, parents are no guide at all; in fact, the adults may not even know of its existence.

One's "reference group," which symbolically looks over one's shoulder, monitoring all actions, is learned early. The reference group influences the individual's behavior even when no group is present. As Redl points out so sensitively, "Even while alone in a room with one adult, the 'group psychological mirror' is omnipresent, and the fear of showing up badly—or the hope of showing up well—if one's group saw one right now may be a strong motivating factor, far beyond anything else. . . ."[1] It is not necessarily formal group membership that influences personal behavior, for, as Redl continues "I have found that . . . youngsters of suburbia, who do not belong to any gang . . . were . . . heavily resistance-encrusted in terms of the 'teenage code of their subsociety' against giving in too easily to parental or psychiatric advice or risking their prestige by being too confidential with the enemy."[2] An adolescent's perception of appropriate behavior is largely formed by his group experiences, and our concern, therefore, is as much with these perceptions as it is with actual group life.

It is important to a child's ego, his sense of self-esteem, to win the approval of peers, even those whom he may secretly despise or publicly ignore. There is a large mass of "others" out there of whom we are dimly or acutely aware and who are important or unimportant to us depending on our upbringing, our ambitions—*and our sex.*

The power of the peer group to influence our lives may in part be a result of the ubiquity of the age-graded school.

Homogeneity of chronological age was not a factor in the older small district school. Children learned to get along as best they could in this extended situation in which they were thrust willy-nilly into partnership with all ages. Today's larger school provides a different kind of social setting for the growing child wherein he constantly compares himself with his peers, and his peers alone. One may ask, seriously, if some of our excessive, almost compulsive, need to conform to our colleagues and our social group may not arise from these early homogeneous groups in which the child was denied the larger vision of how people immediately older and younger did things? Thus he is denied models to strive to emulate and inferiors to protect and excel. All he can do is seek strenuously to keep up with the little Joneses who sit around him—same age, same range of problems, same range of experiences. A vision of the future and of the past is essential in keeping the present in balance. This vision we have taken away from the child. And he does not get it at home. He usually has only one or two siblings, all about the same age. His school days also divide him from them.[3]

We have been trained to be very aware of the assessments of others. We buy clothes not because we like them or find them comfortable, but on the basis of what others will think. We can be persuaded to buy specific items, to vote a certain way, to eat special or different foods, simply because "everyone is doing it."

Which sex is more apt to be influenced by the opinions of others or to assert independence in the face of group pressure? Are men or are women more bound by tradition? We shall look for answers to these questions in this chapter.

Groupie Americans

Many observers have said that Americans have produced the most "organized" culture there is. In America we can find an organization for almost anything; there are clubs for the formerly married; for parents of twins; for parents of children with cerebral palsy; for people with an IQ over 150; and for people from Iowa who migrated to Los Angeles. There are groups for all kinds of social goals: to preserve the bald eagle; to stamp out billboards; to elect Senator Whoosis to Congress; to preserve sand dunes; to guard the separation of church and state. There are alumni groups for those who have been to college or served in the military. There are help-each-other organizations ranging from Alcoholics Anonymous to Synanon to women's lib consciousness raising groups. There are innumerable work-related groups, trade unions, and professional associations. Although it seems there is an endless array of groups to join, no matter what one's vocation or interests, there are far more associations and organizations for men than women, and more for boys than girls.

Groups flourish in America because we have been well socialized to want to belong—to something. From childhood, boys and girls are prepared for group living by the family, by the school, by the church, and by organizations such as Boy Scouts and 4H especially designed to assist in socialization for group life.

One has to pay more than monetary dues for membership in a group: a price is exacted in terms of loyalty to the group and its style; Hell's Angels and the League of Women Voters may not seem to have much in common, but both groups expect certain distinctive behaviors and attitudes of their members. A law-abiding, non-aggressive young man would hardly be likely to seek out Hell's Angels, and vice versa. Passionately partisan political women would find the stringent objectivity of the League of Women Voters uncomfortable.

Out of the House and into the Street

Boys have more opportunity than girls to participate in some kind of organized group life, and their opportunities begin earlier. A boy is encouraged to become part of the street life of his neighborhood, where he quickly learns the importance of the opinion of other boys. His daring, athletic skill, and fiscal resources will help determine the place he wins in the informal social life away from home.

Street life plays an especially important role in the socialization of boys who live in the decaying central core of our cities. The degree to which the youngster can or cannot resist asocial or delinquent group norms will have an influence on the rest of his life.[4] Youth who manage to acquire stable jobs and escape the ghetto and a de-linquent lifestyle are those who accept parental and school norms and who do not identify with neighborhood groups.

At all social class levels, childrearing practices encourage boys to seek their playmates in the street or among neighborhood groups. Neighborhood influences intrude upon them at a relatively early age and are increasingly important each year, often to the despair of parents. And yet a mother or father who kept an active boy penned in the house or backyard (if there were one) while others his age were free to run and play would be thought very odd indeed. Neighbors and relatives would be quick to point out the error of their ways: "Do you want to raise your boy to be a sissy?" Since no parent would admit to this goal, the adults accede to peer group pressure (as they were socialized to do) and let their boy loose to face temptation.

Girls are less likely to be sent out of the house if they show little inclination, and parents are not criticized for keeping a daughter nearby. Playmates are "invited over" to play with daughter and parents can keep an eye and ear open to pick up any subversive influence. At an early age boys must pit their ego against the pressure of others; girls have a longer time for tutelage under adult eyes so that they may internalize parental values and learn appropriate affiliative and dependency behaviors.

One difficulty in discussing group formation among boys and girls is that "practically all of the research concerning group formation has involved preadolescent or adolescent subjects and most of the research deals with boys rather than with girls."[5] A study of delinquent girls found only two girls out of 175 who reported belonging to an organized gang and "only one of these gangs resembled those discussed in the literature describing boy gangs in the large Metropolitan centers."[6]

From an early age, boys' primary interest is in peer relationships, and the groups that they form outside of school carry over into school. In fact, some observers believe that the inattentiveness of boys in the early grades has its roots in early socialization patterns: they are so interested in what other boys are doing that they pay no attention to the teacher. According to McNeil a similar mechanism interferes with their learning to read: they are busy with peer relationships and haven't the time or energy for the self-isolating behavior which learning to read requires.[7]

Girls may engage in some organized play with other girls or, if the neighborhood does not provide enough boys to make up a competing team, boys may "allow" girls to play on boy teams. But typically girls engage in play groups of quite a different order from boys. Girls play house, play school, play nurse, with the active support of adults. The girls are only vaguely aware that in such play they are trying out adult roles, but parents are keenly aware of this connotation. The toys most children are given provide incentives toward sex-appropriate play: group activities for boys—baseball bat, catcher's mitt, football helmet; "pretend" play for girls—tea sets, nurse's uniform, dolls and their equipment. At an early age boys and girls can tell you which toys are appropriate for which sex.[8]

Boys are encouraged to form play groups that are in competition with other groups; you can't have a good game unless you have teams. In contrast, girls' groups revolve around cooperative enterprises: to play school one needs teachers and pupils; to play house one needs mother, father, children. These imaginary roles require complementary support that is far different from the boys' team cooperation for competitive purposes. Girls' greater verbal facility may well be a result of the conversations they carry on in their doll play, requiring the give and take of information and the analysis of alternative lifestyles.

In a revealing comment, Henry notes that when boys enter school their "society pivots on games requiring teams, and there are few boys' games of any prestige that can be played individually," so that young boys cannot avoid group and team life unless they are grossly out of step with their peers. Girls, by contrast, "play with their dolls, their sewing, their cut-outs, or their jacks, and their talk is not about rules of the game, about trying hard and winning, but about the trivia of their semi-isolated play."[9] One wonders on what basis he arrived at the conclusion that girl talk was about trivia, while boy talk concerned important matters.

For most girls, the only opportunity to participate in organized group activity is that presented by clubs such as Girl Scouts or Campfire Girls. The function of these group experiences is to reinforce the lifestyles of the families from which the girls come. Although these clubs do not teach girls how to compete or how to subordinate themselves to group discipline, they do teach girls how to work in structured situations, as part of an organized group, for the achievement of an end. However, most girls do not join these organized youth groups, and those who do, do not remain long. Instead, girls develop close friendships with one or two other girls as early as the primary grades. This social pattern continues into adulthood. The specific girlfriend may change, of course, but the alliance and friendships formed tend to be tight and closed: the typical clique of giggling, gossiping girls.

Let's Join the (Male) Team

Team sports are for boys. Girls have only minimal experience with team sports, in part because such sports are not perceived as an appropriate feminine activity. The adult aversion to organized athletics for girls is almost too vividly expressed by Friedenberg:

Girls also play a form of basketball, of course, as do paraplegics in wheelchairs and, for all I know, purple cows, but I do not know why. Even a culture which can usually convince itself that it would enjoy nothing more than the opportunity to observe scantily-clad young ladies closely for two or three hours seems to find something incongruous in the spectacle and to avoid it. The emotional aura seems wrong; a girls' basketball team is likely to strike an audience as unconvincing, in the same way a bad play does, even if it is technically competent. Dr. Johnson might have compared a girl playing basketball to a woman preacher.[10]

A study of four English-speaking countries found that physical activity was viewed as sex-role specific in all four countries. Females had a positive attitude toward physical activity when it was seen as a social experience, contributing to personal health and fitness, as an aesthetic experience, and as catharsis. Males saw physical activity as a challenge, allowing one to experience risk, thrill, speed, or potential danger (though with the self always in control), and as a means of attaining physical superiority through intensive, even punishing physical training.[11] It is reported that the famous child psychologist, Piaget, "could find not a single collective game played by girls with as many rules and with the fine and consistent organization and codification of these rules as the game of marbles for boys."[12] A cross-cultural study of adult sports activities concluded with this significant statement: "Needless to say, *and perhaps thankfully*, sports and games do not rate anywhere near as high in the women's value structure as in the men's."[13]

Currently, the athletic departments of colleges and universities are being pressured to provide more adequate sports programs for women, and to give equitable financial support for the physical education programs of men and women. The guidelines for Title IX of the Education Amendments to the Civil Rights Act, referring to sex equality in schools (including athletic programs) were published for public review in July 1974. A wave of response followed, with dire predictions from university athletic coaches that the guidelines would ruin intercollegiate programs. Reports citing gross inequities have achieved considerable visibility. Syracuse, New York public schools, for instance, were charged with allocating $90,000 for male sports and $200 for female sports programs. The University of Michigan has no official intercollegiate program for women but spends over $2 million on such activities for men. That there will be considerable debate in schools, colleges, and universities over this issue is certain;

male sports are financially important and they are also a significant source of recreational amusement to major portions of the American public. The debate will be resolved we are sure, so that some kind of equity is achieved, but we are also sure it will be loud, acrimonious, and drawn out.

It is unlikely, however, that organized athletics will ever be as important in the lives and personality development of women as they are for men. Consequently, girls may never really learn what it means to subordinate completely one's individuality to team pressure, team control, and team discipline. We believe this difference to be highly significant for later life.

Most school programs do not provide organized teams until about fourth grade, and by that time many boys have already formed their own neighborhood teams. They form sides in all kinds of semi-organized play. Being accepted to play by one such group against another is coveted; the boy whom neither side wants is a miserable child indeed.

Although the team requires subordination of the individual in order to win, members are taught effective ways of competing within the group as well as against other groups. Boys learn what is required to become a dominant member of the team, and how to secure a strong position in the group. Within-team competition for leadership or for a particular position pits individual against individual. Alliances are formed for mutual promotion and supporters may be cast aside once a goal is achieved; friendships may be fickle within the groups, but team loyalty will override personal antagonisms when the team faces another team.

Boys' participation in organized team activities, sponsored and highly approved of by adults, is both cause and effect of the enduring and ego-involving male interest in sports. Sports and team life dominate males psychologically into adulthood. Since girls typically do not seek to participate in organized team sports, they can relax and enjoy the spectator role. Men in the spectator role are tinged with envy of those still young enough to make the team, or they may nostalgically recall their own past triumphs. After war, team sports are the most masculine activity in our society.

The Great Popularity Game

What happens to boys who do not make the team? Without a team, they may lack an opportunity to get involved, and may not acquire necessary athletic or social skills. The boy is forced to stay an isolate, or he can turn to a gang. The hunch that gangs attract boys who never made the team is behind efforts to wean boys from illegal gang activity by providing athletic coaching and a competitive athletic "league." Such efforts have been sufficiently successful that it is surprising that so few resources have been allocated to this means of reaching delinquent or predelinquent boys.[14]

An interesting question about the role of peer groups among boys has been raised by Toby, who has worked intensively with delinquent youth. He concludes that one of the strongest motives behind gang affiliation is the need for reassurance of masculinity. One major reason for the formation of the gang, particularly the violent gang, is weakness of the family. Because of contemporary family style, "it is less easy for boys to grow up confident of their fundamental masculinity than for boys in the extended families of preliterate societies. One response to doubts about masculinity is *compulsive* masculinity: an exaggerated insistence on characteristics differentiating males from females."[15] This precarious sense of masculinity not only predisposes boys to group action, it also predisposes them toward violence. It is not that most males are insecure, but there are according to Toby, enough insecure males "to influence the cultural ideal of masculinity."[16]

What we see here, then, is a rather dangerous meeting of diverse social forces: young people need to be popular, to be esteemed by their peers. Youth, like other humans, desire group affiliation. For boys, this is preeminently achieved by athletic prowess. But many (most) boys cannot make the team. They seek other ways of finding peer approval and they seek a group to belong to; this may be a gang. The gang will be prone to violence if the neighborhood from which the gang draws its members provides male models who are successfully violent. The fear of loss of self-esteem—of being unmasculine—is so pervasive among boys that pressure to prove masculinity via deviant and even anti-social acts is strong enough to lure vulnerable youngsters into gangs, and in the safety and relative anonymity of the gang the youth may find reassurance—and a criminal career if he is unlucky.

The drive for popularity, for group acceptance, for validation of sexuality, confront the adolescent boy with harsh decisions and agonizing alternatives. Unfortunately, social institutions do not seem able or willing to shift programs despite these rather well known facts. The money spent for athletics is only for the assured athletic geniuses, of whom there are very few indeed. The team, the group that comprise the team, the social and sexual validation achieved through team activity, are thus denied most young males. What are they to do? They do the best they can, the best society lets them do, and often it is not very good at all. The largest number of persons in jails are young males.

Girls gain a sense of validation of their sexual being from other girls, but not in a parallel fashion. Girls are not trained to be independent from parents, especially their mothers. "The girl . . . is encouraged to maintain her identification with the mother; therefore she is not likely to establish an early and independent sense of self."[17] Girls at age eleven or thirteen may have friendships with other girls, but they feel closer to their families than to their friends. With adolescence, a girl wants a friend who is "loyal, trustworthy, and a reliable source of support in any emotional crisis. She should not be the sort of person who will abandon you, or who gossips about you behind your back."[18] When a girl dates, she turns to her girl friends for their approval. "We cannot avoid the impression that the adolescent girl is far more concerned about the opinions of girls than of boys. She wants to be popular with boys, for its effects on her appraisal by the peer group of girls."[19] In early adolescence the girl who dates may have emotional ties both to the boy and to her clique of girl friends. The more popular she is with boys the greater is her popularity with girls.[20]

However, boys do not necessarily gain status with other boys by dating girls. Boys gain status from their sexual exploits, which are basically casual sexual encounters, sometimes occurring in a gang setting. Girls are not present when gang members meet unless they are there for sexual activity. Boys begin serious dating later than do girls, and typically the younger girl dates an older boy. The different dating and group patterns, the different prestige and status needs of boys and girls result in quite different opportunities to learn about others and about groups. The implications for adult family and work roles have been relatively ignored by researchers.

Among boys, peer groups are the primary source of information about the taboo mysteries of life. Most boys receive their sexual information from their peers. This was as true in 1943 as it is today.[21] Girls do not usually find the peer group a useful source of information. Mothers are looked to for information by 75 percent of middle class girls.[22] Because of the strong resistance to adequate sex education in the schools,[23] it is probable that the peer group will continue to be the source of sexual information for boys. One impact of the women's liberation movement may be to provide sex information directly to adolescent girls through such media as the new *Ms* magazine, and increasingly in the so-called women's magazines, such as *McCalls, Cosmopolitan, Redbook, Ladies Home Journal, Family Circle, Woman's Day*. Even *Seventeen* presents information on sex and sexual attitudes. Tremendous pressure is placed on colleges to increase the sex information available to students, with particular stress on educating young women who have not received information from peers. Clearly, peer groups function quite differently for boys and for girls.

◆   **Groups, Gangs, and Friends**

Boy gangs may be casual friendship groups to be found in middle class suburban areas, or they may be highly structured organizations with names, symbols, leadership titles, and territories or "turfs."[24] Most significantly gangs are beyond the control of legitimate adults; they are true natural groups with their own indigenous leadership.

Why are gangs so typically a male activity? If the literature is to be believed, girls rather than boys are socialized to be more affiliative—to need the approval of others and be dependent upon others.[25] If the theory of female socialization holds, one should find more female groups. In fact, however, there are far more male groups; the girl gang is a distinctly rare phenomenon.[26] The power and strength of boys' gangs (and male groups) should be assessed more specifically in relation to socialization and culture. The view that boys are more independent and girls more dependent appears to be contradicted by the intensity of group solidarity among males. What are the psychological and social drives that are operating? Tiger's biological male-bond theory offers one explanation,[27] but it does not seem to explain group behavior in modern America; there is also some question about the biological similarity between human and animal groups.

Douvan and Adelson theorize that gangs are formed among boys and not among girls because of boys' continuous battles with authority. A boy "needs the gang, the band, in alliance with whom he can confirm himself as autonomous and maintain a wall of resistance to authority;" gang membership is also seen as a means of attaining popularity: "boys are more likely to adduce as a cause of unpopularity the unwillingness to 'go along with the crowd.' In their view, the failure to conform to peer standards is a more probable basis for peer rejection than it is for girls."[28]

Summarizing their excellent and far-reaching study of male gangs at several social class levels and among different ethnic groups, Sherif and Sherif conclude that

1. Individuals do not form groups of their own choosing just to be, mechanically, one of a set, or because they want to regulate their behavior in this or that direction. . . . individuals come together because they experience *some* strong motivational basis which is not effectively fulfilled by themselves, individually, or through other existing social channels.

2. . . . the individual looks to fellow members for acceptance and recognition in some capacity. The verdicts of others are not just one among a number of alternative evaluations. They are evaluations which *count* for him. It is through the dynamics of patterned interaction with others that he comes to regulate his behavior voluntarily in line with their expectations of him and with other norms shared by all members.[29]

The Sherifs point out that the strongest impetus to the formation of groups among the boys they studied was that such groups were the major and sometimes only source for feelings of belonging and enhanced self-esteem for these boys. The groups that could claim the greatest loyalty and obedience from members were those that developed where "conditions were most conducive to the members' finding their only locus of pleasurable activity, their only source of personal recognition, their only web of stable relationships, and their only clear personal identity in a group of their peers."[30] Detailed analysis of their home and family life and school experiences illustrate that the boys who needed gangs most were those who were marginal to, if not excluded from, the success and achievement system of society. Boys from middle income and professional families who were successful in school could only be drawn to gang activities as a result of deep but unmet affiliative needs. To give simplistic reasons for gang formation is to miss the fact that groups are formed and survive because they serve a very important function for individuals.

Delinquency among boys is primarily a group phenomenon.

About 75 percent of delinquency among boys has been attributed to group action, although not all of this group-related delinquency derives from gangs.[31]

The evolution of the violent male gang has been viewed as a distasteful and dangerous byproduct of current urban ills. This is debatable, for gangs have flourished in many eras and many places. How violent are youth gangs? Violence, although a dominant theme in gang affairs, is more talked about than consummated. The intergang warfare that has been deplored and, as in *West Side Story*, romanticized, is seen as "predominantly ideological rather than material, and revolves on the concepts of honor and prestige. Gang members fight to secure and defend their honor as males; to secure and defend the reputation of their local area and the honor of their women; to show that an affront to their pride and dignity demands retaliation."[32]

Wars between nations are fought for similar ends: to defend honor, territory, home. Is the solution to the problem of war among men similar to the solution to gang warfare? "At root, the solution to the problem of gang violence lies in the discovery of a way of providing for men the means of attaining cherished objectives—personal honor, prestige, defense against perceived threats to one's homeland—without resort to violence. When men have found a solution to this problem, they will at the same time have solved the problem of violent crimes in city gangs."[33] It is hardly surprising that men socialized in a society in which violent gangs can evolve do not see the inappropriateness of war as a means of resolving international problems.[34]

In those societies where sex roles are least polarized there is less warring, less interest in militaristic activities. Peaceful societies seem to be characterized by 1) an ability to derive pleasure from physical activities which make little distinction between the sexes—eating, laughter, drinking, sex; and 2) relatively little difference between the ideal characteristics of male and female. Such societies do not idealize aggressive masculinity.[35]

In addition to their group affiliation, boys form close "buddy" relationships as they mature into adolescence. A boy will acquire one or two best friends with whom he pals around. Such friendship alliances among boys have received much less study than the cliques that girls form, just as girls' group life has been less studied than boys' group life. Perhaps the more visible male gangs have obscured the phenomenon of close friendships among highly interdependent adolescent boys. Or it may be that fear of the potential homosexuality of such friendships makes researchers nervous.

The "buddy" relationships found among adolescent boys give way to group alliances among young men. Young men seem fearful of too-close friendships with other men. Douvan and Adelson believe that fear of homosexuality "serves to frighten the man away from ties to other men. Men fear more often than women a breakthrough of the homoerotic if they allow themselves too great a degree of intimacy with their own sex."[36] The tension among men, who are on guard for any covert homoerotic elements in a friendship or group, has not, it seems to us, been adequately analyzed or understood. This tension manifests itself in competition for dominance. It seems that among men interpersonal relationships are worked out in terms of leadership and status.[37] Considerable energy is devoted to jockeying for position, and group activities are directed toward daring exploits which serve to deflect any preoccupation with erotic drives.

In an interesting study, Konopka noted an underlying theme of homosexual attraction among delinquent girls. Most of the girls in Konopka's study had been badly hurt in relationships with males; they had suffered "emotional rape" in Konopka's terms.[38] Some of them found females to be a "safer" love partner. "In one of the group discussions the girls wondered how they could ever find 'decent men' who would want something more than just 'sex' from them. One of them dryly suggested that it was simpler to live with girls and get their satisfaction this way. . . . Many of the girls struggle with their bisexual drives and they are not sure which way to turn."[39]

Men's friendships revolve almost exclusively around work and play: the office or the assembly line, the hobby or sport activity. These are legitimate arenas for male friendships, and the talk is legitimately related to the focus of the friendship: office gossip, union politics, the best fly for trout in the North Fork of the Umpqua, or the chances of Slim Whoosis being traded to the Reds from the Blues for the next season. Social class lines determine which aspect of the job is discussed, and which sport or hobby is shared. Social class also determines where these discussions take place: at the neighborhood bar or pool hall, in the locker room of the country club, or over a beer in the recreation room during television commercials while the women are chatting in the kitchen. What seems most noticeable about male friendships is that they rarely include personal, confidential exchanges. Men who have known each other for years may not know anything about each other's family crises or problems.

Such friendships are without a doubt vital and important in the personal and social adjustment of males. The fact that men without jobs or families, such as those described in *Talley's Corner*,[40] congregate around a specific carry-out shop for years on end, where they find others to socialize with—their friends—is evidence of the importance of these male relationships. Small bars in every city neighborhood, on main roads, and in central shopping areas, frequented almost exclusively by men, provide an easy, accessible, and nondemanding group of pseudofriends or real friends with whom to chat about politics, sports, or work.

The friendship patterns of women seem more complex. After the clique or "best friend" stage of childhood and adolescence, the young woman seeks male friends as potential mates, and keeps, on the side, only a few intimate "girl friends." After marriage men are taboo as friends. A young wife home with the first infant finds herself isolated and alone. The result? She finds other women in the neighborhood or apartment house who are alone at home and they gather for morning coffee—if she is lucky enough to find such a group.

Office work attracts many women as much for the companionship and friendship to be found on the job as for the work or money earned. Many women, lacking access to others of the same age, become dependent on their relatives; having a mother nearby can be a hazard for a lonely wife who has no other woman to turn to for social-friendship needs. Not that mothers are to be discarded after marriage, but a grown woman, like a man, may find it hard to perceive herself as an adult when the main source of social feedback is mom.

An interesting commercial phenomenon which seems to feed upon the social needs of women is the selling-club. These groups, in which kitchenware, clothes, cosmetics, baby or household aids are sold, are a peculiar mix of the commercial and the social. Isolated women look forward to their next "Tupperware Party." The proliferation of these hard-sell parties which take place in private homes indicates that they have successfully identified and can exploit the friendship needs of women at home. With the fading popularity of the church social, women have few other opportunities for exclusively female socializing.

There is one means of socializing which women seem to exploit, and that is the telephone. There are many jokes about the female ability to carry on seemingly endless conversations devoted to trivia; but without the phone many women would be isolated and lonely indeed. The popular comic strip, "Blondie," runs many permutations on this theme. For the woman at home who can talk to another person only via the telephone, the jokes are not funny.

Unlike men, women do seem to use their friendships to share crises and ask for help. It is acceptable to admit that a husband is a cranky beast when he gets home in the evening, or that he is stingy with the money, or that junior or junior miss is a terrible worry. As noted previously, the data on the mental health of women are difficult to assess accurately. What is probable is that women reinforce each other by normalizing what is aberrant behavior, or else by evading the development of mature coping mechanisms. Kaffee-klatsch friends may be less than helpful, but they may be all that a woman has.

For both men and women the varieties of friendships available and the function of friendships seem to be sex-role stereotyped. Men need other men to share problems and troubles with; women need others of their sex to share concerns in a mature, nonescapist fashion. The benefits that men derive from sharing office or hobby interests could well be of value to women, while men could profit by learning how to confide in others about problems they find emotionally baffling. Finally, there is the need for a bridge between men and women so that friendships—without sex—could flourish. Today's society makes such friendship rare and suspect, and it is our loss that this is so.

Who Needs Groups?

The literature on sex differences is replete with discussions of the greater affiliative and nurturant needs of women, and the greater male needs for independence, achievement, and aggressiveness. Women are said to be more expressive and men more instrumental in their relationships with others. Since they are perceived as warmer, more expressive, more nurturant, and more affiliative, one would expect females to engage in group activities more than males. But the sex-role training received by females is such as to make peer group affiliation difficult.

In childhood, girls identify with their mothers and women elementary teachers rather than with peers; in preadolescence they begin to realize that their role in life will be dependent on whomever they marry. In early adulthood, the need for affiliation must be directed at males and finally at a particular male. After marriage, other males are *verboten*; only friendships with other women are permitted. After the birth of children, a woman is expected to concentrate on their support and development.

The boy has a different developmental history. At an early age boys are trained to be highly responsive to and aware of the opinions of other boys; at almost any age male behavior can be manipulated by a suggestion that the behavior has a sex-role connotation. *The most powerful word in the English language is "sissy."* Within a group males dare to be nonconforming only when there is no sex-linked factor in the behavior or attitude. If there is any element suggesting that something is masculine or feminine, males will adhere to the "male position."

Girls show less responsiveness to group attitudes, and are responsive to adult suggestions far more than boys. Prior to puberty, girls can rarely be manipulated to change their behavior by being told that something is too masculine or by being accused of tomboyism. During the dating and marriage years, however, women seek to be as feminine as possible, and will respond to pressure to change any unfeminine behavior. It is possible that the desire to reject all unfeminine behavior is responsible for reducing the aggressive achievement strivings of women.

It is clear that the socializing influences at work on boys and girls result in different perceptions of what is appropriate behavior. A great deal of data has been presented, and accepted, indicating that females will shift their opinions toward those of the majority more readily than males. When threatened with social rejection, females are significantly more conforming than when not threatened.[41] It seems girls feel that preserving peaceful social relationships is more important than holding onto an opinion.[42] Girls are high in affiliative needs, but this does not necessarily mean that affiliation is spread over a wide range.[43] The female is socialized to focus her affiliative needs on the members of her immediate family. Even with domineering parents, girls are likely to conform to parents' opinions (whereas boys would respond to such domination with rebellion).[44] Pressures from peer groups are unlikely to make a girl change her behavior.

This is especially true if she has achieved a satisfying or somewhat stable interpersonal attachment. Later in life, women will agree with their husbands more than they will with women friends. A female is so dependent on her family group for the fulfillment of her affiliative needs that she will often accept a lack of self-competence rather than endanger her relationship with the family.[45] Thus Hoffman, summarizing data on childhood experiences and achievement, concludes that, "girls have higher affiliative needs and their achievement behavior is motivated by a desire to please. If their achievement behavior comes into conflict with affiliation, achievement is likely to be sacrificed or anxiety may result."[46]

Men have a choice of public and non-kin social groups to belong to, while women have only the family group. If it is true that the group is the ground we stand on, then women stand on very narrow ground indeed. This may account in part for the lack of independence and assertiveness in women. When one is dependent on a very few individuals for one's safety and security, one cannot afford to strike out in an independent and aggressive fashion.

Are female needs for affiliation adequately met by the family? Has society failed to recognize how much females, just like males, need affiliation with peers? Since the home and neighborhood offer a very limited range of affiliations, many women want to return to work where there is a group of peers.

At work there are people who know if you are sick, who can share the triumphs and tragedies of your life, and who appreciate your efforts, appearance, and skills. It is one thing to matter to an infant (who doesn't "know" you are there anyway) or a school-age child who needs you on an intermittent and fleeting basis, or to an adolescent who only thinly veils his or her contempt and displeasure at your fussing and old-fashioned ways—and quite a different thing to be needed by the "girls" in the office, faculty colleagues, students, the foreman, the boss.

In work situations one is treated like an adult whose personal attributes are the basis for group acceptance and participation; at home one is mom, at the beck and call of dependents who only grudgingly perceive that mom is also a person in the same separate way that everyone is. Women who feel swallowed up by their families may have succumbed because they believed that their only worth was as the family mother. Such women may have tremendous difficulty letting children grow up and leave, and also may be unable to act like adults with their husbands.

On the other hand, women who seek out-of-home activities must continuously appease the nagging conscience that says they should be deriving all their fulfillment from their little family. The suburban nuclear family, cutting women off from a range of adults from whom they could obtain a sense of their identity and worth, is apt to be an unsatisfying arena for girls who have grown up within the fun and games intimacy of peers in school, college, and at work.

The sudden appearance of consciousness raising groups suggests that women are finding the home and family insufficient to meet their personal needs for affiliation or self-expression. The women who join these groups are lonely, unhappy about their view of themselves, and becoming aware that life promised more than it has delivered.[47]

To answer the question "Who needs groups?" one must reflect on the meaning that groups have for boys and girls, men and women. The pervasiveness of the team-athletic-adventure syndrome among males is hardly likely to be changed for some time to come. And young girls are not likely to be encouraged to "act like boys" in forming teams and engaging in adventurous forays. It would be a gross mistake to underestimate the critical importance of differences in group socialization to the development of sex-role differences between male and female. Young boys who look to their peers for personal validation, and young girls who look to parents and teachers for approval and legitimation grow up with rather different expectations of roles in relation to other adults.

Women are pressing to remove barriers for entry into previously all-male sanctuaries: after a long and acrimonious debate, the National Press Club of Washington, D.C. finally admitted women; all-male bars have been successfully integrated. The all-male educational honor fraternity, Phi Delta Kappa, finally succumbed to public opinion and legal pressures and changed its single-sex admission policy. The alternative was to relinquish university support. Now women are appearing aboard Navy vessels!

One can only speculate about the effects of new sexually integrated groups on the male need for peer validation. Will these mixed groups play as important a role in the social, personal, and professional life of men? Will new and different single-sex institutions arise to fulfill the needs developed by early socialization? Or will modification of the single-sex work group in turn influence childrearing practices?

◆   Summary

It is clear that boys and girls have quite different socializing experiences. In their relations with adults, groups, and peers, the two sexes travel very different paths. That much male group experience is negative or dysfunctional shows up clearly in the phenomenon of violent gangs; likewise, the lack of group experience and denial of affiliative needs among females appear to be socially hazardous. Research indicates that both men and women have strong affiliative needs, strong desires for group interaction, and strong dependence on group approval. Although it is generally accepted that women have greater affiliative needs than men, a closer look shows this to be untrue. Men do have very strong affiliative needs, and these needs are nurtured and fostered by gangs, team sports, social groups, and professional groups and associations. Although women supposedly have stronger needs, they do not have access to most of the important groups in our culture, they have little experience in team or group activities, and they are relegated to the small nuclear family for fulfillment of their needs for affiliation.

The power of the group to enforce conformity, to induce members to do things they do not want to do, is almost totally ignored by educators. Schools are planned as though groups and close friendships are unimportant, do not exist, or are dangerous and something to be eradicated. Group and friendship needs cannot be erased from the human psyche; both groups and friendships are essential to sane and whole survival for both males and females.

References

1.   Fritz Redl, "Adolescents—Just How Do They React?" in *Adolescence: Psychosocial Perspectives*, ed. Gerald Caplan and Serge Lebovici (New York: Basic Books, 1969), p. 96–97.

2.   *Ibid.*

3.   Jean D. Grambs and C. W. Hunnicutt, "Trends in the Organization of the Elementary School: Sociological Aspects," in *A Vision for Elementary School Administrators*, 24th Yearbook, California Elementary School

Administrators' Association, ed. Bernadine C. Wilson (Berkeley, Calif.: California Elementary School Administrators' Association, 1952), p. 18.

4.   Larry Cole, *Street Kids* (New York: Grossman, 1970).

5.   Willard W. Hartup, "Peer Interaction and Social Organization," in *Carmichael's Manual of Child Psychology*, ed. Paul H. Mussen, 3rd ed. (New York: John Wiley and Sons, Inc., 1970), p. 370.

6.   Gisela Konopka, *The Adolescent Girl in Conflict* (Englewood Cliffs, N.J.: Prentice Hall, Inc., 1966), p. 90.

7.   John MacNeil, "Programmed Instruction Versus Visual Classroom Procedures in Teaching Boys to Read," *American Educational Research Journal* 1 (March 1964): 113–120.

8.   Louise Tanney, Research paper, Department of Secondary Education, College of Education, University of Maryland.

9.   Jules Henry, *Culture Against Man* (New York: Random House, 1963), p. 276.

10. Edgar Friedenberg, *The Vanishing Adolescent* (Boston: Beacon Press, 1968), p. 28.

11. Gerald S. Kenyon, "Attitude Toward Sport and Physical Activity Among Adolescents from Four English Speaking Countries," in *The Cross-Cultural Analysis of Sports and Games*, ed. Gunther Luschen (Champaign, Ill.: Stipes Publishing Co., 1970), pp 138–155.

12. David B. Lynn, "Determinants of Intellectual Growth in Women," *School Review* 80 (February 1972): 241–260.

13. John P. Robinson, "Daily Participation in Sports Across Twelve Countries," in *The Cross-Cultural Analysis of Sports and Games*, ed. Gunther Luschen (Champaign, Ill.: Stipes Publishing Co., 1970), pp. 138–155.

14. Muzafer Sherif and Carolyn Sherif, *Reference Group* (New York: Harper and Row, 1964), p. 289.

15. Jackson Toby, "Violence and the Masculine Ideal: Some Qualitative Data," *Annals of American Academy of Political and Social Science* 364 (March 1966): 20–27; see also Maynard Erickson, "The Group Context of Delinquent Behavior," *Social Problems* (January 1971): 112–129.

16. Toby, *op. cit.*

17. L. W. Hoffman, "The Father's Role in the Family and the Child's Peer-Group Adjustment," *Merrill-Palmer Quarterly* 7 (1961): 97–105.

18. Elizabeth Douvan and Joseph Adelson, *The Adolescent Experience* (New York: John Wiley and Sons, 1966), p. 188.

19. *Ibid.*, p. 191.

20. James M. Coleman, *Adolescent Society* (New York: Free Press, 1961).

21. G. V. Ramsay, "The Sex Information of Younger Boys," *American Journey of Orthopsychiatry* 13 (1943): 15–19.

22. Mary Breasted, *Oh! Sex Education!* (New York: Praeger, 1970), pp. 304–305.

23. *Ibid.*
24. An extensive literature exists describing boy gangs; see, for example: Albert K. Cohen, *Delinquent Boys: The Culture of the Gang* (New York: Free Press, 1955); Clifford R. Shaw and Henry D. McKay, *Juvenile Delinquency in Urban Areas* (Chicago: University of Chicago Press, 1942); Frederick M. Thrasher, *The Gang*, rev. ed. (Chicago: University of Chicago Press, 1964); William W. Wattenberg, ed., *Social Deviancy Among Youth*, 65th Yearbook, National Society for the Study of Education (Chicago: University of Chicago Press, 1966); M. D. Buffalo and J. W. Rodgers, "Behavioral Norms, Moral Norms and Attachment: Problems of Deviancy and Conformity," *Social Problems* (Summer 1971): 101–113.
25. Lois W. Hoffman, "Childhood Experiences and Achievement," *Journal of Social Issues* 28 (1972): 129–156.
26. Douvan and Adelson, *op. cit.*, p. 195.
27. Lionel Tiger, *The Male Bond* (New York: Random House, 1969), pp. 198–199.
28. Douvan and Adelson, *op. cit.*, p. 194.
29. Sherif and Sherif, *op. cit.*, pp. 243–244.
30. *Ibid.*, p. 240.
31. Lamar T. Empey, "Delinquent Subcultures: Theory and Recent Research," *Journal of Research in Crime and Delinquency* 4 (January 1967): 32–42.
32. Walter B. Miller, "Violent Crime in City Gangs," *Annals of the American Academy of Political and Social Science* 343 (March 1966): 112.
33. *Ibid.*
34. Fran Taylor, "Athletic Politics," *The Second Wave* 2 (1972): 42–45.
35. Gloria Steinman, "The Myth of Masculine Mystique," *International Education* 1 (Spring 1972): 30–35, quoting the British anthropologist Geoffery Gorer.
36. Douvan and Adelson, *op. cit.*, p. 191.
37. Sherif and Sherif, *op. cit.*
38. Konopka, *op. cit.*, p. 97
39. *Ibid.*, p. 102. See also: Feminist Counseling Collective, "Feminist Psychotherapy: A New Method for Fighting for Social Control of Women," *American Journal of Orthopsychiatry* 44 (1974): 187–188.
40. Elliot Liebow, *Talley's Corner* (Boston: Little Brown, 1967).
41. W. C. Carrigan and J. W. Julian, "Sex and Birth Differences in Conformity as a Function of Need Affiliation Arousal," *Journal of Personality and Social Psychology* 3 (1966): 479–483. See also John D. Campbell, "Peer Relations in Childhood," in *Review of Child Development Research*, ed. M. L. Hoffman and L. W. Hoffman (New York: Russell Sage Foundation, 1964), p. 311.
42. Gerald S. Lesser and Robert P. Adelson, "Personality Correlates of

Persuasibility in Children," in *Personality and Persuasibility*, ed. Irving L. Janis *et al.* (New Haven: Yale University Press, 1959), p. 220.

43.   Hoffman, *op. cit.*

44.   Lesser and Adelson, *op. cit.*

45.   Hoffman, *op. cit.*

46.   *Ibid.*

47.   Catherine Breslin, "Waking Up From the Dream of Women's Lib," *New York Magazine*, February 1973, pp. 31–38. See also: Helena Z. Lopata, "The Effect of Schooling on Social Contacts of Urban Women," *American Journal of Sociology* 79 (1973): 604–619.

7

The Sex-Neutral School:

Ideology vs. Reality

The public school has been the American dream factory for generations. Once launched in first grade, sons of even the lowliest could aspire to be president—if not of the country at least of the local bank. Daughters would learn womanly graces, enjoy poetry and the arts, and dream of a happy and financially secure marriage.

The folk view of the school is essentially sexist. With very few exceptions, parents expect, and at crisis times even demand, that schools be quite clear about the fact that boys are boys and girls are girls. They expect the two sexes to be taught different sets of values and attitudes, to achieve mastery in different subjects, and to be socialized into sex-appropriate roles. Female teachers are seen as women first and teachers second; and male teachers are expected to personify male values in the school. Most teachers share parents' attitudes.

Why should this view of schools be any problem? It is patterned after the way society has been organized—males are assigned certain roles and females other roles. Shouldn't the schools reflect this division? Yet the American school system prides itself on its egalitarianism: "equal opportunity for all," and American educators do not admit to any sex bias in general school programs or policies. There are no boys or girls in the classroom—only students. No favors or prejudices are accorded any student (or teacher) on the basis of race, ethnic origin, religion, or sex. But these sex-neutral policies conflict with the realities of the American school system. Students are in fact treated differently on the basis of sex: girls are treated one way and

122

boys another. The schools, like most other institutions, prepare boys and girls for traditional sex roles.

In this chapter we will look at the ways in which the schools make sure that students learn not only their lessons, but also their sex roles. We will look at school practices that enforce behavior considered sex-appropriate. We will learn how schools make it difficult for boys and girls to grow up self-assured and socially adequate by confronting them with conflicting messages regarding what it is to be a good learner, and what it is to be a good male or female in our culture.

◆   **The Impact of School on Boys**

During the first grade, the boy is referred eleven times as often as a girl for social and emotional immaturity, a syndrome characterized by a high rate of absenteeism, fatigability, inability to attend and concentrate, shyness, poor motivation for work, underweight, inability to follow directions, slow learning, infantile speech patterns, and problems in the visual-motor and visual-perception areas. As a school child, he is referred to the school clinic for stuttering (four to one), reading difficulty (five to one), speech, hearing and eye problems (four to one), and eventually to the psychiatric clinic for personality disorders (2.6 to 1), behavior problems (4.4 to 1), school failure (2.6 to 1), and delinquency (4.5 to 1).[1]

Boys may enter school with verbal facility equal to that of girls, but once inside the classroom—lo and behold they are nonreaders![2] Recent studies indicate that the number of boys who read poorly or not at all exceeds the number of girls by ten to one.[3] Students who do not read well may not get promoted, and those who do not get promoted are more apt to become delinquent.[4] Boys are found below the expected grade level much more frequently than girls, and they are less likely to be found above the expected grade level.[5]

Although there is reason to believe that boys are as capable of achievement in elementary school as are girls,[6] there is evidence that teachers don't expect boys to do as well. This may very well create the "self-fulfilling prophecy effect" reported by Rosenthal and Jacobson.[7] It is generally agreed that a teacher's expectations will affect a child's performance. Efforts to manipulate teacher expectancy have shown instead the depth of teacher sex bias. When boys were described to a group of teachers as being superior learners, the teachers rejected this information and instead operated "on the basis of developed attitudes and knowledge about children and tests."[8] Another study found that teachers expecting boys to read well did in fact call forth better performance from boys than did teachers who felt that girls would be more successful.[9] Thus it seems that teacher expectations do influence student performance. It is interesting that the expectations of the school principal may also influence boys'—though not girls'—performance. In a recent experiment involving seventeen classrooms it was demonstrated that a male principal's comments which communicated positive expectations to boys on a first test in arithmetic were followed by improved performance on a second test.[10]

Since mastery of reading is so crucial to later school success, much attention has been given to the reading problems of small boys. Unfortunately, no clear solutions have been found. Some have speculated that women teachers are at fault, while others have concluded that small boys are just more interested in their peers than in the teacher and thus cannot isolate themselves enough to learn to read well. Maturational differences have been said to account for girls' superior achievement, but this superiority is almost entirely restricted to verbal activities; "boys are generally superior to girls in tasks involving numerical reasoning and spatial relationships."[11]

One researcher concluded, "In any case, the educational significance of these differences [in reading ability] does not appear to be exceedingly important—boys for the most part suffer no harm from the initial gap and eventually catch up."[12] Such a conclusion seems to ignore the accumulated data regarding the impact of this early defeat on a boy's self-concept and overall school achievement. In *Reading Rights for Boys* a strong case is made for reorienting many classroom practices in the early elementary school years to exploit male interests and behavioral patterns so that boys would have a better chance of learning to read well.[13] It seems there is a widespread impression that reading is a feminine activity, and "this classification has the effect of lessening boys' motivation to excel in reading."[14]

The American pattern of female superiority in verbal skills does not hold true elsewhere. In Germany, for example, girls had superior arithmetical skills and boys had higher reading skills. Thus the situation among German youngsters is opposite to the American situation. These data cast doubt on any assertion regarding the innate quality of differences in performance.[15] The differences between American and German youth suggest that the way school and culture respond to sex differences between boys and girls contributes to differences in reading performance.

American children report that everyone "knows" that boys are naughtier in school than girls. How do the children get this idea? From teachers, of course! Teachers give boys more attention than girls in elementary school classrooms—but the attention is punitive.[16] Teachers react to the physiological differences that make boys more wriggly by punishing them. And yet throughout their lives boys have been told that it is good to be as active as possible.

Mothers, fathers, and peers make it clear to boys long before they set foot inside a school that only sissies cry and run away from a fight. It is proper and right for a boy to get dirty, to battle for his position, to engage in physical activity whenever possible. But the teacher says that fighting is not nice, that physical activity is less preferred than quiet, sedentary, attentive behavior—things girls do. Although teachers expect passive, obedient, book-oriented behavior, any boy who does not engage in physical activity, who runs away from a fight, or who comes crying to the teacher for protection from persecutors is rejected by teachers and peers alike. How are boys to interpret these conflicting messages? Are boys in fact being told that to succeed in school they must behave like girls?

Fortunately, the secondary school provides some academic pursuits that are clearly identified as more appropriate for boys than girls. Thus, more boys than girls are enrolled in science and math courses, and the boys are expected to excel. Boys do achieve better than girls in many subjects—although their grades do not show this. One school system compared the achievement test scores received by boys and girls with the grades given them by teachers. Girls who received an A in chemistry achieved at the 86th percentile on the standardized test, while boys who earned an A were at the 92nd percentile. A girl achieving at the 64th percentile received a C grade, while a boy only a few percentile points lower would get a D. There was particular irony in the fact that the boys who earned D grades in chemistry in this school system were, according to national norms, scoring better than 61 percent of the boys in the country taking chemistry, while girls who received D grades were in the lowest third of the national group. In history, girls scoring in the 64th percentile received an A grade, but boys receiving A's were in the 84th percentile. Boys earning an A in English achieved at the 92nd percentile, while girls receiving an A scored only at the 76th percentile.[17]

The bias against boys in grading has been documented for over sixty years.[18] One result of such bias is that at almost any junior or senior high school the girls on honor rolls outnumber boys by at least three to one. At one large suburban high school in 1973, eighty-four students were inducted into the honor society—and only eight of them were boys.

Another result of the biased grading system is that in schools students are "tracked" in ability groups, primarily on the basis of teacher grades and teacher recommendations; boys are far more frequently found in the lower tracks, and more girls than boys are in the upper or "honors" tracks.[19]

It is small consolation to know that it is men who are elected president, win the Pulitzer and Nobel prizes, and hold the destiny of the world in their hands if you just happen to be one of the millions of boys whom the system has defeated so thoroughly that you not only cease to aspire, but resent those who have overcome the accumulated hazards of the system. The tremendous ambivalence regarding education which pervades so much of American life may well derive from these irrational educational policies. Is there another country in which society expects one kind of sex-appropriate behavior and the state-controlled educational system demands and rewards the antithesis?

While some might argue that teachers give white girls higher grades because they are presumed to be more orderly, quiet, and clean, the argument is refuted by research.[20] In a junior high school with black and white students, some of whom were advantaged and some disadvantaged, it was found that teachers consistently gave girls higher marks than boys. If school were not such a destiny-shaping institution, one could discount the grades given by teachers, but school is critically important as the gateway to adult achievement. The grading bias does a disservice to girls as well as boys. The boys may feel angry, cheated or stupid. The girls may gain a spurious sense of achievement, or may not know that the grade is phoney; either way they have been as poorly served by the system as have boys.

After receiving poor grades, a boy may be prevented from having access to advanced work. Boys receive assaults on their self-concept by being labeled slow, stupid, or dull. A not-too-able girl can survive in life by finding someone to marry her. A boy labeled stupid, whether he is or not, faces a future with the biggest cards stacked against him. It is astounding that parents and teachers permit such social and personal injustice. Is it that we expect men to have trouble in life, to become deviant, to suffer failure, that we educate them to make these things more likely to happen?

The data so far presented can be read as an indictment of institutionalized bias against boys on the part of the schools. Unfortunately, the school policies which cause the educational difficulties boys face are in fact supported by the public. In school, authority is to be upheld, rules are to be followed, the three R's are to be taught rigorously, and compliance, neatness, and promptness are to be rewarded. The fact that society portrays reading, neatness, and deference as feminine, and rewards boys for aggression, for standing up for their rights, for fighting if necessary, produces an inevitable collision. We can view this situation with alarm, but more importantly we can do something about it. School policies must be reviewed and revised when they cause unnecessary personal as well as educational difficulties for many students. That these difficulties arise from sex-role stereotypes must be brought to the awareness of all policy-makers.

In one sense, those who set some policies are well aware of the schools' bias against boys. For instance, college admissions officers have had to align admissions policies in accordance with boys' lower grade averages. Because of their lower grades, boys occupy the lower ranks when class standing is computed.[21] When the University of California at Berkeley sought to limit freshman enrollment to the very top students in the state, it was found that the cut-off rank for eligibility for entrance had to be lowered from the top 10 percent to the top 15 percent in order to provide a large enough pool of eligible boys.[22] In fact, admissions officers at many colleges acknowledge that if students were admitted solely on the basis of grades, test scores, class standing, and teacher recommendations, girls would be admitted in a much higher ratio than boys. Women have begun to ask for more rigorous application of equal standards to admissions policies, and we predict that this will have very significant consequences for school grades. In fact, we might predict that one effect of the women's demands for equal educational opportunity will be to reduce the bias against boys in precollege schooling!

This dismal picture of an institution thoroughly biased against boys is alleviated somewhat by the opportunity school gives boys to achieve in sports. Making the team is important in college and high school, but it is especially crucial in the junior high school years. These are the years when the adolescent reshapes his view of himself even as his body takes on new dimensions. How lucky the boy who matures early! If he is 6 feet tall by seventh or eighth grade, and has better than minimal coordination and modest ambition, he can make the basketball team. Most of his classmates are 10 to 12 inches shorter. Many of them will catch up in later grades; but so critical is the role of height in the life of a boy that his future may well rest on what nature provided him in seventh or eighth grade.

The early maturing boy is viewed by himself and others as more competent.[23] As a result he becomes more competent. If, along with height, there is adequate muscle development and weight, he can look forward to a competitive advantage in team sports. But he is out of phase, and out of the ball game, if he grows too tall too early. The physically deviant boy who reaches adult height too fast or too slowly has several alternatives: he can withdraw psychologically or literally, he can find approval from his peers by outrageous or dangerous behavior, or he can excel in his studies. If he is lucky, if he is ambitious, if he is bright, and if someone (parent, teacher, group leader, older relative) encourages him, then he may go further and achieve more than his classmates. The luckiest boy, however, is the one who grows to a satisfactory height at the right time, and who is also intellectually able. Boys and girls agree that the good athlete who is not too studious, but makes fairly good grades, is the "best" kind of person. For boys, athletic skills are consistently more valued than academic skills. A brilliant nonstudious boy is preferred over a brilliant studious one, and a nonstudious, nonathletic boy is preferred over a studious boy who is not athletic![24]

In the famous longitudinal study of genius done by Terman and associates it was found that despite a stereotype of the sickly, retiring, frail genius, unusually bright boys were "taller, heavier, more broad-shouldered, stronger in hand grip, larger in the vital capacity of their lungs, and somewhat earlier in their sexual maturity than children in the general population."[25] Could it be that Terman's bright boys were just more visible and therefore received early recognition which stimulated them to greater achievement so that they were more able to be bright than those not so recognized and encouraged? Many late-maturing boys with mediocre high school records achieve good grades in college, for they are competing in intellectual areas where physique is not so important.[26]

Athletic achievement has been an important path of upward mobility for poor white males, and currently for increasing numbers of poor black males. While the emphasis on sports may work to the detriment of boys who are not athletically endowed, it is a very significant area of achievement in school life that is open to boys *only*. Nothing girls do in high school can compare with being on the varsity team and winning the local league championship.[27] Such sweet success is, in fact, so exalting that it may be the peak experience for some boys, after which nothing can compare. Arthur Miller's *Death of a Salesman* and Jason Miller's *That Championship Season* dramatize the corroding impact of such success, too soon and too much.

Boys have a near monopoly on school leadership roles—student body president, editor of the newspaper or yearbook, band leader. Girls may compete for these positions, but it's boys who get elected or selected. However, teacher bias against boys in grading and in applying school rules prevents many boys from participating. Most secondary schools require students to attain a certain grade point average to be eligible to represent the school in clubs, teams, school papers, or elected office. Many boys are disenfranchised by such a system.

The sex-neutral school is a myth. It would almost seem, if one were to take an extreme position, that the public school is set up to make education as difficult as possible for boys, while it pampers and indulges girls. But as girls see it, school offers convincing evidence that it is indeed a man's world. Whose view is accurate?

◆   The Impact of School on Girls

From the earliest grades, most girls do better than boys in school. This may be due partly to teacher bias in grading. But as we have seen girls are socialized to be dependent, obedient, attentive, and careful. This socialization makes them good students and eager learners. However, by adolescence girls have learned that they should not be too smart, should not seek achievement, and should not be competitive.[28] The adolescent girl who is an outstanding student feels selfconscious and embarrassed. One such girl later wrote:

. . . there was a price for succeeding, or rather a double price. Doing well set one off as a "brain," winning respect but not the acceptance one craved. Moreover, it pressured one to compete with one's previous record. . . .

. . . girls were supposed *not* to do what the school prepared them to do, although they were subjected to a very similar education, minus some math and science, and an identical set of values. . . . [For girls] only the achievement of marrying well was completely sanctioned. . . . I am not sure that this situation was a source of conflict for many of my school contemporaries, but it was for me, not because I put less value on marriage—it was the only thing I was sure I wanted—but because I placed a value on school that they in many cases did not.[29]

The competitive climate of the school seems to do a great deal more for boys than girls. Competition makes boys feel more secure about themselves, but girls react with insecurity and a sense of their lack of worth.[30] Studies show there is some relationship between adequacy of a child's self-concept and his achievement; but while this is clearly true for boys it is much less so for girls, particularly at the high school level.[31]

Although boys may resent the school success of girls, most girls are not even aware that they are successful. Asked if they were in the upper quarter of their class, only 14 percent of a group of girls thought they were so placed, when in actuality 36 percent of them were; a very small percentage of boys underestimated their academic standing.[32] A girl who does well in high school is expected to appear surprised: "Gosh I didn't expect an A, I hardly did any work at all," or "I just needed the A for college—I'm not really all that smart," or "Teachers are just prejudiced against boys and that's the only reason stupid little me got an A." A very able girl may be sufficiently adroit to do mediocre work deliberately so as not to appear smarter than boys.[33]

Girls learn that one thing society does *not* reward is smart females. Such learning starts almost in the crib. A study of normal preschool children showed that behavior and IQ and parental discipline result in different correlations for boys and girls. "From an early age, a boy's place in the world is tied to his cognitive abilities, while a girl's value to her parents and herself is enhanced by quite a different set of skills. Indeed, high IQ in a girl may make it more difficult for her to assume her expected passive, conforming role."[34] These researchers are referring to *preschoolers*. If girls are socialized at an early age to consider being smart an undesirable trait, girls who are actually retarded in intellectual development are apt to be overlooked. A study of admissions patterns to mental retardation treatment centers showed a marked sex differential which, in the opinion of the researchers, "suggests that a lower level of sensitivity toward females exists and that many females who might benefit from treatment are not identified."[35]

One experimenter placed junior high boys and girls together in small groups to solve science problems, and observed them as they went about their tasks. Afterwards, the students were asked who contributed most to the solution of the problems. Both boys and girls replied that the boys had; observers noted that in fact the girls provided most of the help solving the problems.[36] Neither boys nor girls recognized the girls' contribution. Boys *do* science; girls *learn* it. How early in school do girls acquire the idea that science is not for them? Does the elementary teacher, in assigning classroom chores, see to it that the girls take care of the "housekeeping corner" while the boys have the "science corner?"

The social etiquette of "ladies first", is inculcated in the early grades. It is standard procedure for classes to line up at the door to go out to recess or the lunchroom; there are separate lines for boys and girls, and of course the girls are allowed out first. Heavy chores are assigned to boys, even when the girls are heavier and more mature. The idea of female fragility is reinforced throughout the school years. The less vigorous sports program for girls is defended because girls are "weaker." By the time they are adolescents, girls are convinced they "need to be taken care of."

Physiological differences during the growth years are of critical importance to girls as well as boys. Prior to the appearance of Lolita and Raquel Welch, the girl whose breasts matured earlier than her peers' hunched over miserably, or bound herself tightly so that she too would look flat. No more! The American breast fetish reaches even into preadolescence—now mothers can buy training bras for their daughters as a kind of psychological assurance of future development.[37] The early maturing girl who grows tall and skinny instead of bosomy will only be pitied, but even with well-developed curves a girl who is too tall is doomed to a desperate wait for a boy who is tall enough if she is to have any dates during her school years. One of the outspoken leaders of the women's movement, Germaine Greer, reports her own school experience: "I was a freak! At six feet, I was too tall for normal sexual relationships. I didn't dance at all. Being six feet tall, it was impossible for me to dance with my head tucked under some boy's chin like a good little girl is supposed to." After several disastrous encounters with older men, the impressionable and unhappy sixteen-year old, " . . . eschewed all dates and decided to concentrate on getting a scholarship to the university instead."[38]

Coeducation places girls and boys together in junior high school, and the early maturing girl towers over the late maturing boy. Through the self-conscious years of adolescence, while critical ideas of self-worth are developed, boys and girls are processed by the school as though none of these things mattered. All the seventh graders move together; likewise all the eighth graders proceed *en masse.* The existence of differences, particularly physiological ones, are not taken into account, because the school is sex-neutral and cannot recognize such differences. Fortunately, the physical discrepancies average out for most boys and girls in high school, when the late maturing boys catch up with the earlier maturing girls. The business of dating and mating is then taken up in earnest. With dating comes greater scrutiny of who is cool and who is not with it. Social class, race, and religion are the most significant factors in determining who is dating material.

Sex-role stereotyping determines which subjects a girl is permitted to excel in. Courses are sex labeled. Although most schools do not say that business-typing and other business courses are for girls, very few boys turn up for such courses. When boys are enrolled in typing classes, they feel less able, clumsy, and out of place.[39] There is research regarding the role of school counselors in "tracking" boys and girls into sex-appropriate courses in high school, and the enrollment figures for these courses seem to reflect accepted policy. Traditionally, girls have been excluded from such courses as auto mechanics and electronic shop, just as boys have been excluded from home economics.

That such sex-segregation in courses is outmoded as well as illegal is now being recognized by school authorities. One sign of changing times is the policy adopted by the Pennsylvania Department of Education eliminating all sex-segregated and sex-stereotyped classes that had not received departmental approval. The policy states that there shall be "affirmative actions . . . taken immediately to achieve equal opportunities for boys and girls in all aspects of the educational program."[40] Equal sports equipment and facilities will be provided for both sexes, girls may enter team sports, boy and girl teams will be integrated if feasible, and students of both sexes will be recruited for previously sex-stereotyped or segregated activities. It will be interesting to see how many school systems follow this lead.

Intellectual discrimination against women is well expressed in the following verse:

> "There, little girl, don't read
> You're fond of your books, I know
> But Brother might mope
> If he had no hope
> Of getting ahead of you.
> It's dull for a boy who cannot lead
> There, little girl, don't read.[41]

That advice was written by Alice Duer Miller in 1915.

Encouragement to go to college is consistently provided to able boys of whatever social class, and particularly to those in the middle and upper socioeconomic strata. Bright girls are not discouraged, but if they fail to go on to higher education it is not considered a major disaster. A girl at the low end of the social scale is less likely to go to college than a boy, no matter how smart she may be.[42]

To what extent does women's liberation effect what girls do in school today? There is little evidence that the average high school girl is aware of shifting social expectancies. The younger teachers who might bring a new view are finding fewer openings in the schools, and older teachers are unlikely to provide new models for youth. The future confronting today's girl seems particularly challenging. Once out of the protection of the provincial high school, the youngster who goes on to college will find new views of appropriate behavior for young men and women. The confusion of values and commitments may well shake the very basis of their identities. Girls will learn that their future is not wholly defined by the man they marry, and boys will be jolted by a new feminism which is competitive, assertive, and intellectually challenging. It is tragic that the public schools so badly prepare our youth for the adult roles that await them. They have failed to prepare youth not only for traditional roles but also for any new definition of what is possible for men and women.

Books and Sex Bias

Reading is a complex act. Although children learn the grammar of their language and develop a large vocabulary with seeming ease in the early years of life, the step into effective reading is a major one.

The building of reading skills is a long process, with mastery at advanced levels achieved by relatively few in the population. The schools' emphasis on the *skill* of reading has obscured the importance of the content of reading. It is implied that reading materials designed to develop reading skills have no significant content, and that values are not transmitted when such elementary materials are read.

Unfortunately, this naive view is shared by many educators and most of the public. Only when the matter touches personal concerns does anyone raise a question about the values conveyed by reading materials. A careful look at primary and early readers as well as at picture books reveals that they are heavily loaded with values, and that they transmit very clear messages about the world, about who people are, what they do, and what is "good" and "bad" about people.

The fact that children's books show men and women in stereotyped roles is so obvious that until recently it was ignored. In fact, books were expected to reinforce cultural values regarding appropriate sex-role behavior. The heavy preachments of the McGuffey readers about good boys and girls was strongly approved by nineteenth century Americans.[43] The message became muted in the early twentieth century, and by the 1950s texts and readers were expected to be neutral, to be in fact a value-free medium of skill learning. But anyone who looks at a book knows that merely by putting three words in a sentence you create a value statement. Which three words? Whose three words? Not only the text but also the illustrations in children's books are heavy with content: as one student commented after examining children's trade books, "Why, even the lady pigs wear aprons!"

Serious studies of book contents have been going on for some years. In 1946 Child and associates published a careful analysis of children's textbooks that clearly identified the different roles portrayed for boys and girls.[44] Girls were passive; boys active. Girls showed greater affiliation needs; boys attempted to solve problems. Female characters were portrayed as "sociable, kind, and timid . . . inactive, unambitious, and uncreative." In 1954, Tannenbaum called attention to the sexist and racist sterotypes in all-white Textbook Town. In the last few years there have been a number of studies of text and trade books published for children. Both text and illustrations have been found to be grossly sex-biased.[45] These studies demonstrate that many more books are directed toward boys than girls, and that while boys are shown doing things, girls are shown watching them. Mothers do housework and girls help them. In Textbook Town children are born but mothers are never pregnant; fathers come home from work carrying a briefcase; and tragedy is the death of a dog.[46]

In stories for preschool children teachers are stereotyped; most of them are female, young, single, and white, and nicely dressed. "Overall, the image of the dumpy, old battleax is missing."[47] If a man appears in these stories he is the principal, the bus driver, or an adjunct person such as school doctor; the men appear older and more mature than the female professionals. The sex-role stereotype and bias "educates" children about school and teachers even before they encounter them.

Parents who might think that sex stereotypes are limited to books for classrooms or children's libraries will find that comic books are no better.[48] Comic books read by students at the elementary, junior high, and senior high levels were examined. Male figures appeared almost three times as often as female figures. Only in the teenage category was there a comic book with more drawings of female than male characters, but here the female was a love-struck girl waiting for her hero. Another significant finding was that the correlation between acts of violence and females was minus .59. Females were rarely if ever present at acts of violence. In contrast, male characters were aggressive, violent, and death dealing. But such is the stuff of heroes.

A study of American history textbooks found that most women are omitted from texts. Little weight is given to the cultural and social restrictions women have faced. Even in the reform movements in which women participate, male leaders are quoted. After analyzing the textbooks' treatment of women in American history, one author summarized their approach thus:

Woman arrived in 1619. They held the Seneca Falls Convention on Women's Rights in 1848. During the rest of the nineteenth century, they participated in reform movements, chiefly temperance, and were exploited in factories. In 1923 they were given the vote. They joined the armed forces for the first time during the second World War and thereafter have enjoyed the good life in America. Add the names of the women who are invariably mentioned: Harriet Beecher Stowe, Jane Adams, Dorothea Dix, and Frances Perkins, with perhaps Susan B. Anthony, Elizabeth Cady Stanton and almost as frequently, Carry Nation, and you have the basic "text" . . . a pattern which presents the stereotyped picture of the American Woman—passive, incapable of sustained organization or work, satisfied with her role in society, and well supplied with material blessings.[49]

One female historian remarked, "Many of my colleagues think women's history is an unimportant exotic specialty. . . . Women are generally not reflected in history because they've not been in the places where what we call 'historically significant' things take place," but "Maybe wars and politics are not the only important things in history."[50]

In order to make amends, one United States history textbook offered the following explanation under the title "History as Fable":

. . . consider the myth that men make history while women wash the dishes. History books have so consistently left half the human race out of account that Henry Adams remarked, "History is useful to the historian by teaching him his ignorance of woman."

The very word "pioneer" conjures up the picture of a man in coonskin cap and leather jacket armed with a rifle. But as you trace the march of the frontier from the Appalachians to the Pacific, remember that there were women pioneers too. Left to himself, the man on the frontier often went savage—witness his treatment of the Indians. It was the women who turned cabins into homesteads, planted flowers outside the doors, and put curtains in the windows. It was usually the mothers and schoolteachers who transmitted to the next generation the heritage of the past.[51]

There is a current and belated effort to find heroines for girls. Books are appearing for all age levels telling the stories of women who have achieved. Eleanor Roosevelt, Florence Nightingale, Queen Elizabeth I, Louisa May Alcott, Mary Mcleod Bethune. . . . How many more? Some famous women are viewed with alarm by conservatives: look at what George Eliot did. Lived with a married man for years, and even wrote under a man's name. And George Sand, who was notorious for her flamboyant affairs. Or Isadora Duncan, who brought new freedom to the dance and to the kind of life women might live. Or Gertrude Stein, whose influence on the writers and painters of her era was profound. How many young women know the searing stories of Margaret Sanger or Dorothea Dix? Emma Goldman, Sojourner Truth, Rosa Luxembourg? Helen Keller, that gentle saint whose life is brought forth as a model for women and the handicapped—neither girls nor boys are told of her passionate fight against the evil labor practices of her day. Who ever heard that she wrote: "We can't have education without revolution. We have tried peace education for one thousand years. . . . Let us try revolution and see what it will do now."[52]

Sex bias in instructional materials and library books was officially recognized in the report *Sexism in Education*, prepared by a task force of the Pennsylvania Department of Education. They found that in the social studies area there were significant weaknesses: "... under-representation of women; representation in limited stereotyped roles— wives, mothers, teachers, nurses, secretaries, and other service-oriented jobs; reinforcement of culturally conditioned sexist characteristics shown as *female*—such traits as dependency, passivity, non-competitive spirit and emotionality; and a very meager appreciation of women's contributions to history, literature, science and other areas of American life."[53]

Guidelines to help authors of social studies textbooks avoid stereotyping were prepared by Burr, Dunn, and Farquhar.[54] Besides commenting on historical omissions, they pointed out that ideas and opinions are typically attributed to men, not women. For example: "Foresighted men saw the need for. . . ." "Men from the north regarded slavery as. . . ." The fragile woman-housewife stereotype should be abandoned. Terminology is especially subject to bias. In many instances the hypothetical person is male; it is recommended that the terms *one* or *person* be substituted. Females are referred to as wives or mothers of important people, rather than called by their own names. There is objection to terminology denoting that an occupation is best suited to men: airman, cameraman, repairman, watchman. Perusing this carefully formulated guide, one is impressed by the extent to which language reflects sex-stereotyped roles.[55] Imaginative teachers could utilize Kotzin's suggestions for studying the mass media for sex bias.[56]

The reading lag boys experience early in their schooling has been attributed in part to the kinds of books available to them. Studies of the reading interests of boys and girls have shown that their interests differ, and that girls will read boy-type material but boys will not read girl-type material. One such study by Byers concludes with the comment that " . . . content should be assessed for its appeal to boys. . ." Boys' interests in outdoor activities such as fishing, vacations and excursions, swimming, horseback riding, and bicycle riding are seldom reflected in first grade readers; nor is there much content dealing with joint activities of father and son.[57] To care for boys' needs in reading, it is suggested that "educators must not shift their positions to the extent that girls' interests are subordinated in the process. One would be well advised to consider, however, that many girls are equally at home in both masculine and feminine environments."[58] Boys, however, are expected to find their needs met only in masculine settings.

The women's movement has stimulated many studies of sex bias in books and its effect on girls. There is no comparable body of analysis regarding the impact of the male stereotype on boys. It has been seen that males are associated with violence, as in comic books, and boys are presented as the doers and makers, the explorers of mystery caves and haunted houses. Boys also read about the great military heroes, from Alexander the Great, through Julius Caesar, Napoleon, George Washington, Grant and Lee, Patton and Eisenhower, to MacArthur. There are the political giants: Henry the VIII, Peter the Great, Louis XIV, Metternich, Thomas Jefferson, Abraham Lincoln, Disraeli, Winston Churchill, Hitler, Franklin Roosevelt. The great money-makers: Carnegie, Rockefeller, Stanford. And the great criminals: Capone, Baby-Faced Nelson, Jesse James. We could study every human endeavor—and locate the men who have made their mark. What a challenge to the young boy! And what a responsibility. A boy learns that *he must achieve.* All the books he reads tell him this. He must have courage, be brave and dependable, support the weak (female), be clever and skillful—the list is frightening. Courage and other positive attributes are accompanied by violence, killing, destruction, death. It is the men who die in battle; who kill not only as hunters but as armed opponents. There is need to examine the literature of instruction to assess the role expectations that are impressed upon boys, which in their way may be as damaging as the stereotypes presented to girls.

Rules, Roles, and Rebellion

The organizational structure of the American school is an accident hardened into tradition. The grade structure based on chronological age cannot be defended by anything known about growth differences among children. The primary victims of an inappropriate school structure are of course our boys and girls. The authoritarian hierarchical organization of the school induces "natural" resistance from boys. A real boy is trained by father, mother, and peers "not to take nothin' from nobody." The American ethos enshrines initiative and independence and questioning of authority as major virtues in men.[59] A boy who challenges authority, whether it be that of the cop on the beat or the teacher in the classroom, wins the plaudits of his peers. But nothing infuriates a teacher more than a boy who talks back, is sassy, or shows contempt for school rules.

As schools have grown larger, rules have proliferated. To the average boy, rules are made to be tested and if possible bent or broken. Teachers, counselors, and administrators report more trouble with boys than girls. Not unexpectedly, boys report more trouble with the system. Boys are far more apt to be suspended or expelled from school than girls. Boys get into fights and are more likely to be physically disruptive in school. And boys challenge the system. They are the editors of underground newspapers; they lead peace strikes and sit-ins; they confront administrators with group demands. Girls follow. A careful study of boy dropouts showed that those who were going to leave school before graduation from high school had demonstrated in the early elementary grades their dissatisfaction with the system, and their conflict with authority.[60] Girl dropouts, on the contrary, had no such predictable behavior. The causes behind their dropout lay not in dissatisfaction with the system, but rather in social and personal relationships outside of school.

School authorities are outraged by the way boys flout school regulations. Once it was pants that were too tight, then pants worn too low, then pants worn without belts, then hair that was too long, then beards, then . . . . The 1960s could be characterized as the decade of hirsutism. The intense reaction to hair on boys and, incidentally, on men teachers, called forth many a confrontation.[61] Why are hairy boys so menacing, such a threat to law and order, to peace and intellectual activities? The real cause of the intense reaction probably lies in the fact that long hair is a challenge to old bulls from young bulls; for hair is above all a symbol of virility.

There are so many unreasonable rules and regulations governing mass education: students must have passes to hall lockers, permission to go to the bathroom (an eighteen-year-old has to ask?), permission to phone home, excuses from parents for tardiness or absence. Not to mention the hassling of students through boring classes in huge schools where intermission between classes is cut to the barest minimum and lunchrooms are hazards to physical and mental health. Not surprisingly students, specifically boys, have objected to the proliferation of rules. The militance of college youth has been seized by high school boys who have discovered that a few determined people can close down the whole operation.

The initiative required to close down a school, to go out on strike, to develop and print an underground newspaper, to stage a sit-in, to boycott a school cafeteria, is in the spirit of the American frontier. Most fathers and mothers are appalled and frightened when it is *their* son in the thick of this kind of outrage against authority. Yet what parent does not also comment admiringly, "I must say, that took a lot of gumption." Gumption is a valued trait for American males.

The confusion among youth is understandable. Is it good to obey? Or good to challenge? Am I a sissy because I did not go out on strike with the others? Am I a traitor because I did not uphold law and order?

Research has found that the leaders of campus rebellions were those whose parents were most idealistic.[62] The system is rough on those who dare express either their parents' idealism or their own brand of American gumption: they are suspended or expelled from school. A suspension or expulsion is forever engraved on the school dossier, for the FBI to find years later. The organization of the school creates an atmosphere that challenges boys to test the system, and then the same school will punish boys for demonstrating the very aggressiveness which in America is traditionally associated with masculinity. How can boys be anything but losers?[63]

The schools neglect to assess the impact of structure of methodology on the productivity of youngsters. There are very few studies which show how school *programs* affect creativity, for example. Classroom and school climate can influence boys and girls, as one study demonstrated. An elementary school that instructed children in a traditional fashion with clear-cut expectations enunciated by teachers produced a greater sense of challenge and satisfaction among boys; an elementary school which was progressive in its orientation, allowing and encouraging different kinds of behavior, produced a higher level of expressiveness in girls.[64] There is little question that certain teaching methods encourage divergent or creative thinking, whereas other methods induce convergent and conforming thinking. It seems that some boys respond better to a structured situation against which they must test their mettle, and that some girls respond better when there is more ambiguity and freedom. Our great number of male poets, novelists, composers, inventors, and political leaders are the products of traditional schooling. We do not now know what latent talents in girls are systematically suppressed by the school, but we suspect there are many.

◆   Summary

Is there such a thing as a nonsexist school? The evidence so far shows a consistent sex bias which favors boys for some activities and girls for others, and distributes punishment on a sex related basis. We probably will never know the true potential of our children until students are seen as persons, as well as male and female.

        The revolution in school practices necessary for truly nonsexist schooling is probably far in the future. Ingrained notions of what is right for boys and what is right for girls must be modified; many old policies and old leaders must pass from the scene. And many parents, fearful of change, must be helped to see that nonsexist education is more beneficial for boys and girls than the present practices which punish boys for being boys and deflect and demean the talents of girls.

References

1.   E. James Anthony, "The Behavior Disorders of Childhood," in *Char-michael's Manual of Child Psychology*, ed. Paul H. Mussen (New York: John Wiley & Sons, 1970), p. 722 (see also p. 782).

2.   J. D. McNeil, "Programmed Instruction Procedure in Teaching Boys to Read," *American Educational Research Journal* 2 (1964): 113–119.

3.   *Phi Delta Kappan* (April 1971), p. 502.

4.   Sheldon Glueck and Eleanor T. Glueck, *One Thousand Juvenile Delinquents* (Cambridge: Harvard University Press, 1934).

5.   White House Conference on Children, *Profiles of Children*, Chart 124, (Washington, D.C.: U.S. Government Printing Office, 1970), p. 72.

6.   Kenneth M. Parsley, Jr. and Marvin Powell, "Achievement Gains or Losses During the Academic Year and Over the Summer Vacation Period: A Study of Trends in Achievement by Sex and Grade Level Among Students of Average Intelligence," *Genetic Psychological Monographs* 66 (1962): 285–342.

7.   Robert Rosenthal and Lenore Jacobson, *Pygmalion in the Classroom* (New York: Holt, Rinehart & Winston, 1968).

8.   Elyse S. Fleming and Ralph G. Anttonen, "Teacher Expectancy and My Fair Lady," *American Educational Research Journal* 8 (March 1971): 241–252; see also Fleming and Anttonen, "Teacher Expectancy as Related to the Academic and Personal Growth of Primary-Age Children," *Monograph of the Society for Research in Child Development* 36 (1971): 1–32.

9.   J. Michael Palardy, "What Teachers Believe, What Children Achieve," *The Elementary School Journal* 69 (1969): 370–374.

10. Doris R. Entwistle, Evart Cornell, and Joyce Epstein, "Effect of a Principal's Expectations on Test Performance of Elementary-School Children," *Psychological Reports* 31 (1972): 551–556.

11. Thomas L. Good and Jere F. Brody, "Do Boys and Girls Receive Equal Opportunity in First Grade Reading?" Series No. 24 (Austin, Texas: Research and Development Center for Teacher Education, 1969). Carol A. Dwyer, "Sex Differences in Reading: An Evaluation and Critique," *Review of Educational Research* 43 (1973): 455–467.

12. Good and Brody, *op. cit.*

13. David Austin, Velma Clark, and Gladys Fitchett, *Reading Rights for Boys: Sex Role in Language Experience* (New York: Appleton-Century-Crofts, 1971).

14. Dwyer, *op. cit.*

15. Ralph C. Preston, "Reversals in Reading and Writing Among German and American Children," *Elementary School Journal* 57 (March, 1957): 330–334.

16. Pauline S. Sears and David H. Feldman, "Teacher Interactions with Boys and Girls," *National Elementary Principal* 46 (November 1966): 30–35.

17. Fairfax County, Virginia, Public Schools, Department of Instruction, Office of Psychological Services, "A Study of the Relations Between Grades and Standardized Tests, July 1970," Unpublished report; see also: Mary C. Winkler, "High School Ability Patterns: A Backward Look," *Journal of National Association of Women Deans and Counselors* 29 (Summer 1966): 177–179; David C. Lavin, "Sex Differences in Academic Performance," *The Prediction of Academic Performance* (New York: Russell Sage Foundation, 1965), pp. 128–131; 135.

18. Leonard P. Ayres, *Laggards in Our Schools* (New York: Russell Sage Foundation, 1909); see also C. H. Judd, *Measuring the Work of the Public Schools* (Cleveland, Ohio: Survey Committee of the Cleveland Foundation, 1916).

19. Phyllis R. Arvest and Ronald L. Mittall, "The Effects of a Teaching System on Student Satisfaction and Achievement," *American Educational Research Journal* 7 (May 1971): 511–520. See also: Walter E. Schafer and Carol Oleya, *Tracking and Opportunity* (Scranton: Chandler Publishing Company, 1971)

20. Boyd R. McCandless, Albert Roberts, and Thomas Starnes, "Teachers' Marks, Achievement Test Scores, and Aptitude Relations With Respect to Social Class, Race, and Sex," *Journal of Educational Psychology* 63, No. 2 (1972): 153–159.

21. Denise B. Kandel, "Race, Maternal Authority, and Adolescent Aspiration," *American Journal of Sociology* 76 (May 1971): 999–1020; see also Patricia Sexton, *The Feminized Male* (New York: Random House, 1969), pp. 62–66.

22. Dorothy M. Knoell, "Inter-Institutional Studies Leading to Changes in

Freshmen Admission Requirements," mimeographed (Sacramento, California: State Department of Education, 1961).

23. William W. Hartup, "Peer Interaction and Social Organization," in *Manual of Child Psychology*, ed. Paul Mussen, 3rd ed. (New York: John Wiley & Sons, 1971), pp. 394-395.

24. Gudelia A. Fox, *Attitudes of Prospective Teachers Toward Student Characteristics* (DeKalb: Northern Illinois University, 1968); Abraham J. Tannenbaum, *Adolescent Attitudes Toward Academic Brilliance* (New York: Teachers College Press, 1962); James S. Coleman, *The Adolescent Society* (New York: Free Press, 1961).

25. Richard Herrnstein, "I.Q.," *Atlantic Monthly*, September 1971, p. 52.

26. Victor G. Cicirelli, "Sibling Constellation, Creativity, I.Q. and Academic Achievement," *Child Development* 38 (June 1967): 481-490.

27. Sexton, *op. cit.*, pp. 115-132.

28. An excellent summary of findings of sex discrimination against girls in school is: *A Look at Women in Education: Issues and Answers for HEW*, a Report of the Commissioner's Task Force on the Impact of Office of Education Programs for Women, mimeographed (Washington, D.C., HEW, Office of Education, November 1972).

29. Phyllis LaFarge, "An Uptight Adolescence," *Daedalus* 100 (Fall 1971): 1172-1173.

30. Emmy A. Bepitone, "Comparison Behavior in Elementary School Children," *American Educational Research Journal* (Winter 1972): 45-63.

31. Wilbur B. Brookover, Shailor Thomas, and Ann Paterson, "Self-Concept of Ability and School Achievement," *Sociology of Education* 37 (Spring 1964): 271-278.

32. Kandel, *op. cit.*

33. James S. Coleman, *Adolescents and the Schools* (New York: Basic Books, 1965).

34. Diana Baumrind and Allen E. Black, "Socialization Practices Associated with Dimensions of Competence in Preschool Boys and Girls," *Child Development* 38 (1967): 291-327.

35. Benjamin D. Singer and Richard W. Osborn, "Social Class and Sex Differences in Admission Patterns of the Mentally Retarded," *Journal of Mental Deficiency* 75 (1970): 160-162.

36. E. Paul Torrance, "Developing Women's Natural Gifts," *Women's Education* 4 (March, 1965): 1-4.

37. Grace Hechinger and Fred M. Hechinger, *Teenage Tyranny* (New York: Wm. Morrow & Co., 1963).

38. Claudia Dreifus, "Freeing Women's Sexuality: An Interview with Germaine Greer," *Evergreen* 15 (October 1971): 25-27+.

39. Martha Mead, unpublished research study, University of Maryland, College of Education, 1971.

40. Joseph F. Bard, ed., *Sexism in Education: Joint Task Force* (Harrisburg: Pennsylvania Department of Education, 1972).
41. *Ibid.*, p. 10.
42. William H. Sewell, V. P. Shaw, "Socio-Economic Status, Intelligence and the Attainment of Higher Education," *Sociology of Education* 40 (Winter 1967): 1–23; see also C. E. Werts, "Sex Differences and College Attendance," *National Merit Scholarship Corporation Research Reports* 2 (1966): 1–11.
43. Richard D. Mosier, *Making the American Mind: Social and Moral Ideals in the McGuffey Readers* (New York: King's Crown Press, Columbia University, 1947); see also Ruth M. Elson, *Guardians of Tradition: American School Books of the Nineteenth Century* (Lincoln: University of Nebraska Press, 1964).
44. Irvin L. Child *et al.*, "Children's Textbooks and Personality Development: An Exploration in the Social Psychology of Education," *Psychological Monographs* 60 (1946): 1–53.
45. Aileen P. Nilson, "Women in Children's Literature," in *Women in English Departments*, ed. Susan McAllister (Urbana, Illinois: National Council of Teachers of English, 1971), p. 72–80; Marjorie B. U'Ren, "The Image of Woman in Textbooks," in *Women in Sexist Society*, ed. Vivian Gornick and Barbara K. Moran (New York: Basic Books, 1971); Lenore J. Weitzman *et al.*, "Sex-Role Socialization in Picture Books for Preschool Children," *American Journal of Sociology* 77 (May 1970): 1125–1150; Janice M. Pottker, "Female Stereotypes in Elementary School Textbooks" (Research paper, University of Maryland, College of Education, 1971); Rita R. Campbell, "Need for Studies of Sex Discrimination in Public Schools," Washington, D.C. Citizens' Advisory Council on the Status of Women, Department of Labor Building, Room 1336, 20210; see also "Dick and Jane as Victims: Sex Stereotypes in Children's Reading," *Women on Words and Images*, P.O. Box 2163, Princeton, New Jersey, 1972; Feminists on Children's Literature, "A Feminist Look at Children's Books," *School Library Journal* 17 (January 1971): 19–24; Katherine Rogers, "Liberation for Girls," *Saturday Review*, June 17, 1972; *Little Miss Muffet Fights Back* (New York: Feminists on Children's Media, P.O. Box 4315, Grand Central Station, 1971); Lenore J. Weitzman and Diane Rizzo, "Sex Bias in Textbooks," *Today's Education* (January-February 1975): 49–52.
46. Abraham Tannenbaum, "Family Living in Textbook Town," *Progressive Education Association* 31 (March 1954): 133–141.
47. Joanne Bernstein, "The Image of Female Teachers as Portrayed in Fiction for Young Children," *Women's Studies Abstracts* 1 (Fall 1971): 5–6+.
48. Raymond E. Spaulding, "Another Look at Comic Books" (Research paper, University of Maryland, College of Education, 1970).
49. Janice Law Trecker, "Woman in U.S. History High School Textbooks," *Social Education* 35 (March 1971): 249–261.

50. Jeanette Smyth, "Women's History: Exotic Specialty?" *Washington Post*, April 16, 1972.

51. Henry W. Bragdon and Samuel P. McCutchen, *History of a Free People*, 6th ed. rev. (New York: Macmillan, 1967).

52. Jonathan Kozol, "Look What They've Done to Helen Keller," *Teacher Paper* 6 (December 1973): 19–24.

53. Bard, *op. cit.*

54. Elizabeth Burr, Susan Dunn, and Norma Farquhar, "Equal Treatment of the Sexes in Social Studies Textbooks: Guidelines for Authors and Editors," mimeographed (Unpublished report available from BDFR Associates, 12709 Dewey Street, Los Angeles, California, 1972).

55. *Ibid.*

56. Miriam Kotzin, "Women, Like Blacks and Orientals, Are All Different," *Media and Methods* 8 (March 1972): 18–26; see also Susan Rice, "Women in Film," *Media and Methods* 8 (March 1972): 10.

57. Loretta Byers, "Pupils' Interests and Content of Primary Reading Texts," *The Reading Teacher* (January 1964): 227–233.

58. David Austin, Velma Clark, and Gladys Fitchett, *Reading Rights for Boys: Sex Role in Language Experiences* (New York: Appleton-Century-Crofts, 1971), p. 7.

59. Gordon B. Forbes and Dale Dykstra, "Children's Attribution of Negative Traits to Authority Figures as a Function of Family Size and Sex," *Psychological Reports* 28 (1971): 363–366.

60. Solomon Lichter *et al.*, *The Drop-Outs* (New York: Free Press, 1962); see also Edgar Z. Friedenberg, *The Vanishing Adolescent* (Boston: Beacon Press, 1962).

61. Jane Jones Aubrey, "The Beard," *Liberty* 67 (May-June 1972): 3–5; Daniel Zwerdling, "Unshaven, Unshorn, Unacceptable?," *Today's Education* 57 (November 1968): 23–24; Irving C. Hendrick and Reginald I. Jones, *Student Dissent in the Schools* (Boston: Houghton-Mifflin, 1970), pp. 191–202.

62. Jeanne H. Block, Norma Haan, and M. Brewster Smith, "Activism and Apathy in Contemporary Adolescents," in *Understanding Adolescence*, ed. James F. Adams (Boston: Allyn and Bacon, 1968), pp. 198–231.

63. Friedenberg, *op. cit.*; see also Patricia Sexton, *The Feminized Male* (New York: Random House, 1969).

64. Patricia Minuchin *et al.*, *The Psychological Impact of School Experience* (New York: Basic Books, 1969), pp. 396–398.

8

Is Learning Sexless?

Some school practices that perpetuate sex-role stereotypes were outlined in the preceding chapter. But there are still difficult questions about learning to be considered. Are the differences in treatment accorded boys and girls by the school due to real differences in intelligence? The school as currently organized is failing to free boys and girls from stereotyped sex roles. How, then, should it be reorganized? Would it be preferable to have male teachers or female teachers? Should classes be sex-segregated? Solutions to the problems of a sex-biased institution may sometimes be found in the people who run it. Thus we will examine the teaching profession and look at the kinds of people who go into it.

◆   **Sex Differences in Learning: An Open Question**

Problem solving and cognition are at the center of intellectual activity, whether that activity involves answering a question in the classroom, analyzing the platform of a political party, rebuilding an automobile engine, or borrowing money from a bank.

Everyone develops certain cognitive strategies, that is, ways of thinking by which they handle, organize, store, and recall information. Cognitive strategies determine and govern the amount as well as the organization of information that is available to a person. Although we know something about what goes into cognition, we know very little about what might affect differences in cognition between the sexes.[1] Cognitive strategies evolve, at least in part, as a function of individual personality development, so we infer that the differential socialization of males and females has the net effect of predisposing

146

each sex toward certain cognitive strategies rather than others. Strategies for learning become enduring aspects of the manner in which individuals solve problems. The greater aggressiveness of the male is presumed to be a strong contributing factor underlying the better analytical skills of men and boys. Early in life aggressiveness is built into the personality makeup of the male; this is probably why boys initiate more queries and make more declarative statements in the classroom.[2] If one of the goals of the school is to develop analytical thinking skills then teachers should assist girls in acquiring this so-called unfeminine behavior.

As a group, girl babies talk earlier than boy babies; in school girls talk more than boys. The verbal skills that girls bring to school are demonstrated in almost all testing situations.[3] Do girls have an innate capacity for superior verbal skills, or do they develop this skill because the home or school rewards them for it?

One study found girls from the fifth through seventh grades to be superior to boys in language usage—grammar—and to have better study skills. In vocabulary and reading comprehension girls were ahead of boys in the fifth grade, but not in the sixth or seventh.[4] The boys, however, excelled in tests of arithmetical skill. Are these differences a result of a true sex difference or simply a reflection of cultural attitudes? The cultural view of intellectual differences was strongly supported by Kagan and Moss at the conclusion of their longitudinal studies:

> Each individual has a cognitive picture of the person he would like to be and the goal states he would like to command—an idealized model of himself. . . . It would appear that the desire to be an *ideal male* or *ideal female* as defined by the individual, comprises an essential component of everyman's model. Thus the position of a response on a cognitive dimension ranging from *highly masculine* to *highly feminine* is a primary determinant of its acceptability and, therefore, of its probability of occurrence.[5]

Since boys expected to be better problem solvers than girls they are expected to excel in arithmetic.[6] But studies of arithmetic achievement give highly conflicting—and confusing—results. Some recent tests of arithmetic achievement show either no difference between boys and girls, or only a slight superiority for boys—depending on the test and the grade in which it was given. Tests in one suburban school system showed boys to be significantly superior to girls in understanding arithmetic concepts in seventh grade[7] and better than girls in high school.[8] In knowledge of the vocabulary of mathematics, girls out-scored boys in grades four, five, and six. In arithmetical computation the girls again outscored boys, but in arithmetical concepts and applications the fifth and sixth grade boys did better than girls. An interesting sidelight of this analysis was that both boys and girls did less well in computational skills in 1968 than in 1930, thus raising questions as to whether the "new math" is increasing some kinds of understanding at the expense of proficiency in ordinary arithmetical computation.[9]

A careful and heavily studied program designed to identify youngsters with a very high aptitude for mathematics, and to determine what kinds of instructional procedures would encourage the development of their extraordinary potential showed that, in any pool of candidates, there were far more boys than girls. The fact that there were many more boys than girls in this exceptionally able group must not obscure the fact that there were some girls as able as the most competent boys. But why were there more boys than girls? The researchers say that the predominance of boys might be attributed to the differential treatment accorded boys and girls. ". . . parents give boys such gifts as microscopes, telescopes, science kits and reference books more often than they give such presents to girls." And furthermore, "There is evidence in the published research that girls tend to avoid mathematics courses partly because they do not perceive such training as relevant to their anticipated vocational activities." The researchers conclude that "a full-scale investigation of what makes individual girls excel in mathematics may hold the key to understanding the dynamics of female psychological development in our culture."[10]

It seems that many factors play a part in the development of quantitative reasoning. Over a number of years, studies of entering freshmen at the University of California have shown that students of either sex from two child families have higher quantitative scores if the sibling is male. Other studies, too, have shown that "having a brother for a sibling helped both younger and older in a two child family."[11]

Parental attitudes appear to play a significant role in a child's mathematical achievement. Boys were found to like mathematics if their parents approved of mathematics education for them, and if the parents felt that learning mathematics aided their intellectual development. Even if their parents valued mathematics education, girls' attitudes were negative, but approval of competition in schooling produced positive attitudes toward math in both boys and girls.[12] Among boys, fathers' expectations of high achievement was a more significant factor than mothers' expectations. There appears to be an association between fathers' views of masculinity and sons' achievement in mathematics.[13] The absence of the father for extended periods of time during early childhood has been shown to be related to lower mathematical scores for both sexes. But if the father was absent for a short period during the son's adolescence, the boy's scores in mathematics were higher than if the father was always at home.[14]

There seems to be a significant relationship between boys' attitudes toward arithmetic and teachers' style of classroom presentation, regardless of the teacher's sex. One study showed that the more theoretically oriented and the more involved the teachers were, the better were boys' attitudes toward mathematics.

This study also reported that the cumulative effect of teacher on student was greater when the teacher and pupil were the same sex.[15] If the identification hypothesis holds, then the fact that most elementary teachers dislike arithmetic—and that most such teachers are women—has implications for girls' negative attitudes and poorer scores in arithmetic.[16]

Whether influenced by the attitudes of parents, peers, or teachers, many girls see mathematics as a subject for boys. This cultural bias affects girls' achievement in mathematics, and may be the cause of the average lower scores in quantitative reasoning skills among females. Kagan summarizes the data regarding the role of personality in the development of quantitative reasoning skills when he says:

It is well documented that problems requiring analysis and reasoning, especially spatial reasoning, science, and mathematics problems, are viewed by both sexes as more appropriate for boys than for girls. As might be expected, girls perform less well on such materials. . . . The typical girl believes that the ability to solve problems in geometry, physics, logic, or arithmetic is a masculine skill, and her motivation to persist with such problems is low. Her decreased involvement reflects the fact that her self-esteem is not at stake in such problems. In some cases she is potentially threatened by the possibility that she might perform with unusual competence on such tasks, for excellence is equated with a loss of femininity.[17]

The idea that something is more feminine than something else has been the basis for developing measures of femininity and masculinity. That feminine and masculine are dubious grounds for measuring patterns of behavior is increasingly clear to researchers. Nevertheless, one effort to see if masculinity was related to problem solving showed that male students who majored in science had higher masculinity scores than women science majors, but men nonscience majors also had higher scores than the female science majors.[18] One intriguing study reported that femininity scores for women math majors in college were higher than for female education majors.[19]

Cognitive functioning does not take place in a vacuum. If one is disturbed or troubled, one's problem solving ability is apt to be impaired. The influence of psychological state on cognition differs according to sex and age. In preadolescence or early adolescence psychological difficulties seem to interfere with boys' cognition, while girls seem not to be so affected until middle adolescence. Researchers reporting these findings also noted that boys and girls seemed to respond to different cultural expectations.

Although both sexes may think an equal number of "bad thoughts," the threat to the individual's concept of self-worth instigated by these thoughts may be far from equal for boys and girls. If morbid and aggressive fantasies tend to be less threatening to boys, their occurrence would be less likely to set off a chain of introspective events interfering with rational cognitive functioning. Girls on the other hand, might be less capable of ignoring this "internal disorder," and accordingly there would be greater interference with rational cognitive functioning.[20]

An alternative hypothesis might be that it is permissible for girls to admit morbid thoughts, and even to dwell on them, while boys would think it unmanly to be introspective about such fantasies.

In a study of differences between the sexes in applying knowledge, it was found that high school boys had superior scores but that this was not due to practice effects, reading preference or activities, IQ, previous knowledge, personal traits, or reading comprehension. The boys' higher scores reflected their superior ability to apply knowledge or skill when confronted with a new situation. One might suppose that this superior ability to transfer learning would cause males to achieve better in the educational environment. Yet, we know that this is not the case, at least as far as their grades are concerned.

Investigation of the level of conceptual reasoning attained by boys and girls from different socioeconomic groups revealed that 1) higher social class was associated with ability to conceptualize at a higher level, and 2) female scores were significantly higher than male scores. At the same time, there was a wide variation in male scores on conceptualization among middle class junior high students.[21] The results of a study conducted by Buddeke indicate a sex difference in patterns of conceptualization. In this study one hundred high school boys were equated with one hundred girls on the basis of identical scores on standardized algebra tests.[22] While the girls tended to keep content areas relatively separate from each other and perceived direct relationships among the elements of a given area of algebraic study, the boys solved problems through a recognition of broad relationships *among* content areas. This study demonstrates that males and females seem to put ideas together differently. We are nagged, of course, by questions raised by Kagan's remarks: is it the task that produces the different strategies? If boys and girls were given other kinds of problems would they differ as much?

Differences in cognitive patterning may be an important clue to male superiority in applying knowledge. One investigator found that, when given verbal tasks requiring the synthesis of ideas, boys were always better than girls.

On a test measuring inferences drawn from maps, girls were better than boys in all-black groups, while in lower class white groups only the more disadvantaged girls were superior to the boys; boys from a suburban environment were superior to all others. Contradictory results by social class and racial group suggest that environmental factors may play as great a role as any innate differences in the development of cognitive skills.[23] Stafford studied the relative influence of heredity and environment on differences in quantitive reasoning ability. After examining a vast amount of data regarding achievement and attitude, he looked at cross-cultural studies and found consistent male superiority. Twin studies revealed similar sex differences. His conclusion:

In general there is an underlying hereditary component for a proficiency in quantitative reasoning which fits the sex-linked recessive model fairly well. This "have" or "lack" quality results in two normal curves. . . . Whether an individual is placed in the top curve or the bottom curve would, therefore, depend largely upon the effect of a host of environmental components. . . . We, therefore, cannot discount the very important interaction effects of environment (such as home life, choice of school, adequacy of teacher, proper attitude, and family support) with genetic endowment which result in students with varying degrees of quantitative reasoning ability.[24]

The influence of the genetic component is not understood. In persons with an extra X chromosome, or in those having only one X chromosome and no Y chromosome, the larger "female" component leads to lessened ability in quantitative reasoning, even though those studied had an IQ range similar to that of the normal population. Persons with only one X chromosome and no Y had a distinctive deficit in perceptual organization, a kind of "space-form blindness."[25]

    In this section we have presented a wide range of conflicting data and divergent hypotheses about sex differences in learning so that the reader might be aware that this remains a highly controversial area. So far the researchers have provided only inconclusive evidence about the causes of any intellectual or cognitive differences that may exist between the sexes,[26] but they have learned a good deal about the way schools mark some ways of thinking as masculine and others as feminine. As young people learn their sex-identity, they perforce take up the sex-appropriate intellectual strategies which may in fact have little to do with any innate predisposition to think or solve problems in one way or another. Schools must do a far better job of supporting intellectual ability in boys and in girls, so that both may feel free to explore the world of ideas freely and productively. So far, intellectual vitality and curiosity seem to be male prerogatives.

Tests and Test-Taking

In school, college, business, and even in the armed services, tests are critical measures of success. The person who does well on tests usually has a wider range of choices and alternatives available to him or her. One must be wary of accepting test scores at face value, however. Many tests of aptitude or achievement are biased in favor of one sex or the other. The bias may inhere in the test itself (for example, in the kinds of questions asked), or it may derive from the manner in which the test scores are interpreted. For instance, a test manual for one standardized test allowed the combining of scores for boys and girls into one table of norms in the areas of verbal, numerical, and abstract reasoning, as well as language usage. This despite the manual's statement that in every grade girls score higher than boys in language usage.[27] Clark used the California Test of Mental Maturity and the California Achievement Test to ascertain if there were differences in abilities and achievement of children in grades three, five, and eight.[28] The former test was supposed not to be biased in favor of either sex, but analysis of test scores in language, mechanics of English, and spelling revealed consistently higher scores for girls. This was true even after he removed from the data such differences as could be attributed to chronological age and mental age.

In addition to bias in tests and test scoring, the conditions of test taking may distort the results. Boys do less well than girls in certain stress-producing situations. Reduce the threat of the test situation, and boys' scores would go up. Girls, on the other hand, may need the spur of anxiety to perform well in test situations; numerous studies indicate that girls and women express more anxiety in many situations.[29] Males, however, seem to hide their anxiety, for they believe it is not masculine to indicate this state.

But many factors inhibit girls from trying to do their best. Over a decade ago McClelland, who has contributed some of the major theoretical and experimental findings about achievement, commented:

Women do not show an increase in Achievement scores as a result of achievement-involving instruction. . . . Why then don't women's scores increase under experimental arousal? This is the puzzler. Two possible explanations—invalidity of the scoring for women, scores too high to go higher—have been eliminated. Apparently the usual arousal instructions simply do not increase achievement striving in women. . . .[30]

An experiment was designed to produce higher achievement scores among girls selected for outstanding achievement. These girls were aroused only in response to pictures of girls achieving, not boys. But girls who had not been successful in school work showed an increase in their achievement scores in response to pictures of males. The conflicting evidence can hardly be explained, say the researchers, by any simple theory based on a single motive.[31]

The drive to achieve inevitably leads to competition with others, and competitiveness is an attribute which is not generally rewarded among girls. Thus girls may deny their actual achievements and may consistently choose their life goals in terms of a stereotype of the passive, dependent, slightly stupid women. Males respond to achievement motivation quite differently, and are willing to engage in combat and competition at a very early age. Yet under great pressure as in test-taking, boys demonstrate more anxiety and lower achievement.[32] Men may get further because of their greater drive, but it is a fragile and vulnerable personality attribute. Women may not get as far, but they have far lower expectations of themselves—in fact, negative expectations. For a girl, to succeed is to fail. No wonder some able students regard their test scores with cynicism. *They* realize that these are not true measures of what they know—or what they could know.

Is It True That Boys Are Smarter Than Girls?

If being smarter means getting good grades in school, then girls are smarter than boys; if intelligence is measured by achieving recognition through leadership in government, the arts, business, or almost any other field of endeavor, then there is no question that men far outdistance women. Yet no one believes that school grades or positions of leadership are sufficient evidence to judge one sex as more or less intelligent than the other. Girls appear to win the IQ race early in life, and boys win later on. If achievement is not a reliable measure of intelligence, what then is? Is the IQ test an objective measure that we can rely upon?

IQ tests were carefully constructed to eliminate items which favored one sex over the other. When Terman undertook to refine the intelligence testing procedures of the French psychologists, Binet and Simon, he excluded items which might demonstrate that either sex was superior or inferior; his basic assumption was that intelligence was equally distributed regardless of sex. Although subsequent studies have shown that IQ is not constant over time, that it is difficult to identify "inborn" mental abilities, that cultural, academic, and other experiences can influence IQ, test makers continue to measure IQ as they did in Terman's time.[33]

. . . there is still not available any test of over-all "intelligence" which will permit except accidentally of differential performance by the two sexes, although it is readily apparent that boys and girls of normal upbringing in our society have different sorts of experiences and we have different expectations of them, even in the schools. It is not likely that an item would be dropped from a mechanical assembly test because girls performed less well on it than boys, yet the intelligence test-constructors will not permit us to discover whether there are important differences we should know about in the intellectual functioning of the two sexes. . . . Terman simply stated that he eliminated tests which would be "relatively less fair to one sex than the other," seeing no need for further justification. . . . Would it not have been equally appropriate to eliminate items on which there was differential performance for Negro and white children?[34]

If this rationale were accepted, any item which differentiated among ethnic groups or groups of different socioeconomic status would be eliminated. As the authors cited above say rather testily: "The continuing attempt of test makers to obscure differences in performance by boys and girls runs counter to the constant and conscious effort of parents, teachers, and society at large to instill in growing children the very different attitudes, motivations, and behaviors expected of each sex."[35] Longitudinal data show that IQ tests require an empathetic relationship between an examiner and the one being tested, a situation with different meanings for boys and girls. Analysis of IQ data can be misleading because patterns of intercorrelations among subtests vary by sex. "It is likely that many studies in literature or in a file drawer would have led the investigator to draw different conclusions if separate analysis had been made for males and females."[36] If one sex is "smarter" than the other, IQ tests are the last place to find the evidence.

School-administered tests of IQ are probably the least reliable measures of ability. Generally the tests given in school are group tests, administered to a large number of pupils at one time in one place. Since we know that boys and girls have a rather different orientation to school tasks, it is not surprising that girls perform better on these tests. They pay attention to the directions, are less easily distracted, and in general have a higher level of verbal functioning. Thus any aspect of the test that involves reading would automatically favor the girls. As boys learn the school game, and as slower youngsters drop out, measured intelligence of boys equals and sometimes exceeds that of girls. Such factors as a child's dependency on the teacher or development of autonomous behavior may affect test results.[37]

In the early school years girls do better on tests of general intelligence, but by adulthood males do better or females test less well.[38] During late childhood and adolescence developmental differences show up: girls who started out as the brightest slow down in their mid-years, while boys who started out being quite clever get smarter as they go along, according to one longitudinal study. There is some question as to whether the very bright girls found out that being bright did not pay, and suppressed their real ability, but tests do not yet tell us this.[39]

After doing extensive longitudinal studies, Kagan and Moss concluded that boys' scores at age ten are a better indicator of intellectual abilities in adulthood than the scores obtained when they are six years old. Boys with a strong desire to master intellectual skills gained in IQ score during the early years of school, while those with low mastery motivation remained stable or showed slight decreases in IQ score. This difference in the predictive power of the IQ test at age six versus age ten did not occur for the girls. ". . . twice as many boys as girls had major increases in IQ scores during the school years."[40]

If this research is correct, then parents and teachers would be well advised to treat IQ scores, particularly those of young boys, with extreme skepticism. Any kind of tracking or grouping system used by a school must be scrutinized with care, since neither IQ tests nor grades appear to be very reliable indicators of student ability; this is particularly true among younger boys.

There is striking evidence that the adult pattern of achievement is decisively and perhaps irreversibly influenced by parental attitudes during very early childhood. Longitudinal studies show that a girl benefits when her mother does not dominate or oversee too closely, but a close and warm relationship with mother is very beneficial for a boy, particularly in regard to verbal test scores. Girls are more apt to have lower tested aptitudes if their early family life was marred by parental conflict. Boys showed higher aptitudes when their fathers demonstrated concern about their educational achievement, when both parents were satisfied with the father's occupation, and when the father's income was relatively high. A girl's mental development appears to flourish when she has a father who is friendly but not overly demonstrative.[41] One study showed that even among ninth grade girls who achieved good grades there was a belief that their parents had higher educational aspirations for boys than girls.[42]

Boys are referred for special attention due to "mental retardation" more often than girls,[43] but there is no convincing evidence that there are more stupid boys than girls. There is greater variability in intelligence among boys than girls. That is, there will be a larger spread between very bright boys and very slow boys. Does this mean that girls—even very slow ones—put their intelligence to work, but are not motivated to push themselves to their limits at the highest end of the continuum? Boys start off with built-in handicaps—frailer physique, less verbal stimulation, physiologically behind girls until after adolescence which may reinforce tendencies to lag behind. But as the boy matures, social and physiological forces support his motivation to excel.[44]

To some extent, intelligence lies in the eye of the beholder. In one recent study, young men and women were presented with an "authoritative" statement about matters of fact. For one group of subjects the author of the statement was said to be a woman, while the other group was told it had been authored by a man. Both men and women subjects had more confidence in the report supposedly written by a man.[45] Both sexes think men are better at almost any intellectual task, even in traditionally female activities.

There may be food for thought in the research that found that boys and girls react differently to success or failure. Boys are inclined to consider academic success to be due to their own efforts, but to see failures as the result of bad luck or external causes. Girls express feelings of greater control over their academic performance, but this is apt to be related to failure rather than success. Girls feel guilty and blame themselves for failure, but consider outside forces or luck more significant when accounting for success.[46]

If one assumes that children learn their sex roles through a process of identification with persons of the same sex, then it would follow that boys adopt "male" modes of thinking and girls "female" modes. After studying the data on sex-role models and the theories of sex-role identification, Lynn asserts that, with the proper models available at the right time and in the right way, "The little girl acquires a cognitive style that primarily involves (1) a personal relationship, and (2) imitation rather than restructuring the field and abstracting principles. In contrast, the little boy acquires a cognitive style that primarily involves: (1) defining the goal, (2) restructuring the field, and (3) abstracting principles."[47] To substantiate this view, Lynn points out that girls can learn about life around them by observing their mothers; they do not have to make any special effort to restructure the field. Boys, however, must learn to be boys through a specific intellectualizing—they must figure out what kind of behavior is acceptable and what is "being a sissy." The masculine learning method inculcates restructuring the field as a learning principle.[48] What kind of cognitive style would boys learn if they were raised by men only? Would the necessity for learning how to restructure the field disappear?

In answer to our original question, "Are boys smarter than girls?" it would appear that females may be the more intelligent sex, and that there are more males with low IQs. Girls receive higher grades than boys, and consistently outperform them scholastically, but boys have a greater sense of personal power.[49] In adult life, one might therefore conclude that intelligence may be less important than the conviction one can succeed.

Who Is More Creative?

The absence of women from among those who have achieved greatness through creative pursuits has been attributed to lack of opportunity, although some observers believe that there may be an innate difference in creativity between the sexes.

Though there is considerable interest in creativity and its nurturance, little research has been done on sex differences in creativity. Torrance reviewed 142 studies, and found only one that indicated any analysis by sex.[50] The limited amount of research regarding creativity and sex differences has not, however, limited speculation on the subject.[51] Neither sex appears to be consistently superior in creativity during childhood. Teachers report that during adolescence boys are far more resistant than girls to many kinds of "creative endeavors such as writing poetry. Girls are heavily represented in school orchestras and art classes. But in adulthood, males dominate the graphic arts and performing arts. Clearly, something other than "innate" capacity or even interest is at work here.

In school boys receive more encouragement for creativity than girls. Teachers reward boys almost three times as much as girls for divergent contributions. A cross-cultural study found that boys, whether living in Bombay or Minneapolis, have more opportunities to develop their creativity than girls.[52] Even if girls are not as creative as boys, they show a much higher correlation of IQ with creativity.[53] Experimental efforts to raise girls' aspiration levels suggest that boy-girl differences in creativity might be affected by changed treatment.[54] So far there is no hard evidence that boys and girls are innately different in the *potential* for creativity.

So far in this chapter we have reviewed the evidence regarding sex differences in learning, intelligence, and creativity. The evidence is murky. The findings of researchers indicate that only minimal differences in ability and achievement between the sexes can be attributed to physiology. We find that the human animal, male or female, is almost infinitely flexible. If we want intellectual boys and girls and creative girls as well as boys, then institutions and parents must make it possible.

♦   **Teaching: A Sexless Profession?**

"The children were entering the elevator—girls first, then boys—a game started previously. One boy turned and said, 'Teacher is a girl and should enter first,' 'No, a teacher is not a boy or a girl,' said Harry. 'She's just a teacher,' "[55] In the view of parents, however, there is a difference between men and women teachers. But consistent with the sex-neutral stance of educators is their refusal to acknowledge any difference. Few studies are available which show classroom teaching differences, although there is abundant evidence that the men and women who enter teaching come from different backgrounds, have different motives, perceive their role differently, and participate differently in school, community, and professional activities.

No matter how bright or able they may be, women are encouraged by relatives and friends to choose teaching. Men are less apt to be encouraged to select public school teaching; the more able they are the more likely are they to be recruited into other fields.[56]

The teaching careers of men and women differ.[57] The men who leave teaching are apt to be brighter than those who remain.[58] Most men select secondary school teaching not only because of its higher social status, but also because the emphasis is on subject matter first and students second. There appears to be consistent social disapproval of a man who is more interested in young children than in ideas; hence recruitment of men into elementary schools, particularly the lower grades, has been difficult.

Once in the system, men are more aggressive and more militant.[59] If there is a large proportion of men on a school faculty it is likely that there will be militant professional organizations; the strength of the American Federation of Teachers local is directly related to the number of men on a faculty.[60] The reason advanced for the greater militancy of male teachers is interesting:

Because they are much more likely than women both to carry weighty financial burdens and consider themselves relatively deprived, male teachers have the greater incentive to join organizations that evince militancy and the willingness to fight hard for monetary gains. Consequently, schools dominated by males are more likely to encourage aggressive behavior while those dominated by females tend to promote submissiveness. [However] by the time an organization reaches maturity and membership becomes rather commonplace, things pretty well even out and male-female differences recede in prominence.[61]

Although they may be less aggressive politically, women teachers are more progressive educationally. It has been found that 60 percent of male high school teachers are willing to use corporal punishment, while only 40 percent of the women would do so; although 25 percent of the women reported no disciplinary problems, only 13 percent of the men reported this. Male teachers are more rigidly routinized, and much more apt to be opposed to change in school practices than women.[62] Men teachers, particularly in secondary schools, are often interested in out-of-school politics and active in community affairs while female teachers are more active in professional groups.[63]

Even though women teachers have been characterized as more "professional" by their support of school programs and policies and their participation in teacher organizations, the leadership positions in such organizations are held by men. The National Education Association alternates between the sexes in its choice of president, but the job is more honorary than powerful. The executive secretary, who really runs the show, has always been a man. The top leadership in the American Federation of Teachers has been male. In purely professional organizations, men dominate. One study of the science teachers' professional group showed far more men on committees, holding office, and attending meetings.[64] At the local level in teachers' associations, men hold most offices. Only in sponsorship of Future Teachers of America did women have an edge.[65] Analysis of the articles written over a thirty-year period in *Social Education*, the official journal of the National Council for the Social Studies, an affiliate of the National Education Association, showed that the proportion of female authors declined from a high of 28 percent in 1937–38 to a low of 12 percent in 1957–58. In 1967–68 the proportion of articles authored by women rose to 14 percent.[66] The findings may reflect a change in the ratio of male to female social studies teachers; they may also reflect greater professional activity on the part of men, and a bias against school teacher authors. A most disturbing study now underway is a test of the bias of the scholar-reviewers for a mathematics education journal. The preliminary findings indicate a very grave bias against authors purported to be female, and a strong tendency to believe that if an article is written by a male professor it is significantly more acceptable than if written by a female, or by a school teacher.[67]

Differences between the sexes in the teaching profession are consistent with many findings about men and women in the general population. To what extent these differences do in fact make a difference in school practice is still under debate.

The Teacher Stereotype

In the public mind the teacher is an ambitious, domineering, managing, fussy, tyrannical woman who has powers that enable her to see more of people's motives than they wish to reveal. She has few friends; she is not interested in people's problems; social mingling is not to her liking. When things go wrong, she rarely blames herself. Set in her ways, bound up in routine, she hesitates to do the unconventional.[68]

The teacher stereotype is almost always a women, often wearing eyeglasses, neatly groomed, respected by the community, married, and a church member.[69]

The stereotype of the spinster school teacher, immersed in syrup in *Good Morning, Miss Dove* is still with us.[70] Sex-starved, left out, respected neither as an intellectual nor as a female, she is a dismal person indeed. In a novel published in 1970, there is a conversation between a woman and a bus driver that reveals the persistence of the stereotype:

"How 'bout you, Red? You got a husband?"
"No. No. I'm not married, Ed."
"That ain't right."
"Well . . . right or not, that's the way it happens to *be*. I. . . ."
"I know. You're a schoolteacher."
"Do I make it so obvious?" (She wondered why admission to being a schoolteacher was tantamount to an admission of sexual failure.)
"Uah! If you're not married. A girl like you."[71]

In the words of Waller, whose study of the schools has become a sociological classic, the male teacher is assimilated into the "female character ideal" that isolates him from normal male activities. Waller remarks: "It has been said that no woman and no Negro is ever fully admitted to the white man's world. Possibly we should add men teachers to the list of the excluded.[72] In attempting to identify those aspects of the teaching role which produce the "teacher stereotype" Waller comments: "Spinster teachers sometimes present a sorry picture and one rightly diagnosed as a picture of frustration. But, then, so do the men who teach; and men teachers are free to marry. It is something in the teaching itself, or something in the life of the teacher, which frustrates."[73] "Teaching," says Waller, "does something to those who teach."[74] "Teaching, along with the ministry, is known as one of the sheltered occupations, as an occupation where those persons who shrink from the daily battle of life, often very estimable people, by the way, may find refuge."[75]

Today's teachers find the classroom far from tranquil, and the battles of the secondary school and the inner city classroom demand persons of aggressiveness and strength, yet the persistent stereotype may keep such persons away from teaching. Is there something in the teacher ideal which recruits a certain kind of person? Is it the training which produces a "teacher type" or does living the teacher role turn both males and females into "teacher types?"

Teaching illustrates very clearly how a profession's prestige and status are related to the sex that has achieved predominance within the profession.[76] Since most teachers are women, teaching is accorded relatively little status. Historically in America the common school was in the hands of women.[77] In the twentieth century most public elementary school teachers have been women, and boys do not see many men as teachers. Teaching is viewed as a feminine activity, and few "real" men can see themselves in this role. Furthermore:

There are often not enough male models or idols among their teachers whose performance will convey the sense that the world of the mind is legitimately male, who can give them masculine examples of intellectual inquiry or cultural life, and who can be regarded as sufficiently successful and important in the world to make it conceivable for vigorous boys to enter teaching themselves as a livelihood. The boys grow up thinking of men teachers as somewhat effeminate and treat them with a curious mixture of genteel deference (of the sort due to women) and hearty male condescension. In a certain construct, the male teacher may be respected, but he is not "one of the boys."[78]

The feminization of the school is accepted by young children.

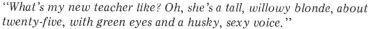

"What's my new teacher like? Oh, she's a tall, willowy blonde, about twenty-five, with green eyes and a husky, sexy voice."

Drawing by Chon Day; © 1970 The New Yorker Magazine, Inc.

When asked to identify common objects found in classrooms, second grade children identified them as feminine rather than masculine.[79] Articles and books which talk about the elementary teacher invariably refer to the teacher as "she," while articles and books about secondary school teachers, administrators, and college professors use the pronoun "he." Able men are attracted to public school teaching at the elementary level only on the premise that they will swiftly move into leadership and managerial roles as school administrators.

Far from being a sexless profession, teaching is a profession filled with females. This fact has served to restrict the entry of the

other sex. "The very factors which lead women to flow into education in large numbers are factors which make the professionalization
of education all but impossible," says one vehement spokesman for
professional education.[80] Only when the proportion of men teachers
is increased and the number of women decreased will it be possible
to eliminate teaching from the "occupations which are not regarded
as life careers. . . ."[81]

Efforts to attract men into teaching, and thus raise the status
of the profession, have included elimination of the restrictive contracts which plagued women teachers, contracts which specified
where they must live, whom they could visit, and the hours they
must attend church. These contracts prohibited them from dancing,
smoking, drinking, or dating, and fired them if they dared to get
married. Men were paid higher wages than women until only recently; by 1953 all but a very few states had provision for equal pay
for teachers in accordance with experience and training. But despite
equal pay provisions bonuses, for family men, veterans, and coaches,
have been and continue to be common.[82]

Like the stereotypes of the old maid school teacher and of the
classroom dominated by a female, there is a reverse stereotype which
identifies all administrators as males. The ogre male principal who
stands ten feet tall and is ready to inflict swift punishment on some
shivering boy culprit, is a standard theme of cartoons. Who ever
heard of a female school superintendent? Who, indeed! In 1971
there were only seven. Though at one time elementary principals
were apt to be women, now 80 percent are men. And 96 percent of
secondary school principals in the United States are men.[83] Male
control of school affairs extends to our school boards—women constitute only 10 percent of school board membership.

The lack of women in administrative positions in education reflects not only the need to keep the career ladder open to men in
order to attract them to the profession, but also perhaps a negative
view of women administrators. Such a view is held by women as well
as men. As one study commented, ". . . women may usually be, in
fact, less effective administrators than men" because both sexes
agree that "women should not give orders to men," and therefore
women "may not feel at ease if they have to do so."[84] A study of
male and female elementary principals, however, showed that on the
average the female principals exercised firmer leadership and were
able to get their teachers to make a greater effort on the job. They
were also more apt to know what was going on in the school.[85]

If one accepts the idea that teaching is a feminine profession then one must conclude that the men who choose teaching are somewhat feminine, or that they become less masculine because of their teaching and administrative roles. Men in education would of course protest this characterization. Personality studies of male and female teachers are far from conclusive. In some respects male teachers resemble their female counterparts, and in others they are like men in the general population.

What Can Be Done?

The school as it is constituted today is not a sex-neutral institution. Teachers, like others in our society, are socialized as male and female. Parents want teachers to carry on the same socializing function for boys and girls, to demand sex-appropriate behavior at all times.

But sex-appropriate behavior leads boys and girls into difficulties because the structure of the school makes success easier for girls in some situations and for boys in other situations. It is felt that boys are discriminated against by women teachers, and that they suffer when their more aggressive and exploratory behavior is compared to that of docile girls. Two solutions worthy of study have been advanced. These solutions are 1) provide more male teachers in the early elementary grades to help boys and reduce their learning problems, and 2) separate boys and girls for academic instruction (it is believed that this would be of particular benefit to boys).

Are More Male Teachers the Answer?

At one time there was a strong movement to get more men into teaching. The few studies that have examined them show that male and female elementary teachers are more alike than they are different, and that the men are similar to women in their attitudes toward and view of children.[86] Because the structure of the educational system prevents effective decision-making at the teacher level, the occupation may change the male teacher's view of what kind of assertive activities are appropriate. As a result, he becomes more passive, accepting the traditional "feminine" teacher role—at least in communities in Oregon studied by researchers.[87] People-oriented values seem to characterize both men and women teachers, and both view high monetary rewards as less important than people in general.[88]

An examination of the propensity of teachers to give failing grades showed no difference by sex of teacher or by subject taught. The most important factor seemed to be attitude toward students; teachers with a poor classroom atmosphere who were more interested in covering the subject matter than in the feelings of students, were far more apt to fail students—irrespective of teacher age, sex, or subject taught.[89]

Given these similarities between male and female teachers, what advantage would there be to having more men in the schools? One study pointed out that male sixth grade teachers saw boys in a less positive light than did female teachers! Male teachers, especially the younger male teachers, were reported more ready to punish boys than female teachers.[90] On the basis of this evidence, which is certainly far from definitive, one would not recommend more male elementary teachers! Boys would have an even harder time of it than they do now. It is possible that male sixth grade teachers are more like secondary school teachers in their response to the challenge to authority presented by preadolescent boys. Since many of them are undoubtedly planning to leave elementary teaching for administrative positions in the educational system, they may be individuals who are more authoritarian to begin with.

One views with some dismay this cavalier statement by one authority: "... many female teachers put up with low salaries and poor working conditions, since they are married or plan to get married, and their salary is only a secondary source of income. Since teaching is a lifework for many male teachers, they are more concerned about better salaries, more status, and better working conditions."[91] The above statement parallels the kind of offensive remarks made about immigrants who were willing to work at poor wages and did not care about better working conditions!

In a conference on training of teachers for elementary schools there was a consensus that more men teachers are needed in the elementary school. In the conferees' words, "Girls are teacher pleasers, while boys are difficult to deal with and need men's leadership."[92] The suggestion that recruitment of more men elementary teachers would solve boys' school problems comes from a wide variety of observers. The reasoning behind the suggestion seems weak and often fallacious. Some educators do not even follow their own findings. For instance, one study found teachers of grades four, five, and six to be very similar with no significant differences between the sexes. Nonetheless, the study concludes, "Men are needed in elementary schools to serve as models for sex identification and to lend their masculine influence to the curriculum and child."[93] The sociologist Boocock observes: "For boys, the feminine atmosphere of the school and the emphasis on obedience and conformity, instead of upon more active learning, overshadows their first years in school, and they do not catch up with girls in performance until the clear linkages of academic achievement with occupational and other kinds of adult success make school and learning more relevant."[94] Boocock notes that school climate decreases girls' intellectual potential as well as boys', and cites an experiment in Akron, Ohio which "aims to increase the number of male teachers in the elementary schools, and thereby reduce the incidence of reading and other learning difficulties among girls."[95] Boocock does not see the possible fallacy of this approach. Women high school or college teachers, who presumably have been effective in the competitive and intellectually aggressive world, have not provided girls with effective role models to influence the way they perceive intellectual tasks. How will more men in elementary schools do this for boys?

It has been asserted that male teachers could serve as role models for poor boys: "Boys more readily identify with male teachers than with female teachers. This is especially true among lower class or disadvantaged boys, who are becoming an increasing problem in public schools today."[96] Yet a study of children from lower socioeconomic backgrounds showed that they did least well with black male teachers; black boys and girls did better with female teachers in arithmetic and with male teachers in reading.[97]

It has been suggested that "male teachers might be able to facilitate certain types of cognitive functioning in paternally deprived children as well as contributing to their interpersonal development . . . through providing special incentives to males to teach in lower grades, or having older boys or male paraprofessionals in the school."[98] Although no data are given to support the hypothesis upon which the above recommendation is made, many studies indicate that sex of adult does make a difference to children. For instance, young girls try to get adult attention in an experimental situation when the adult is a male, but boys are more apt to seek attention if the adult is female. Girls respond better to adult approval from a male experimenter and give more correct responses. Boys respond best to a female experimenter.[99] A number of studies have shown that adults of the opposite sex provide more effective social reinforcement than adults of the same sex. When the role of the adult was neutral, children appeared to be facilitated by adults of the opposite sex.[100] In an elaborate study to assess cross-sex versus same-sex preference among children, it was found that age, social class, and role of adult as well as sex were determiners of preference. For instance, middle class girls and lower class boys preferred an adult of the same sex if this person were seen as taking a supportive role. Interestingly, this study showed that the most and the least preferred women were rated on physical characteristics, while men were evaluated in regard to social attributes.[101]

The notion of solving the educational problems of boys by adding more males to elementary school faculties is very simplistic.[102] There is far more to the interaction between child and adult than merely the sex of either. It is probable that both boys and girls would benefit if they were to have teachers of either sex at any grade level from kindergarten through graduate school. It may be as vital for boys to see male teachers in first grade as for girls to know that women can be full professors. But if male and female teachers are equally insistent upon instilling sex-role stereotypes in children then the sex-biased school will not be materially altered by any change in the composition of the educational staff—at any level.

Are Sex-Separated Classes the Answer?

Another popular answer to the problems that sex-biased schools cause for boys is sex-separated classrooms. There have been several experiments at the elementary school level, where such problems might be more easily prevented. Few of these experiences have been researched thoroughly, though the proponents report enthusiastic acceptance by parents and teachers.[103] One school reported success when separating boys and girls in grades four and five. "The programs were designed in each classroom with the idea of giving the boys a male environment to work in, and an opportunity to act like boys with no negative repercussions. The girls' program had the same basic philosophy from a female standpoint."[104] The report of the first year's experiences showed that all students made the expected gains in mastery of subject matter. A majority of the boys and girls liked the separate classes, though boys liked the situation somewhat more than girls. The parents were overwhelmingly in support of the program. Interestingly enough, discipline problems in the playground and classroom decreased dramatically: from a high of 244 referrals the year before to a low of fourteen during the first year of separated classes. Other factors such as parent supervision of playgrounds and parent aid to teachers in solving discipline problems may account for the decrease in referrals. The school principal reports that the program must continue for three years before a true evaluation can be obtained.

In an experiment segregating boys and girls in first grade for one year, there were favorable results for boys in spelling and reading; first grade girls did better than boys when separated and when in mixed classes. The teachers' subjective evaluation was that there were distinct advantages for the boys when they were separated by sex, since "without the presence of girls, the boys were freer to be themselves." Furthermore, in mixed first grade classes, the exploratory and physically active behavior of the boys was directed toward the girls, creating classroom discipline problems. The girls tended to dominate the boys in playground activities, in some instances being "little mothers" to the less mature boys. The authors of the report felt that girls were more task-oriented: "Girls seem to need more structure. They want the teacher to say what comes next."[105]

Sex separation may not be the only factor causing changes in achievement among these children. Two different approaches to reading readiness were utilized with matched kindergarten groups. The more active program resulted in significantly higher scores for boys; the girls did well by both methods.[106] Similar changes in program may accompany the experiments with sex separation.

In a suburban junior high school, eighth grade boys and girls were placed in separate social studies and English classes. No significant changes in achievement were noted. The only important finding was that both male and female teachers were more restrictive with the all-boy classes; they allowed them to move around less and they lectured to boys more than to girls. In all-girl classes the grades of girls were somewhat lower, too.[107] In another junior high school class students were randomly placed in mixed or sex-segregated classes in science, mathematics, social studies, and English. Since they were already effectively separated in physical education and home economics/shop, for five-sixths of the day the students were separated by sex. The achievement levels and attitudes of the students were compared to those of students in coeducational classes. Grades and achievement levels were similar for both coeducation and sex-separated students. In both situations the girls received higher grades, had higher achievement test scores, and liked school better than boys did; but they were more negative toward the sex-segregated school situation.[108]

One educator has been conducting a series of studies of attitudes and achievement in the secondary schools of England for many years. These are comparative studies of sex-separated and mixed schools, and the findings were only recently reported. In a society where the best schools, the public schools, were always separated by sex, as were the "good" universities, it is interesting to find overwhelming support for coeducation among students, teachers, and adults who have experienced both kinds of schools. Dale reported that both boys and girls felt that sex-separated schools were harsher in their discipline, and permitted less freedom intellectually as well. In these schools there was much greater preoccupation with sex than in the coeducational schools.[109]

The trend toward approval of coeducation appears to be world-wide. A UNESCO survey showed the following acceptance of coeducation at all levels: schools were 100 percent coeducational in the USSR; 35 percent in Europe; 33 percent in South America; 28 percent in North America; 25 percent in Oceania; 12 percent in Asia, and 7 percent in Africa. The interest in increased coeducation reflected the pressure for more education for women. Sex segregation tended to be greatest at upper educational levels, with access for women severely limited. Segregation by sex is considered to be detrimental to the achievement of equal opportunity for women.[110]

Adequate childrearing and support for improved social conditions can only come when women are allowed to share the same intellectual climate as men. That this effort may destroy the basis for family organization and cultural control is something that social planners in developing countries have ignored. Coeducation which allows men and women to share taboo areas of tribal life could well destroy the tribe.

Another vote against sex-segregated schooling comes from the possibility that this procedure may be one way of dealing with racial desegregation. In the case of *Irma J. Smith, et al. & United States of America* v. *Concordia Parish School Board, et al.* the judge ruled that ". . . where black students perceive sex separation as racially motivated such would have a positive detrimental effect on their willingness to learn and general educational motivation. . . ." The

Court thus concludes that the separation of the sexes in the schools is educationally detrimental for black students and, as a result, educationally unsound and unconstitutional for the system as a whole.[111]

The research to date does not present a compelling argument in favor of sex separation as the answer to the sex-biased school. It is probable that more studies, with more rigorous controls and more adequate followup would reveal some critical times and places when boys and girls do benefit from separate educational treatment.

The American school system has the difficult task of showing boys and girls, adolescents and young adults that sex-appropriate roles can be defined within a very wide spectrum and that there is no danger of loss of sex identity. We still have a long way to go to achieve a sex-neutral school which supports security within one's own sexual identity.

◆   Summary

Boys and girls have been studied and researched, and yet no convincing evidence has been produced to demonstrate that one sex is brighter or more creative than the other, or that there are innate differences in cognitive functioning. Teachers respond to children in terms of sex-role stereotypes, and both male and female teachers consistently uphold sex biases.

The educational system is clearly biased, yet solutions such as recruitment of more male teachers or establishment of sex-separated classes have yet to be assessed. Meanwhile, parents and educators must see beyond the myths of sex differences in order to provide consistent and appropriate schooling for boys and girls.

References

1. Irving E. Sigel and Frank H. Hooper, eds., *Logical Thinking in Children: Research Based on Piaget's Theory* (New York: Holt, Rinehart and Winston, 1968).

2. O. L. Davis and June J. Slobodian, "Teacher Behavior Toward Boys and Girls During First Grade Reading Instruction," *American Educational Research Journal* 4 (1967): 261–269.

3. Leona E. Tyler, "Sex Differences," in *Encyclopedia of Educational Research*, ed. Robert E. Ebel (New York: Macmillan, 1969), p. 1218; see also Jeremy D. Finn, "Expectations and the Educational Environment," *Review of Educational Research* 42 (1972): 387–410.

4. Victor Rice, "An Appraisal of the Predictive Value of Patterns of Sub-test

Scores in Achievement Test Patterns," (Ph.D. diss., American University, 1967).

5. Jerome Kagan and Howard A. Moss, *Birth to Maturity* (New York: John Wiley & Sons, 1962), p. 9 (italics in original).

6. E. J. Sweeney, "Sex Differences in Problem Solving," (Ph.D. diss., Stanford University, 1954).

7. Rice, *op. cit.*, p. 55.

8. Lewis R. Aiken, "Attitude Toward Mathematics," *Review of Educational Research* 49 (October 1970): 551-596.

9. Herbert T. Olander and Charles L. Ehmer, "What Pupils Know About Vocabulary in Mathematics—1930 and 1968," *Elementary School Journal* 71 (April 1971): 361-367.

10. Julian C. Stanley, Daniel P. Keating, and Lynn Fox, eds., *Mathematical Talent: Discovery, Description and Development* (Baltimore: Johns Hopkins University Press, 1974), pp. 95-96; see also chapter 4.

11. William D. Altus, "Birth Order and Its Sequelae," *Science* 151 (1966): 44-49.

12. Aiken, *op. cit.*, p. 569.

13. J. P. Hill, "Similarity and Accordance Between Parents and Sons in Attitudes Toward Mathematics," *Child Development* 38 (1967): 777-791.

14. L. Carlsmith, "Effect of Early Father Absence on Scholastic Aptitude," *Harvard Educational Review* 34 (1964): 3-21; see also Elizabeth Herzog and Celia E. Sudia, *Boys in Fatherless Families* (Washington, D.C.: Childrens Bureau, Office of Child Development, 1971).

15. Aiken, *op. cit.*, p. 574.

16. Wilbur H. Dutton, "Attitudes of Prospective Teachers Towards Arithmetic," *Elementary School Journal* 52 (October 1951): 84-90.

17. Jerome Kagan, "Personality and the Learning Process," *Daedalus* 94 (Summer 1965): 553-563.

18. George D. Young, "The Use of Masculinity-Femininity Measures to Account for Sex Differences in Problem Solving," *California Journal of Educational Research* 12 (November 1961): 208-212.

19. Aiken, *op. cit.*, p. 569.

20. Philip W. Jackson, Jacob W. Getzels, and George A. Xydis, "Psychological Health and Cognitive Functioning in Adolescence: A Multivariate Analysis," *Child Development* 31 (1960): 285-298.

21. David E. Hunt and John Dopyera, "Personality Variation in Lower Class Children," *Journal of Psychology* 62 (1966): 47-54.

22. Sr. Rita Buddeke, *Differential Factoral Patterns of Boys and Girls in Algebraic Computation* (Washington, D.C.: Catholic University of America Press, 1960).

23. Sylvia Farnham-Diggory, "Cognitive Synthesis in Negro and White Children," *Monograph* of the Society for Research in Child Development 35, No. 2 (March, 1970): 75.

24. Richard R. E. Stafford, "Hereditary and Environmental Components of Quantitative Reasoning," *Review of Educational Research* 42 (1972): 183–201.

25. John Money, "Two Cytogenetic Syndromes: Psychologic Comparisons 1: Intelligence and Specific-Factor Quotients," *Journal of Psychiatric Research* 2 (1964): 223–231.

26. Eleanor E. Maccoby, "Sex Differences in Intellectual Functioning," in *The Development of Sex Differences*, ed. Eleanor E. Maccoby (Stanford: Stanford University Press, 1966), p. 51.

27. Psychological Corporation, *Academic Promise Test Manual* (*Grades Six to Nine*) (New York: Psychological Corporation, 1962). For a fuller statement see: Carol K. Tittle *et al.*, *Women and Educational Testing* (Princeton: Educational Testing Service, 1974).

28. W. W. Clark, "Boys and Girls—Are There Significant Ability and Achievement Differences?" *Phi Delta Kappan* 41 (1959): 73–76.

29. S. B. Sarason *et al.*, *Anxiety in Elementary School Children* (New York: John Wiley & Sons, 1960); see also John C. Cowen *et al.*, "The Relation of Anxiety in School Children to School Record Achievement and Behavioral Measures," *Child Development* 36 (1965): 685–695.

30. D. C. McClelland *et al.*, *The Achievement Motive* (New York: Appleton-Century Crofts, 1953), p 178.

31. Gerald S. Lesser, Rhoda N. Krawitz, and Rita Packard, "Experimental Arousal of Achievement Motivation in Adolescent Girls," *Journal of Abnormal and Social Psychology* 66 (1963): 59–66.

32. Sarason, *op. cit.*

33. Richard L. Masland, Seymour B. Sarason, and Thomas Gladwin, *Mental Subnormality* (New York: Basic Books, 1958), p. 261.

34. *Ibid.*

35. *Ibid.*

36. Kagan and Moss, *op. cit.*, p. 175 (italics added).

37. Walter Emmerich, "Continuity and Stability in Early Social Development: Teacher Ratings," *Child Development* 37, No. 1 (1966): 17–27.

38. Eleanor Maccoby, *The Development of Sex Differences* (Stanford: Stanford University Press, 1966), p. 26.

39. John Kangas and Katherine Bradway, "Intelligence at Middle Age: A Thirty-Eight Year Follow-up," *Developmental Psychiatry* 5, No. 2 (1971): 333–337.

40. Kagan and Moss, *op. cit.*, p. 152.

41. Marjorie P. Honzik, "Environmental Correlates of Mental Growth: Prediction from the Family Setting at 21 Months," *Child Development* 28 (1957): 338–364.

42. Sarane S. Boocock, *An Introduction to the Sociology of Learning* (Boston: Houghton-Mifflin, 1972), p. 83.

43. Masland, Sarason, and Gladwin, *op. cit.*, pp. 263–264.

44. Maccoby, *op. cit.*, pp. 47–48; see Boocock, *op. cit.*, p. 83 for schematic diagram; see also Ralph D. Norman, Betty P. Clark, and David W. Bessemer, "Age, Sex, I.Q. in Achieving and Nonachieving Gifted Children," *Exceptional Children* 29 (November 1962): 116-123.

45. Philip Goldberg, "Are Women Prejudiced Against Women?" *Trans-Action* 5 (1968): 28-30.

46. Doris R. Entwisle and Ellen Greenberger, "A Survey of Cognitive Style in Maryland Ninth-Graders; III. "Feelings of Control Over Academic Achievement," mimeographed (Baltimore: Johns Hopkins University Center for the Study of Social Organization of Schools, August 1970).

47. David B. Lynn, *Parental and Sex Role Identification* (Berkeley: McCutchan Publishing Company, 1969), p. 37.

48. *Ibid.*

49. Elyse S. Fleming and Ralph G. Anttonen, "Teacher Expectancy as Related to the Academic and Personal Growth of Primary-Age Children," *Monograph* of the Society for Research in Child Development 36, No. 5 (1971): 1-32.

50. E. Paul Torrance, "Can We Teach Children to Think Creatively?" *Journal of Creative Behavior* 6 (1972): 114-143.

51. Nathan Kogan, "Creativity and Sex Differences," *Journal of Creative Behavior* 8 (1974): 1-14.

52. Jacqueline H. Straus and Murray A. Straus, "Family Roles and Sex Differences in Creativity of Children in Bombay and Minneapolis," *Journal of Marriage and the Family* 30 (February 1968): 46-53.

53. Anne Anastasi and Charles E. Schaefer, "Notes on the Concepts of Creativity and Intelligence," *Journal of Creative Behavior* 5 (1971): 113-116; Linda Nochlin, "Why Have There Been No Great Women Artists?" *Artnews* 69 (January 1971): 22-39; Gary A. Davis and T. L. Belcher, "How Shall Creativity Be Measured? Torrance Tests, RAT, Alpha Biographical, and I.Q.," *Journal of Creative Behavior* 5 (1971): 153-161.

54. E. Paul Torrance, "Developing Women's Natural Gifts," *Women's Education* (AAUW) 4 (March 1965): 1.

55. Kenneth D. Wann, Miriam S. Dorn, and Elizabeth Ann Liddle, *Fostering Intellectual Development in Young Children* (New York: Teachers College Press, 1962), p. 77.

56. D. Auster and J. Modstad, "A Survey of Parents' Reactions and Opinions Concerning Certain Aspects of Education," *Journal of Educational Sociology* 31 (October 1957): 64-74; Haskin R. Pounds and Michael L. Hawkins, "Adult Attitudes on Teaching as a Career," *Journal of Teacher* 20 (Fall 1969): 339-342.

57. Ronald M. Pavalko, "Recruitment to Teaching: Pattern of Selection and Retention," *Sociology of Education* 43 (Summer 1970): 340-353; see also Jean D. Grambs, *Schools, Scholars and Society* (Englewood Cliffs, New Jersey: Prentice-Hall, 1965), p. 139.

58. Robert L. Thorndike and Elizabeth Hagan, "Characteristics of Men Who Remained in or Left Teaching," Project No. 574 OE23016 (Washington, D.C.: Office of Education, Cooperative Research Program, 1959-1960).

59. Andrew Fishel and Janice Pottker, "Women Teachers and Teacher Power," *Urban Review* 6 (November-December 1972): 40-44.

60. Alan Rosenthal, "The Strength of Teacher Organizations: Factors Influencing Membership in Two Large Cities," *Sociology of Education* 39 (Fall 1966): 359-380.

61. Alan Rosenthal, *Pedagoges and Power: Teacher Groups in School Politics* (Syracuse: Syracuse University Press, 1969), p. 45.

62. Harmon Zeigler, *The Political Life of American Teachers* (Englewood Cliffs, New Jersey: Prentice-Hall, 1967).

63. *Ibid.*

64. Kenneth V. Fast, Research Paper, College of Education, University of Maryland, 1972.

65. *Ibid.*

66. June R. Chapin and Richard E. Gross, "A Barometer of the Social Studies: Three Decades of Social Education," *Social Education* 34 (November 1970): 788-794+.

67. Henry Walbesser, Study in progress, University of Maryland, College of Education.

68. Joanne W. Saltz, "Teacher Stereotype—Liability in Recruiting?" *The School Review* 68 (Spring 1960): 105-111.

69. John H. Chilcott, "A Community Study of the Teacher Stereotype," unpublished paper, 1965.

70. Frances Gray Patton, *Good Morning, Miss Dove* (New York: Dodd, Mead and Company, 1954).

71. William Inge, *Good Luck, Miss Wyckoff* (Boston: Little, Brown and Company, 1970; Bantam Books Edition, 1971), p. 103.

72. Willard Waller, *The Sociology of Teaching* (New York: John Wiley and Sons, 1932), p. 50.

73. *Ibid.*, p. 409.

74. *Ibid.*, p. 375.

75. *Ibid.*, p. 379.

76. Arthur Foff, "The Teacher as Hero," in *Readings in Education*, ed. Arthur Foff and Jean D. Grambs (New York: Harper and Row, 1956); see also George Gerbner, "Smaller Than Life: Teachers and Schools in the Mass Media," *Phi Delta Kappan* 44 (February 1963): 202-205.

77. Bernard Bailyn, *Education in the Forming of American Society* (Chapel Hill, North Carolina: University of North Carolina Press, 1960); see also Richard A. Foster, *The School in American Literature* (Baltimore: Warwick and York, 1930); Dan C. Lortie, "The Balance of Control and Autonomy in Elementary School Teaching," in *The Semi-Professions and Their Organization*, ed. Amitai Etzioni (New York: Free Press, 1969), p.

21; "School Victims," *Saturday Evening Post*, April 6, 1918; Richard Hofstadter, *Anti-Intellectualism in American Life* (New York: Alfred A. Knopf, 1963), pp. 316–317, 320; and Amitai Etzioni, "The Women's Movement—Tokens vs. Objectives," *Saturday Review*, May 20, 1972, pp. 31–35.

78. Hofstadter, *op. cit.*, p. 320.

79. Jerome Kagan, "The Child's Sex Role Classification of School Objects," *Child Development* 35 (December 1964): 1051–1056.

80. Myron Leiberman, *Education as a Profession* (Englewood Cliffs, New Jersey: Prentice Hall, 1956), p. 249.

81. Albert J. Huggett and T. M. Stinnett, *Professional Problems of Teachers* (New York: Macmillan, 1956), p. 19.

82. Joseph A. Kershaw and Roland N. McKean, *Teacher Shortages and Salary Schedules* (New York: McGraw-Hill, 1962).

83. Catherine D. Lyon and Terry N. Saario, "Women in Public Education: Sex Discrimination in Promotions," *Phi Delta Kappan* 54 (October 1973): 123–130.

84. Ida H. Simpson and Richard L. Simpson, "Women and Bureaucracy in the Semi-Professions," in *The Semi-Professions and Their Organization*, ed. Amitai Etzioni (New York: The Free Press, 1969), p. 230.

85. Helen Morsink, "Leader Behavior of Men and Women Principals," *National Association of Secondary School Principals Bulletin* 54 (September 1970): 80–87. For summary of data on women as leaders in education and their influence on schooling see: Jean D. Grambs, "Sex Role and Educational Leadership," *Social Studies Journal* 2 (Winter 1973): 21–31.

86. Ward S. Mason, Robert J. Dressel, and Robert K. Bain, "Sex Role and the Career Orientations of Beginning Teachers," *Harvard Educational Review* 39 (Fall 1969): 370–383.

    While it can be shown that many male elementary teachers have masculinity scores as high as the average male secondary teacher, many of those with such scores were men who really did not want to teach in elementary school, were interested in moving into administrative jobs, or had a background in physical education and were certified for secondary teaching rather than elementary. Mildred S. Biedenkapp and Jacob D. Goering, "How Masculine are Male Elementary Teachers?" *Phi Delta Kappan* 52 (October 1971): 115.

87. Robert B. Carson, Keith Goldhammer, and Roland J. Pellegrin, *Teacher Participation in the Community* (Eugene, Ore.: University of Oregon, 1967), pp. 55–56; see also Donald J. Willowe, Terry L. Eidell, and Wayne K. Hoy, *The School and Pupil Control Ideology* (University Park, Pa.: Pennsylvania State University, 1967), p. 30ff.

88. *Ibid.*

89. Patrick D. Rocchio and Nolan C. Kearney, "Teacher-Pupil Attitudes as

Related to Nonpromotion of Secondary School Pupils," *Educational and Psychological Measurement* 16 (1956): 244-252.

90. Donald T. Schaeffer, *op. cit.*

91. Carl F. Backman and Paul F. Secord, *A Social Psychological View of Education* (New York: Harcourt, Brace and World, 1968), p. 144.

92. The Report of a Symposium on the Training of Teachers for Elementary Schools, an I.D.E.A. Occasional Paper, Melbourne, Florida, I.D.E.A., n.d.

93. Rodney N. Tolbert, "Should You Employ That Male Elementary Teacher?" *National Elementary Principal* 47 (February 1968): 40-43.

94. Boocock, *op. cit.*, p. 95.

95. *Ibid.*

96. Backman and Secord, *op. cit.*

97. Hjordis G. Ohberg, "Does the Black Child Need a Black Teacher?" *Integrated Education* 12 (March-April 1972): 27-28.

98. Henry B. Biller, *Father, Child and Sex Role* (Lexington, Mass.: D. C. Heath, 1971), p. 131.

99. Lewis P. Lipsitt and Charles Spikes, "Cross Sex Effect of Child and Adult," *Advances in Child Development and Behavior* (New York: Academic Press, 1965), 2: 101-103.

100. K. T. Hill and H. W. Stevenson, "The Effects of Social Reinforcement vs. Non-Reinforcement, and Sex of E on the Performance of Adolescent Girls," *Journal of Abnormal and Social Psych* 63 (1961): 147-154. K. T. Hill, "The Effects of Social Reinforcement and Non-Reinforcement Following Success and Failure as a Function of Test Anxiety of Subject, Sex of Subject, and Sex of Experimenter," (Ph.D. diss., University of Minnesota, 1965).

101. H. W. Stevenson, G. A. Hale, K. T. Hill and B. E. Moely, "Determinants of Children's Preferences for Adults," *Child Development* 38 (1967): 1-14.

102. Patrick C. Lee, "Male and Female Teachers in Elementary Schools: An Ecological Analysis," *Teachers College Record* 75 (September 1973): 79-98.

103. Thomas B. Lyles, "Grouping by Sex," *National Elementary Principal* 46 (November 1966): 38-41.

104. Donald Cooks, unpublished communication to the author, Kirchgater Elementary School, Sacramento, California, Segregated Classes Evaluation, 1971.

105. Emily Kernkamp and Eleanor Price, "Co-education May Be a 'No-No' for the Six-Year-Old Boy," *Phi Delta Kappan* 53 (1972): 662-663.

106. W. Paul Blakely and Erma M. Shadle, "A Study of Two Readiness for Reading Programs in Kindergarten," *Elementary English* 38 (November 1961): 503-505.

107. John K. Fisher and Walter B. Waetjen, "An Investigation of the Relation-

ship Between the Separation by Sex of Eighth-Grade Boys and Girls and English Achievement and Self-Concept," *Journal of Educational Research* 59 (May-June 1966): 409–412.

108. Joseph R. Ellis and Joan L. Peterson, "Effects of Same Sex Class Organization on Junior High Student's Academic Achievement, Self-Discipline, Self-Concept, Sex Role Identification, and Attitude Toward School," *Journal of Educational Research* 64 (July-August 1971): 456–464.

109. R. R. Dale, *Mixed or Single-Sex School?*, 2 vols. (London: Routledge and Kegan Paul, 1970).

110. Richard Greenough, "Coeducation as a World Trend," *School and Society* 98 (January 1970): 31–32.

111. Scott W. Kester, "Sex Separation—New Strategy for Discrimination," *Integrated Education* 11 (November-December 1971): 30–33.

9

Beyond High School

Most American youth finish high school. By the time they graduate they have accumulated twelve years of education. This twelve-year progress through the American school system is a widely variable experience: for some students schooling has been marred by fear and failure; for others it has been a steady accumulation of honors and recognition. For most it has been an emotionally confusing mixture. By the time youth graduate from high school they are able to vote; in many states they can make critical decisions without parental consent. They are free at last to be grown up, to be masters of their own fate.

◆ The College Experience

But the end of high school is not the end of education. A very large portion of American youth complete the twelve-year cycle knowing that ahead of them lie at least four more years of education. To be college educated does not mark one as a member of an elite group, but only as someone more fortunate than one's peers. Do young men and women respond differently to the college experience because of their sex? Are men and women more alike or more divergent as a result of a college education?

Who Goes to College?

The likelihood of a given student going to college—any college—is related to three major factors: sex, income, and ethnic origin. If the individual is white, from an above-average income home, and male, then he is very likely to go to some kind of college. If, in addition,

179

he is moderately intelligent, his chances of going to a four-year college or university are about 100 percent. Only a very determined youngster who fits these criteria can manage to avoid college. He has been tracked for college from his earliest school experience. If he shows no intellectual interests and does poorly in his course work the full academic armament is brought to bear: special counseling, testing, conferring with parents. As young dropouts will testify, it takes tremendous ego strength and determination, if you are male, bright, affluent, and white, *not* to proceed to college.

If the student is female, white, rich, and intelligent, she too is highly likely to go on to some kind of college, but if she decides not to, the world does not cave in. Since seventh grade this girl has been pressured to select college preparatory curricula. She may make good grades—very good grades compared to those of many college-bound males. But the rate of college attendance among this female group, while high, is not as high as among males.

If a student is male, white, bright but poor, his chances of getting to college are decreased substantially; this is even truer for the female. At the lowest socioeconomic levels, boys have a 26 percent advantage over girls in getting to college, an 86 percent greater chance of completing college, and a drastic 250 percent greater chance of attending graduate or professional schools. Among the very affluent, boys still have a great advantage over girls. Boys have a 20 percent greater chance of attending college, a 28 percent greater chance of finishing, and a 129 percent better chance of obtaining post-college education.[1] The influence of intelligence does not counteract the overwhelming contribution made by economic status and sex in determining who will get to college, remain there, and advance into professional work.[2] Equal educational opportunity, indeed!

Higher education for blacks has been one of the disgraces of America.[3] It was years after the Civil War that the first southern colleges were open to Negroes. Some few blacks were able to obtain higher education in northern universities, but these were a very small minority. The hallmarks of black colleges have been 1) grossly inadequate financing and 2) rigid restrictions on students. The biased financing of land-grant black colleges is another story, but it certainly accounts for the disparity between the aspirations and achievements of poor black and poor white students. The data show that more black females than males have sought higher education and completed college.[4] The reasons for this are various. The low income of black families has made it imperative that all who could work should do so. Until very recently, the opportunities available to black college educated males were highly restricted. In the 1950s one Negro mother explained her lack of enthusiasm about her son's ambitions: "His uncle is a college graduate, and he is a Pullman porter; why should my son break his heart on college and end as a day laborer?" A black girl could almost always count on a teaching position in a black school, or a job as a nurse in a black hospital or ward.

With the emphasis on equal occupational opportunity the patterns of black college enrollments have shifted. Increasing numbers of black students, particularly males, are attending college, and their vocational goals are high. The black community is aware of the acute shortage of black lawyers, doctors, engineers, and scientists of all kinds, plus middle and upper echelon business and government personnel. White colleges and universities are under heavy pressure to recruit black youth, and regularly bid for the top black students with scholarship aid.

Other minority groups have fared less well in attaining higher education. The Mexican-American group has been extremely marginal, with very few attending college or completing degree work. The Mexican-American male is more apt to be interested in higher education than is the female, for the culture supports his ambition and his entry into a wider community. However, the female is not encouraged to pursue higher education. A similar situation exists among the Puerto Rican and American Indian groups. When family resources are allocated, it is the males who are favored.

Sex and College Careers

Just as high schools and poor families discriminate against bright girls in favor of boys who want to go to college, so the colleges themselves have discriminated against girls by setting limits on the number of girls to be admitted. One's sex has been at least as important as one's intelligence in determining admission to college. In July, 1970, testimony before a special subcommittee on the House Subcommittee on Education and Labor revealed:

We know that many colleges admit fixed proportions of men and women each year, resulting in a freshman class with fewer women meeting higher standards than it would contain if women were admitted on the same basis as men. At Cornell University, for example, the ratio of men to women remains three to one from year to year; at Harvard/Radcliffe, it is four to one. The University of North Carolina at Chapel Hill's fall 1969 "Profile of the Freshman Class" states, "admission of women on the freshmen level will be restricted to those who are especially well qualified." They admitted 3,231 men, or about half the male applicants, and 747 women, about one-fourth the female applicants. Chapel Hill is a state supported institution.[5]

Women's groups have mounted a vigorous attack on all such discriminatory policies, and the response has been visible: for instance, in 1973 Stanford University announced the abandonment of all quotas on the admission of women.

The colleges' traditional discrimination against women is in part derived from a general lack of enthusiasm for higher education for women at all. The early American colleges defined their task as preparing students for law, medicine, and the ministry. A few "select academies" were founded to educate "gentlewomen" in the household arts, needlework, music, and etiquette. Oberlin College was the first to allow men and women to study together for a baccalaureate degree.

The issue of coeducation in college, as in high school, was hotly debated during the nineteenth century. It was considered unseemly to educate women because it made them think like men, and they were thought presumptuous to want a professional career. In 1869 the United States Supreme Court upheld the Illinois State Bar's refusal to admit a woman, on the grounds that "the natural and proper timidity and delicacy which belong to the female sex evidently unfit it for many of the occupations of civil life."[6]

Although women were allowed to attend institutions of higher learning along with men in the latter half of the nineteenth century, it was felt more appropriate that special colleges be established for women. The prestigious Seven Sisters women's colleges that paralleled the Ivy League men's colleges were an attempt to provide women with the equivalent of men's education.

Bryn Mawr, for instance, was founded by Quakers who believed that "women must be sensible and able; they should be equal to taking part in the thought and discussion of the vital things with which Friends were constantly occupied. [Thus they established] . . . a college for the advanced education and care of young women and girls of the higher and more refined classes of society."[7] M. Carey Thomas, the president of Bryn Mawr during its most formative years fought to make the college as rigorous and intellectually substantial as Harvard. Her demand that the faculty have Ph.Ds and that the entrance examination be as selective as that of Harvard brought ridicule—but she won. She used the college as a means of opening professional opportunities for her select student body. But as times changed, and more women went to every kind of college, Bryn Mawr, like the other elite women's colleges, "capitulated utterly to society's regressive view of women," so that today's graduates are merely "intellectual decorations."[8] There were some women's colleges who saw their mission as preparing upper class women for their family role and for responsible public spirited volunteer work. The finishing school was extended for four years instead of the earlier two.

Men's colleges have had no such identity problems. They have had a clear awareness of their function and role. Men's colleges were established to prepare their students for the world of business, for the professions, and to be intelligent patrons of the arts. Men's colleges have been the source of faculty for universities, funneling the best students, or those least interested in business, into graduate specialties.

The future of sex-segregated colleges is uncertain.[9] Each year several join the ranks of coeducational institutions. This may be due in part to financial difficulties, but it may also reflect acceptance of the belief that men and women fare better if they share intellectual experiences. Arguments against coeducation are that in the coed institution women are underrepresented in leadership roles, and that in mixed sex classes men do most of the talking.[10] But women are quiet even in all-female classes; instructors at women's colleges have complained about the passivity of their students.[11] It has been argued that it is valuable for both men and women to see women faculty members in coed colleges as role models.

Except in Catholic women's colleges, most college presidents are men. A study of the governing boards of institutions of higher learning showed that in 1969 a majority of college trustees were male, at least fifty years old, and white.[12]

Although women are pressing for greater academic encouragement and support, college girls will find relatively few women as role models to emulate on the typical college campus. The percentage of women obtaining advanced degrees has consistently declined.[13] Women who manage to complete a graduate program and obtain the final graduate degree face limited job opportunities at the college

level. Just as colleges have discriminated against female students in
their admissions policies, so they have also discriminated against wom-
en in their hiring policies. Male colleges traditionally had all-male
faculties, and by the mid-1960s even the faculties of female colleges
were predominantly male.

Once on the faculty, women advance significantly more slowly
than men. Almost two-thirds of all full professors are men. At lower
ranks, with less prestige, women outnumber men: 34.8 percent of
college faculty at the instructor level (a nontenured rank) are female,
and only 16.3 percent are male.[14] Women must wait longer for those
promotions which do come. Furthermore, they are paid less than
men at every professorial rank in most colleges and universities.[15]
A case study of women in sociology shows how the system works.
Relatively few women are on the faculties of those "prestige" colleges
or universities producing the "best" sociologists. Of those women who
are teaching in such institutions, a much higher proportion than men
are also degree holders from the institution. Even with comparable
rank, women are more apt to teach undergraduate courses than men.
The author of this case study comments,

The components of career advancement are the same for men and women: (1)
individual prestige and (2) organizational treatment and rewards. Men, as their
careers advance, gain more organizational rewards, which leads to more individual prestige; the more their prestige advances, the more their careers advance . . . and so on in an ascending spiral. Rewards are cumulative . . . with
additional rewards going to those who already have the prestige of previous
awards.

For women, the same circuitous relation becomes a vicious circle: Because
women do not have high prestige they do not advance in their careers; because
they do not advance in their careers, they do not receive organizational rewards;
and because they do not receive organizational rewards, their prestige remains
low. Thus, the system of sponsored mobility in academia systematically excludes
women from organizational rewards.[16]

Recognition of the barriers facing women who seek to advance
their careers has caused many professional organizations to form special committees on the status of women. Committee W of the American Association of University Professors has come to life on many
campuses. Achievement of parity in access to higher education and
equal treatment within the system are the goals of academic women.[17]

The Impact of the College Experience

Traditionally parents send their children to colleges that convey an image of education (and of society) congruent with their own view. Most students are relatively unchanged by their college experiences: they choose the college that most fits what it is they have already become, in terms of attitudes and values and goals in life. That is, girls or boys who choose liberal, permissive colleges tend to be that way before the college experience; those who choose denominational, engineering, or teacher education institutions also reveal significantly homogeneous traits. This is not to imply that the four-year college experience is of little significance in the young adult's life. It is during these years that vocational choice usually becomes explicit; a marital partner may be chosen, and general values are solidified. However, most of these decisions are in keeping with what the student was like on entry. If the student was conservative, he or she will remain relatively conservative; if previously liberal, they will retain this stance.[18]

Although much research shows that the college experience has little impact on a student's political views, other research indicates that there is a considerable difference in the political opinions of those who go to college and those who do not. College educated adults tend to have more liberal political views, and they accept divergent views more readily.[19] In 1970 college educated young people were much more likely to have liberal or radical political views than young persons who have not yet gone to college or were not going to go. The group who had no college goals were the least liberal.[20]

According to some studies women change more than men as a result of the college experience. The greatest changes are reported to occur among women enrolled in humanities programs.[21] Women become less stereotyped in their thinking after four years of college, less rigid and authoritarian than males.[22]

Prejudice toward other groups is a complex matter, and when studied in the college context such things as membership in a Greek house as well as courses selected may make a difference in the amount and direction of change over four years, but here again women appear to be more influenced by their education. A study of white women undergraduates showed that they developed greater tolerance toward persons outside their group, such as Jews and blacks, than did men.[23] Personality tests find college women to be more conforming and more sociable than men, and the change in attitudes may be due to the impact of peer culture in college, rather than the result of a "real" personality shift.[24] While males become more homogeneous in their values as they progress through college, females develop wider differences. A study by Stewart[25] found that most of the reported changes took place during the freshman year or early in the sophomore year. A little bit of college, it would seem, may be quite a dangerous thing!

There have been major efforts to determine if the college experience changes ideas. The data show increased tolerance, a shift from conventional views to more open views. However, a study of the way students spend their time at one rather typical campus indicates that most students are not engaged in serious intellectual endeavors.

> . . . the informal, peer-group aspect of student life in the university does not generally support the intellectual-academic objectives which are the manifest educational function of the university. This observation is scarcely new, but the study does provide a body of concrete evidence that the interests supposedly cultivated in the classroom and its adjuncts are not carried over into peer-group interaction to any significant extent . . . intellectual activities (other than regular academic work) took up only about . . . half an hour a day of student time.[26]

And the faculty are as little interested in what students do outside of class as students are interested in what faculty do! There are no sex differences in these findings.[27]

Who Gets the Rewards of the System?

Going to college requires some effort, some interest in achieving— something. Studies of the achievement push show that it is a strong drive in men. How much achievement women seek, in what direction, and under what kind of stress remains relatively unstudied. One research effort, already a classic, was provided by Horner. She asked a sample of freshman and sophomore men and women to project their personal response to a hypothetical situation. The women responded to this statement: "After first-term finals, Anne finds herself at the top of her medical school class." The name John was substituted in the version given to the men. The women responded in three ways: most frequently there was fear of being rejected, of losing friends and dates which required that one keep success a secret or pretend it had nothing to do with being smart. The second type of response indicated a feeling of guilt, questioning whether it was normal for a girl to be so smart, to get so far ahead. The third type of response was a denial of the success, a refusal to recognize it. Two-thirds of the women responded in one of these three ways; only 10 percent of the men gave responses that fell into one of these categories.[28]

Analysis of achievement records of men and women during the college years shows that women consistently receive higher grades than men. The pattern of higher grades for girls continues from elementary and secondary school into college. In one large university women obtained higher grades no matter how the pie was sliced: by class level, dormitory residents versus commuters, Greeks versus non-Greeks, and by area of study. Although the differences were not great, they were all in the same direction. One would assume that a good grade point average would increase any student's self-esteem. But women seem not to be influenced by the grades they attain: their perceptions of themselves are independent of their academic achievement. Is this because getting the man is more important than getting the grade?[29]

Although they may achieve higher grades, women do not typically fill the leadership roles in college, a pattern evident in precollege education. In coeducational colleges, 95 percent of the student body presidents were male and 94 percent of class presidents were male. Men were far more likely than women to hold such offices as student union board chairman, debate team captain, judicial board chairman, activities committee chairman, and freshman orientation committee chairman. Women held 25 percent of the newspaper editorships, 49 percent of the yearbook editorships, and 30 percent of literary magazine editorships. The smaller the college the more likely were women to have an opportunity for leadership, but even then most positions were held by men.[30] Like blacks, who lose their opportunity to emerge as leaders when they are a small minority in a college, women are submerged in coed schools.

As in high school, the focus of school spirit on athletics means that the men who succeed in competitive interscholastic athletics garner many of the rewards available within the system: recognition, scholarships, special educational attention. For many poor white boys, and for many disadvantaged black males, college athletics have been a very significant and even necessary conduit to upward mobility. Without the extensive programs of grants-in-aid it is doubtful whether

many black athletes would have succeeded in college or later in professional sports. It is unfortunate that this huge subsidy is limited to
the small group of students who are athletically talented. The greatest
subsidy goes to those in the major intercollegiate sports: football,
basketball, track, swimming, baseball. Except in large schools, such
sports as archery, golf, wrestling, and lacrosse may receive no aid.

　　Until very recently, discrimination against women in the athletic
domain provoked no comment, although the bias was extreme. In one
university, athletic scholarships for men amounted to nearly a half
million dollars, with almost the same amount allocated to salaries of
thirty-one full and part-time coaches. The women's athletic director
pointed out that in her ten sport program, including Olympic cham-
pion competition areas, no coaches were provided; all had to be volunteers, and there was no money for recruitment or scholarships.[31]

　　In June 1974, guidelines for implementing the ban against sex
discrimination in education, the famous Title IX of the Educational
Amendments of 1972, were issued. These guidelines were submitted
for public review and response;[32] the extent to which they will detail
specific discriminatory acts to be remedied will be determined some
time in 1975. The response to the guidelines by men and women, by
educators and special interest groups, has been most vociferous regarding the call for equity in athletic activities. According to some
college spokesmen, providing equity for women will ruin men's athletics, as there are not funds for both sexes, particularly if scarce
money must be used to upgrade facilities and staff for women. The
prospect of women in coed sports and on coed teams has outraged
many. Prior to the issuance of these guidelines, the Association for
Intercollegiate Athletics for Women was opposed to any athletic
scholarships for women in order to avoid the abuses that such scholarships had brought to male athletic programs, but finally "women began to suspect the zeal with which men in sports encouraged women
not to get entangled in the scholarship program."[33]

　　The impending struggle for equality in education, particularly
higher education, now buttressed by legal guides and sanctions, will
undoubtedly have a major impact on the achievement patterns of
both men and women in the years ahead. What women are finding
out, however, as in the case of athletic equity, is that men will not
easily give up their privileged positions, nor willingly share the goods
of higher education. On campus after campus women are beginning
to gather data, to organize, and to sue.

The effect of efforts to equalize educational opportunities are already evident. The number of women applying to law schools and medical schools has increased greatly. Dental schools, veterinary schools, and graduate business schools have more women applying. Although previous admissions procedures utilized quota systems of all kinds—limiting the number of out-of-state applicants, Jews, Catholics, alumni—all such systems are under legal attack. Any quota system, even one designed to rectify previous discriminatory acts, may be unconstitutional.[34]

Another significant shift in educational opportunities for women is the decision of almost all the Ivy League colleges to become co-educational. Amherst announced that the freshman class of 1975 would be open to women. The prestige associated with a Yale or Princeton degree gives an individual added points when applying to graduate school or professional school, and has traditionally worked against women. In a few years women will have degrees from Amherst or Williams, and the final bastions of male privilege will be thrown open.

College has traditionally provided men with models to emulate. Courses in the social sciences, literature, or business administration describe the activities of successful men. The influence of such models is significant. Psychologists made an important contribution to our understanding of human motivation by pointing out the role of models in affecting individual decisions. If a person knows that others like himself have achieved recognition, status, power, or wealth, then he has some hope that he too may achieve such eminence. Lacking any model of achievement, one may work hard to succeed, but the burden of doubt regarding one's possible success may become too much to bear. This has been the situation for women, and college courses have done nothing to alleviate it. Social science courses deal with the achievements (as well as the pathologies) of men, not women. Political histories tell about kings, generals, and revolutionaries; sociology details the lives of male criminals, while psychology spends much of its time experimenting with male subjects. Thus the system lets the male student learn about who he is and what he can become. Women, on the other hand, have learned next to nothing about female psychology, sociology, or history. They have found few models in the subject matter they have studied. In an effort to change this situation, courses in women's studies have been established at many institutions in the last five years.

"The Board of Education requires me to give you some basic information of sex, reproduction and other disgusting filth."

There are reports that approximately four thousand courses in women's studies are being taught in colleges and universities across the country. These courses are primarily attended by women. They will provide their students with models, and will give them some knowledge about themselves. If some of these students choose academic careers and incorporate their specialized knowledge about women into general courses for all students, there may be a readjustment in the balance of who learns what about whom.

For the present, men remain the primary beneficiaries of the academic system. Men continue to be favored in hiring and promotion. And the achievements of men remain the subject of most courses. This state of affairs is open to challenge from women. It is highly probable that in a few decades the imbalance will be lessened, and equal educational opportunity may be nearer at hand.

Some Don't Make It

For many young men and women the four college years present an opportunity to clarify their identity and determine their direction in life. Away from home, a college student can be independent most days of the year, and yet dependent on family for financial support. If necessary, the student can return periodically to a secure haven— his own room, a full refrigerator, and solicitude over his health. That all is not rosy, however, is demonstrated by the statistics on suicide among college youth. Among the men, suicide is a tragically high cause of death. Although many more young women attempt suicide, very few succeed.[35]

The separation from home is difficult for both men and women. A college dropout may be a student in the throes of a "separation crisis" and unable to leave home either psychologically or physically. Recognizing this fact, a few innovative colleges have recently accepted students on a "deferred admission" basis which allows them a year to adjust to being out of high school and to test the strength of the umbilical cord.

The girl, who may show her distress by suicidal calls for help, may be coping with different problems. The college years may be providing her with an unwanted "psychosocial moratorium," to borrow a phrase from Erik Erikson. "Women are psychologically prepared to start on their life task sooner than men. A four-year college moratorium cannot realistically be expected to detain the young woman in her anxious hopes for marriage and a family."[36]

The girl in college may feel ambivalent about her goals and purpose, unsure whether it is wise to postpone marriage in order to seek academic achievement. A study of campus culture points to a particular problem area for women:

We would hypothesize that identity seeking is high in the first years of college because American culture creates identity problems for girls about the time they enter college. About 20 percent of the girls in the present sample fitted into the identity-seeker social type. While the role conflict for college girls that was celebrated in the writings of two decades ago has probably been blunted, the resulting situation has been less one of clarification of the female role than diffusion of ambition. The middle-class girl entering college now assumes that she is going to be a wife and mother but she also feels that she must have some stopgap vocation to fill in a few years just in case she does not marry by the time she leaves college. . . . But she has also been encouraged by her society to think that she should do something independent and exciting for a few years before settling down. . . . College is generally her first occasion to play that role out from under the protective cover of the home. . . .[37]

Colleges and universities are increasingly sensitive to the personality upheavals that college precipitates; almost all offer psychological counseling and psychiatric referral. A higher proportion of women than men seek such help. One interesting finding was that of those seeking help, over two-thirds were either first born or only children, and this was true of both men and women.[38] About three-quarters of this group dropped out of college, but very few because of academic failure.[39]

Numerous studies show more women than men seeking help, psychological or medical, reporting more personal adjustment problems, and indeed having a higher rate of institutionalization for mental illness (see Chapter 3), but studies indicate that it is easier for a girl to admit having a problem. In view of the number of suicides among males, as against the suicide attempts of women, college personnel have begun to ponder the ways in which institutional arrangements reinforce the reluctance of troubled males to obtain help.

Colleges have been justly criticized for having little significant impact on many students or for having a negative and disturbing effect on others. The agonies of the troubled campuses of the sixties made many thoughtful educators reassess the impact of college.[40] The questioning and discontent of both men and women, erupting violently on many campuses, seemed to reflect deep dissatisfaction with the prevailing view of the purpose of education. Both men and women wanted more than a certificate leading to a job. They wanted preparation for life.

✦   The Revolutionary Generation

It was in the colleges that young people were exposed to the "new radicalism" of the sixties. The phenomenon of student militance has become familiar to the general public. It is not restricted to the United States, but is observable in universities in Japan, France, Spain, Chile, Germany. Is it the fault of the colleges that youth are revolting? Or is it the times that have tried the souls of youth?[41]

The widely publicized disruptions of colleges and universities that occurred between 1964 and 1973 produced a tremendous volume of study and comment, and considerable reevaluation of the purpose of higher education.

The Hard Revolution

Segregating large groups of young people in highly concentrated areas can easily produce an explosive situation. Dissent is contagious. Never before have so many people of a single age group been gathered in so few places. Often, twenty thousand or more young adults are concentrated on one campus and they have sophisticated means of communication available to them. Campus newspapers, radio stations, television stations, mobile sound trucks allow a few articulate and determined leaders to be heard by thousands of students. And in the 1960s there were four major factors provoking American students to outrage and violence: 1) uncertainty over the draft and the unpopularity of the war; 2) the blacks' dissatisfaction with the slowness of the "political" solution to social and economic inequities, a dissatisfaction that attracted the sympathy and support of idealistic white youth; 3) an unprecedented state of national affluence and high rates of employment; 4) growing disillusionment with government and its leaders. These several factors explain a good deal of the student unrest of the last decade. Of even greater significance, perhaps, is the fact that all these young people learned at about the same time that authority was vulnerable: one clear voice could indeed bring the whole works to a screeching halt. A speech by Mario Savio has often been quoted as the spark which precipitated the contagious University of California disturbances: "There is a time when the operation of the machine [the university] becomes so odious, makes you so sick at heart that you can't take part. . . . You've got to put your bodies upon the gears and upon the levers, upon all the apparatus and you've got to make it stop."[42] Such rhetoric is heady stuff, and when combined with deep anger over individual mistreatment and social injustice, it can compel students to abandon slow political methods for achieving change.[43]

Most of the students involved in campus disturbances were white, middle class, above average in academic standing and intelligence, and *male*. The men described themselves as ". . . significantly more critical, curious, idealistic, individualistic, impulsive, informed, moody, perceptive, rebellious and restless than did those in a randomly selected sample."[44] Most anti-war demonstrators were male. The few young women involved in the anti-war movement were not students, and thus had more time to give to "the cause."[45]

Why were the young men the leaders of the student revolts? The answer lies in the traditional roles of men and women in our society. Not only was it unlikely that a young women would express violent opposition to the status quo, it was also unlikely that anyone would listen if she did. Male leadership in the student revolts was consistent with the role expectations of young men—and women. Whatever the activity—voter registration, desegregation of transportation, marches to demand legal redress—the young women found themselves performing traditional tasks of cooking, caring for children, doing the secretarial work. The women who were asserting their right to stand with the men in bringing Columbia University to a halt found themselves relegated to traditional roles: ". . . a call went out for women volunteers to cook for the hungry strikers. One young female revolutionary protested that 'women were not fighting the revolution to stay in the kitchen,' and the call was amended to ask for *people* to man the kitchen."[46] Dissatisfaction with treatment of women in the civil rights movement prompted Ruby Doris Smith Robinson, co-founder of SNCC, to write a statement protesting their subservient role: "It was laughed at and dismissed."[47] In commenting on the New Left movement, one of the emerging leaders in the women's movement noted, "From the beginning, it was clear to me that the Movement didn't really make room for women. A lot of women came in expecting a radically new scene. Like, here was a group of young people with a new politics, a new lifestyle, a new sexual honesty and freedom. And still, the notion of a liberated woman was someone who is indiscriminate about whom she sleeps with, not a realization that women don't want to be objects. A lot of Movement women might just as well have gone to Scarsdale."[48]

While the campus revolution was carried by men, the very fact that they treated movement women in stereotypic fashion may have radicalized the women into creating their own freedom movement.

Despite the expectation that women would not be leaders, the questioning of traditional ways of doing things was irresistible.

An interesting by-product of the hard revolution was its impact on other aspects of college life. Language has been "liberated," and four-letter words are used commonly. The shock value of the words reached a peak about 1970; few adults react any longer with instinctive anger at a well-placed obscenity. Symptomatic of the changed attitude toward language was the reception accorded the publication of the transcripts of President Nixon's confidential White House conversations. The term "expletive deleted" very quickly became a signal for laughter. When unexpurgated versions of the transcripts were finally published, the response was surprise that they were in fact so mild! It is probable that Nixon was responding to his own upbringing when such words were never used in public and uttering them in the presence of a woman was inconceivable. How have times changed! What we are witnessing is the passing of the double standard, and the demise of the lady. One linguist reported that women's swearing in general has increased drastically in the last ten to fifteen years. Women not only swear more freely, but "the stronger taboo against using words referring to bodily functions also is crumbling—more so on the East and West Coasts than in the Midwest. . . ."[49]

College students expressed their new freedom with an abandonment of "nice" clothes as well as "nice" language. Both men and women adopted sandals and jeans as classroom and dating attire. On some campuses the battle of pants for women almost paralleled the intensity with which males fought for the right to wear their hair long. By 1970 it was not uncommon to see female faculty members wearing pants, and soon secretaries and clerks found that pants were more economical and more comfortable. Both young men and women have come to dress in ways which they perceive as expressing their own personalities. On some campuses, the new conformity is to be nonconformist.

The dissent of black youth has taken its own distinctive form. The Afro or so-called natural hairdo marked the revolutionary black student. Although few Africans wear their hair in this style, the fact that straightening hair is an effort to imitate whites made it inevitable that the flaunting of fuzzy unstraightened hair would become a symbol of "black is beautiful." In the 1970s "corn-rowing" became the radical black hair style. In the sixties it was possible to assess the radicalism of a black audience by the number of persons with Afro hair styles. In the south these were rare; anyone with an Afro might be seized by police for provoking to riot. In the north and west youth who did not wear Afros might be called Uncle Toms by their peers. Some black youth leaders had to obtain Afro wigs in order to become believable to their followers. Blacks openly denigrate whites on college campuses, particularly at large state universities and urban colleges. The black movement on campus has taken other forms as well: demands for black studies, separate dormitories, separate clubs and meeting rooms, special counselors, and remedial programs if needed. Black male students provide leadership. Although Ms. Angela Davis has provided a singularly interesting model for assertive black intellectual women, the typical dissident black student group finds women in supportive rather than aggressive roles—as long as there are black men to fill the latter.

One manifestation of the hard revolution that most adults find difficult to comprehend has been the popularity of drugs and "mood-changing" pills. Campus youth discovered marijuana. LSD was invented (more or less) on a university campus. The extent of drug use and abuse by college students is difficult to assess, since self-report data which might prove incriminating are not easily obtained. Estimates vary wildly as to the number of students involved. It is probable that at no time has the number of youth partaking in the drug culture been anywhere near the number who are part of the alcohol culture. There is a sex differential in the use of illegal drugs. Males are far more apt to be involved in the more serious kinds of drug use, and to require hospitalization from a "bad trip." The familiar pattern repeats itself: males are educated to be more daring, to take risks to prove their masculinity. College men are more anxious about life, and often experience an acute crisis in self-esteem during the early college years; drug-induced euphoria or oblivion seems a desirable escape. Women are more fearful about risks, and far less responsive to the dare. College women show an interesting contradiction: although usually more open to suggestion than men, in a serious situation they do not respond to peer group pressure. The socialization that girls have received seems to make them more immune to the lures of the drug culture.

A study of marijuana use at one large institution found that more females than males reported never using it, slightly more females than males said they had smoked it five times or less during the previous months, and a larger percentage of males than females had smoked five times or more. Only 5 percent of those classed as "hippies" said they had never smoked it, while 68 percent of those who were typed as "succeeders" or highly motivated students stated they had never used marijuana. Freshmen were more likely to try it than seniors, and students majoring in the humanities were more likely to try it than those in the natural sciences. Students from affluent families were more likely to smoke pot. Among those not using drugs, males were more likely than females to plan to study further after graduation. In summarizing the data, the researchers note: ". . . the use of drugs such as marijuana is highly associated with a subcultural normative system which has taken on the proportions of a social movement in attracting many students (and school dropouts) to what may be a radically redefined world view. It is probably participation in this ill-defined but obviously important student subculture rather than drug use itself that accounts for the findings that were summarized above."[50]

One product of the hard revolution was the "hippie" scene of the late 1960s. At first the lifestyle of the so-called counterculture was interesting, in the sense that the youth who congregated in Haight-Ashbury or Greenwich Village expressed a desire for a new kind of freedom—to love, to be themselves, to put spiritual gratification above material things, to engage in genuine communion with each other, to partake of enhanced religious experiences. For a year or so the new movement seemed to be succeeding: it produced a sense of brotherhood, companionship without hangups, a blossoming of creativity in the arts, music, and dance, a discovery of the excitement of natural things—the woods, home grown food, nongadgeted homes—and there was a contagious euphoria. College youth flocked to these centers, and tried out all these new things.[51] For some it was a good experience; for others it was a "bad trip." The drug scene turned ugly; exploiters appeared quickly, and violence or extreme apathy took over.[52] Many aspects of the counterculture filtered out, however, into lifestyles that are apparent on most college campuses today, and have influenced what we call the quiet revolution among college youth.

The Quiet Revolution

Disruptive behavior, whether rioting, using obscenities, wearing odd clothes with extra long hair, taking drugs, comprised what we called the hard revolution. The majority of students on any campus are *not* part of the hard revolution. Their hair may be somewhat longer, they may find sandals comfortable, may try a "joint" once or twice, but few engage in direct confrontation with society's norms, or with university authority.

But many college youth are experiencing what we call, for want of a better term, the quiet revolution. These youth make a virtue of appearing to be poor; if they live off campus their rooms and apartments are decorated with candles and India prints, and are sparsely filled with furniture bought at flea markets or the Salvation Army. The ethos is for remaining independent and away from home, and only a few of their classes "turn them on." They may be active in "free university" classes, attend film classic series, collect records of some special group or era (depending on what is in at the moment), and support such causes as free birth control information, food co-operatives, and doing your own thing. Students have turned toward orthodox religious groups on campus, and these have responded by putting on rock music masses, and other nontraditional worship services.

The attitudes of these students are not very different from those of the "square" types. Toward sex, for example, there is a genuine liberalizing of attitude on the part of all students. Even that bastion of conservatism, the middle western small town, has not been impervious to changing sexual mores. One study of a college group composed of students from such towns produced findings which surprised even the researcher: ". . . the most unexpected finding . . . was that the girls in this sample tended more consistently to take the 'liberal' position on controversial issues than the boys did." The boys were much more anti-divorce where children were involved, although they were more supportive of sexual permissiveness than the girls.[53] These students were very much aware of their professors' views on sex, marriage, and divorce, and it is probable that they were highly influenced by their professors' views.[54]

While fewer women are virgins at the end of four years of college,[55] nearly half the men continue to prefer a wife who is a virgin at marriage. The women may be moving toward acceptance of premarital sexual relationships, but many men hold onto the double standard.[56] One researcher commented, ". . . while male attitudes may be changing, they may not be changing as rapidly as the sexual behavior of college women. Consequently, this discrepancy may result in male attitudes which are out of step with changes in the behavior

of college women and point to an area which will cause some difficulty and conflict between sexes."[57]

Other data do not indicate greater liberality on the part of wom-
en. In their attitudes toward abortion, for instance, undergraduate
males are more liberal than females, and upperclassmen are more
liberal than sophomores or freshmen: "men may see abortion as a
more acceptable part of the sex act rather than an undesirable con-
sequence of it."[58] Even the most liberally oriented women differ
from men. Careful analysis of data shows that women perceive sexual
relationships to be meaningful and significant, with very few holding
the "sex is for fun" attitude considered typical of the young male.
Sexual intimacy is acceptable, say the women, if there is also a love
relationship; and though over the four years of college there may be
a number of "love" relationships, there is not the general kind of
female promiscuity that adults fear.[59]

Influenced in part by the new movement toward equality, the
sexual revolution "has weakened, though not demolished, the double
standard," says one observer, "and reduced, though not ended, male
preoccupation with virility. There is somewhat less boasting about
sexual conquest. . . ." And, as one graduate student said, "Now that
girls are living with their boy friends in the dorms, it's pretty hard to
sit around with them and talk like a stud. Male bull sessions of sexual
braggadocio have been replaced by coed bull sessions of sexual traumas."[60] Although the new freedom may test youth before they are
ready, it is a healthy sign that they can even admit to having such
problems.

That the colleges and universities have accepted this sexual revolution is evidenced by the publication of a pamphlet entitled *How to
Have Intercourse Without Getting Screwed: A Guide to Birth Control,
Abortion and Venereal Disease*, produced by the women of the University of Washington, and distributed with official sanction.[61]

The colleges' more liberal attitudes toward student sexuality,
and their general loosening of restrictions, especially those on wom-
en, may account for the decline in the number of runaway girls in
the seventies. If a girl desperately wants to get away from home, she
need only wait out her high school years and get into college, and
she has the same unrestricted freedom that her brothers had before
her.

Another phenomenon associated with campus change has been
the new assertiveness of women. The influence of the women's lib-

eration movement itself is relatively recent; what is most impressive is its swift acceptance by women across the country. In a fashion similar to the establishment of black studies courses in the sixties, women's studies courses have proliferated in the seventies. With almost none a decade ago, there were seven hundred such courses in 1971, and more than four thousand in 1974.[62] A few colleges are offering B.A. programs in women's studies and at least four colleges have M.A. programs in this field.

Women's caucuses have been formed on campus, paralleling the black caucus model. For the young woman who had not previously been exposed to the ideas conveyed by the women's liberation movement, a college course or caucus meeting could be an enlightening experience. Most women's studies programs enroll both men and women, though the latter are overwhelmingly in the majority. The women's caucus groups are sex-segregated on most campuses. Some of the militant tactics of the blacks have been copied by women. Male students were physically ejected from a class meeting in a women's studies course which had been designated for women only; a university official was bodily removed when he refused to leave an institute session on his campus which was devoted to considering the status of women in society.[63] On one campus the women staged a sit-in to demand childcare facilities. In another institution women crowded into the offices of the chairman of the history department when word circulated that a popular female instructor and her courses on the history of women were being dropped. They were reinstated.

While these activities are bound to influence college women, another aspect of the movement is becoming equally if not more significant. Women have been applying to professional schools in increasing numbers, and with some prodding from civil rights groups, the number of women accepted into professional schools has increased rapidly. Women who have learned that it is permissible to aspire to careers will enter traditional male occupations.

The communes which have sprung up over the last few years, attracting many college age youth, present models of different kinds of relationships among men and women and children. Some have attempted a "no marriage" kind of commune, but these have not succeeded too well; others have developed a balance between individual privacy and common enterprises.[64] Communes can be found around most major colleges and universities. Some of the communes are, in lifestyle and in the way members relate to each other, merely small heterosexual dormitories, student-run. Others have a mystique of "community," and efforts at honesty and openness are made. The techniques of encounter groups are often used, with leaders imported from outside.[65] The values prevailing in these communes force members to question traditional attitudes about family, security, job, success, and ambition. Of most relevance to our inquiry, the communes seem to assert the equality of the "selfness" of men and women—a truly revolutionary social concept.

Although the general public perceives the average high school student to be obnoxiously sophisticated, college faculties feel quite the reverse: most students have lived sheltered, narrow lives, knowing something about their own family difficulties, but with little insight into the larger world or the sources of the confusions that beset themselves and their friends. College is often a shocking experience. It is at college that young men and women encounter for themselves the startling fact that sex-role stereotypes may not be immutable; that not all women are solely interested in settling into a comfortable marriage, nor are the bright career-minded females arrogant nonsexual beings. Women are meeting young men who question the achievement-at-all-costs rat race, and who are struggling to find a secure, albeit new, masculine identity. On campus many students discover groups seeking to achieve a respected and accepted place for male and female homosexuals. Colleges are providing neutral medical advice and services for venereal diseases, pregnancy prevention, and abortion counseling. All of these are drastic changes from the controlled, inhibited, censored world of the average high school. Major segments of college courses are devoted to analysis of changing values—including, of course, new appraisals of male and female relationships, and of the family within society.

Greater numbers of youth are attending institutions of higher learning; what will be the impact of this experience on sex-role perceptions, behaviors, and stereotypes? Will we enter the new world of uni-sex, whatever that may be? Certainly higher education will play a major role in opening up new life options to men and women.

The apathy regarding social issues which seems to have replaced the activitist atmosphere of the late 1960s and the early seventies may mislead those who think that students are returning to traditional views of life and of themselves. Issues such as black studies seem to have faded since the courses have been accepted as standard fare. Freedom from restrictive college or university supervision has been achieved, and there is nothing to protest about in that area. Dress styles which once differentiated the radical from the conservative have become common; all students are dressed more or less like "radicals."

Colleges and universities seem to have satisfied most of the student movement's demands. The remaining area of unrest, if it can be called that, is the slowly mounting drive for equity in all educational matters for women. As noted, women's studies are increasing in number. Women graduate students are not taking rejections politely; they want to know why. Women faculty are gathering data about salaries, promotion decisions, and tenure, and are asking for their share of administrative positions. Unlike the movements which preceded it, the women's campus agitation has not produced sit-downs or marches except in a very few places. What the women have learned is the lesson of legal redress, or the threat thereof, with powerful Federal legislation as a bulwark.

The campus is becoming a model of the coming society in which women and men are perceived first as persons for whom a gender designation is only as important as hair color or height or weight.

◆ Summary

The years immediately beyond high school are crucial for youth who go directly to work as well as for those who go on to higher education. Noncollege youth become seriously involved in dating, marriage, and parenthood, and are concerned with jobs. College-bound youth look ahead to two, four, or more years of intellectual stimulation in an age-segregated setting with unclear ideas of what may be expected, and fears about what they themselves have to offer.

Most youth emerge from college relatively unchanged in terms of basic values and aspirations. Some have shifted their specific career interests, others have become somewhat more liberal politically and sexually, and more tolerant of racial, ethnic, and religious differences. For some, college is a testing ground where they face failure and damaged self-esteem. Others find college classes boring, tests irrelevant, sports activities juvenile, and commuting or dormitory living a daily unrewarding hassle. And after college, what?

Colleges and college youth have been through trying years in the past decade. Student unrest has caused painful self-assessment by faculty and administrators. Though colleges and universities have not changed in many respects, some of the verities of institutional form have been questioned. New social rules, new courses, alternative grading practices, more questioning of the sacred four year B.A. requirement are symptoms of change. Is it enough? Youth and their parents today wonder more seriously than ever whether college is worth it. Youngsters may learn too much—or too little. College remains the pathway toward occupational prestige for ethnics, blacks, and women. La Raza, the black revolution, and the women's movement are potentially the forces which, via college, may challenge the monopoly on power and status now held by white males. How will society fare then? What kind of college education can be designed to provide educational opportunities that are not sex biased, allowing men and women to achieve equally on the basis of a healthy, personal, sexual identity?[66]

References

1. William M. Sewell, "Inequality of Opportunity for Higher Education," *American Sociological Review* 36 (October 1971): 793-809.

2. Melvin M. Tumin, *Social Stratification: The Forms and Functions of Inequality* (Englewood Cliffs, New Jersey: Prentice-Hall, 1967); see also Ronald M. Pavalko and D. R. Bishop, "Socioeconomic Status and College Plans: A Study of Canadian High School Students," *Sociology of Education* 39 (Summer 1966): 288-298; W. H. Sewall and V. P. Shaw, "Socioeconomic Status, Intelligence, and the Attainment of Higher Education," *Sociology of Education* 40 (Winter 1967):1-23; C. E. Werts, "Sex Differences and College Attendance," *National Merit Scholarship Corporation Research Reports* 2 (1966): 1-11; Margaret C. Dunkle and Bernice Sandler, "Sex Discrimination Against Students: Implications of Title IX of the Education Amendments of 1972," *Inequality in Education* (October 1974): 12-35.

3. Christopher Jencks and David Riesman, *The Academic Revolution* (New York: Doubleday, 1968), pp. 406-479; see also "The Future of the Black Colleges," *Daedalus* 100 (Summer 1971): 593-899 (whole issue); E. Earl Baughman, *Black Americans* (New York: Academic Press, 1971), pp. 88-89; Robert L. Crain and Carol S. Weisman, *Discrimination, Personality and Achievement* (New York: Seminar Press, 1972); "How Separate? How Equal?" editorial, *Change* 6 (September 1974): 11-12.

4. Esther Peterson, "Working Women," *Daedalus* 93 (September 1964): 671-699.

5. U.S., Congress, House, Special Subcommittee on Education of the Committee on Education and Labor, "Are Women Equal Under the Law?" 91st Cong., 2nd Sess., H. Rept. 16098, part 2; see also *Women's Stake in Low Tuition* (Washington, D.C.: American Association of State Colleges and Universities, 1974).

6. Cynthia Fuchs Epstein, *Woman's Place* (Berkeley: University of California Press, 1970), p. 154; see also Eleanor Flexner, *A Century of Struggle* (New York: Athenaeum, 1968).

7. Liz Schneider, "Our Failures Only Marry: Bryn Mawr and the Failure of Feminism," in *Woman in Sexist Society*, ed. Vivian Gornick and Barbara Moran (New York: Basic Books, 1971), p. 427. See also: Catherine R. Stimpson, "Women at Bryn Mawr," *Change* 6 (April 1974): 24–31; Andrew Silk, "Bryn Mawr and Haverford: Competition vs. Coeducation," *Change* 6 (April 1974): 32–33.

8. Schneider, *Ibid.*

9. *Chronicle of Higher Education* March, 1971, p. 1; George R. LaNoue, "The Future of Antidiscrimination Enforcement," *Change* 6 (June 1974): 44–45+.

10. Sandra Acker Husbands, "Women's Place in Higher Education?" *School Review* 30 (February 1972): 261–274.

11. David Boroff, *Campus U.S.A.* (New York: Harper and Brothers, 1958), p. 144.

12. *Chronicle of Higher Education*, January 1969, p. 8

13. *Chronicle of Higher Education*, November 1970, p. 4.

14. "Women: The Fight for a Fair Shake on Campus," *New York Times*, October 8, 1972. See also: John A. Centra, "Women with Doctorates," *Change* 7 (February, 1975): 49, 61.

15. Jack Magarrell, "Who Earns How Much in Academe," *Chronicle of Higher Education* IX(No. 19, 1974).

16. Cathleen M. Kubiniec, "The Relative Efficacy of Various Dimensions of the Self-Concept in Predicting Academic Achievement," *American Educational Research Journal* 7 (May 1970): 1321–1336.

17. W. Todd Furniss and Patricia A. Graham, *Women in Higher Education* (Washington, D.C.: American Council on Education, 1974). See also, Jill K. Conway, "Coeducation and Women's Studies," *Daedalus* 103 (Fall, 1974): 239–249.

18. Philip E. Jacob, *Changing Values in College* (New York: Harper and Brothers, 1957); Alan E. Eayer, "Sexist Students in American Colleges: A Descriptive note," *Journal of Marriage and the Family* (forthcoming, 1975).

19. Warren B. Martin, "Cultural Values on Campus," *Change* 4 (June 1972): 8–9+.

20. "The *Real* Opinion Gap," *Trans-Action* 8 (November-December 1970): 8–9.

21. Harold Webster, Marvin Freedman, and Paul Heist, "Personality Changes in

College Students," in *The American College*, ed. Nevitt Sanford *et al.* (New York: John Wiley & Sons, 1962), pp. 811–846.

22. *Los Angeles Times* as quoted in *The Spokeswoman*, July 1, 1972; Joseph Katz, "Four Years of Growth, Conflict and Compliance," in *No Time for Youth*, ed. Joseph Katz *et al.* (San Francisco: Jossey-Bass, 1968), p. 67.

23. Charles H. Stember, *Education and Attitude Change* (New York: Institute of Human Relations Press, 1961), p. 177; for additional discussion of impact of living arrangements in college on personal development (of males), see Marjorie M. Lozoff, in *No Time for Youth*, ed. Joseph Katz *et al.* (San Francisco: Jossey-Bass, 1968), pp. 255–317.

24. Lawrence H. Stewart, "Change in Personality Test Scores During College," *Journal of Counseling Pyschology* 11 (Fall 1964): 211–219.

25. *Ibid.*

26. Charles D. Bolton and Kenneth C. W. Kameyer, *The University Student* (New Haven: College and University Press, 1967), pp. 252–253.

27. *Ibid.*

28. Matina Horner, "Fail, Bright Women," *Psychology Today*, November 1969, p. 36. For follow up on this study see Adeline Levine and Janice Crumvine, "Women and the Fear of Success: A Problem in Replication," *American · Journal of Sociology* 80 (Jan. 1975): 964–974.

29. Kubiniec, *op. cit.*

30. *Chronicle for Higher Education*, November 1970, p. 5.

31. *Los Angeles Times* as quoted in *The Spokeswoman*, July 1, 1972.

32. *Federal Register* 39, no. 120, part III, June 1974.

33. Margaret Dunkle, "College Athletics: Tug-of-War for the Purse Strings," *Ms*, September 1974, pp. 114–117; see also Katherine Ley, "Women in Sports: Where Do We Go From Here, Boys?" *Phi Delta Kappan* 56 (October 1974): 129–131; George H. Hanford, *An Inquiry into the Need for a National Study of Intercollegiate Athletics* (Washington, D.C.: American Council on Education, 1974).

34. Alexandra P. Buek and Jeffrey H. Orleans, "Sex Discrimination—A Bar to a Democratic Overview of Title IX of the Education Amendment of 1972," *Connecticut Law Review* 6 (Fall 1973): 1–27.

35. Marshall B. Clinard, *Sociology of Deviant Behavior*, 3rd ed. (New York: Holt, Rinehart, Winston, 1963), pp. 506–509.

36. Karen J. Monsour, "Education and a Woman's Life," in *Education and a Woman's Life*, ed. Lawrence E. Dennis (Washington, D.C.: American Council on Education, 1963), p. 10.

37. Bolton and Kameyer, *op. cit.*, pp. 204–205.

38. Ellis Ving, "Students Who Seek Psychiatric Help," in *No Time for Youth*, ed. Joseph Katz *et al.* (San Francisco: Jossey-Bass, 1968), pp. 318–347.

39. *Ibid.*, p. 322.

40. Nevitt Sanford, *Where Colleges Fail* (San Francisco: Jossey-Bass, 1967);

Sheldon S. Wolin and John H. Schaar, *The Berkeley Rebellion and Beyond: Essays on Politics and Education in the Technological Society* (New York: New York Review Books/Vintage Books, 1970); Paul Heist, *The Creative College Student: An Unmet Challenge* (San Francisco: Jossey-Bass, 1968).

41. Jacob R. Fishman and Fredric Solomon, "Youth and Social Action: An Introduction," *Journal of Social Issues* 20 (October 1964): 1-28.

42. Jerome F. X. Carroll, "Understanding Student Rebellion," *Adolescence* IV (Summer 1969): 163-180, who quotes it from still another secondary source.

43. Richard Flacks, *Youth and Social Change* (Chicago: Markham Publishing Company, 1971); other commentators on student dissent can be found in: Kenneth Keniston, *Young Radicals* (New York: Harcourt, Brace and World, 1968); Immanual Wallerstein and Paul Starr, *The University Crisis Reader*, 2 vols. (New York: Random House/Vintage Books, 1971); Lewis S. Feur, *The Conflict of Generations* (New York: Basic Books, 1969); A. W. Astin, "New Evidence on Campus Unrest, 1969-70," *Educational Record* (Winter 1971): 41-46; Harry Edwards, *Black Students* (New York: The Free Press, 1970); Edward E. Sampson and Harold A. Korn, *Student Activism and Protest* (San Francisco, Jossey-Bass Publishing, 1970); Peter Davies, *The Truth About Kent State* (New York: Farrar, Straus, Giroux, 1973).

44. James H. Block, Norma Haan, and M. Brewster Smith, "Activism and Apathy in Contemporary Adolescents," in *Understanding Adolescence*, ed. J. F. Adams, 2nd ed. (Boston: Allyn and Bacon, 1973).

45. Stanley J. Morse and Stanton Peele, "A Study of Participants in an Anti-Vietnam War Demonstration," *Journal of Social Issues* 27, No. 4 (1971): 113-136.

46. Epstein, *op. cit.*, p. 34.

47. Robert Morgan, *Sisterhood is Powerful* (New York: Random House, 1970), p. xxi.

48. Julie Ellis, *Revolt of the Second Sex* (New York: Lancer Books, 1970), p. 127.

49. Kenneth Goodall, "Tie Line: The Liberated Lady Has a Dirty Mouth," *Psychology Today*, August 1972, p. 16.

50. Mark Messer, "The Predictive Value of Marijuana Use: A Note to Researchers of Student Culture," *Sociology of Education* (Winter 1969): 91-97.

51. Donald Barr, "A Parents' Guide to the Age of Revolt," *McCall's*, October 1969, p. 73+; Bernard Bard, "College Dropouts: Sabotage on the Home Front," *Mademoiselle*, January 1969, p. 105+; John Robert Howard, "The Flowering of the Hippie Movement," *Annals of the American Academy of Political and Social Science* 382 (March 1969): 43-55; Joe David Brown, *The Hippies* (New York: Time/Life Books, 1967).

52. Nicholas Von Hoffman, *We Are the People Our Parents Warned Us Against* (Greenwich, Connecticut: Fawcett Publishing, 1968).

53. Richard K. Kerckhoff, "Value Stance in Family Life Education," *The Family Coordinator* 19 (July 1970): 253-260.

54. *Ibid.*

55. Lester Graham, *No More Morals: The Sexual Revolution* (New York: Pyramid Books, 1971), p. 140.

56. John H. Hudson and Lura F. Henze, "Campus Values in Mate Selection: A Replication," *Journal of Marriage and the Family* 31 (November 1969): 772-778.

57. Gilbert R. Kaats and Keith E. Davis, "The Dynamics of Sexual Behavior of College Students," *Journal of Marriage and the Family* 32 (August 1970): 390-399.

58. Joseph W. Maxwell, "College Students' Attitudes Towards Abortion," *The Family Coordinator* 19 (July 1970): 247-252.

59. Midge Decter, "Toward the New Chastity," *Atlantic Monthly*, August 1972, pp. 42-55.

60. "Teen-Age Sex: Letting the Pendulum Swing," *Time*, August 1972, pp. 34-40.

61. Lynn K. Hansen, Barbara Garner, and Diana Hilton, *How to Have Intercourse Without Getting Screwed* (Seattle: Associated Students of the University of Washington Women's Commission, June 1971).

62. *Project on the Status and Education of Women* (Washington, D.C.: American Council on Education, November 1974).

63. Elaine Showalter and Carol Ohmann, "Female Studies IV: Teaching About Women," prepared for the Modern Language Commission on the Status of Women, mimeographed (Pittsburgh: Know, Inc., 1972).

64. Flacks, *op. cit.*, pp. 110-114; see also Kenneth Westhaus, "Hippiedom 1970: Some Tentative Hypotheses," *Sociology Quarterly* 13 (Winter 1972): 81-99.

65. Eleanor Links Hoover, "The Age of Encounter," *Human Behavior* 1 (January-February 1972): 8-15.

66. For description of a new college program of promise see: Franklin K. Patterson, *The Making of a College* (Cambridge: The MIT Press, 1969).

10

Sex and Occupational Choice

"No Boy of Mine is Going to Become a Ballet Dancer . . ."

Choice of occupation is determined by one's sex as much as by knowledge and ability. Women select from a cluster of "typical" female occupations: nursing, teaching, library work, social work, secretarial work. Men have a broader field to choose from, and are expected to pursue their careers more vigorously than women.

The insistence that men take an aggressive role in public affairs and that women stay behind the lace curtain has made many men and women feel out of place and out of tune. Not all men are aggressive; not all women are passive. For those who do not fit the mold, the cost is high. Society's definition of men's work and women's work, it's views regarding who shall be boss and who the assistant may well influence every major decision in an individual's life.

◆ Sex-labeling of Occupations: Inevitable?

The sex-labeling of occupations is a matter of tradition and history. That women can do heavy physical labor is borne out by reports of female slave work in the pre-Civil War south and by observations of contemporary Japanese and Russian women who work on road building and heavy construction.[1] Among migrant families in the southwest or Florida (or anywhere else in the country) there is equal exploitation of men and women and boys and girls in arduous and ill-paid work.[2]

The jobs men do are not intrinsically "masculine." However, the claim that many jobs require more strength than women possess has

208

rarely been challenged in America. The Western world, particularly the urbanized United States, supports an etiquette that discourages women from carrying heavy burdens. The law has consistently limited the weights that women can lift and the hours they can work, and it specifies that women must not be employed in this or that "hazardous" occupation. Some labor unions presented their opposition to the Equal Rights Amendment as a desire to retain such "protective" legislation. Women's groups claim, however, that the abandonment of protective legislation would allow women to earn overtime and would make them eligible for many higher paying jobs.

Even in those cultures where women share heavy labor with the men, other work remains sex-specific. Men are still the chiefs, directing the work to be done, in Communist Russia the party leadership is overwhelmingly male, as is the governmental structure of all countries.

Is the sex-typing of occupations a reflection of a true difference between men and women, or is it due to social prejudice? It would seem that both factors play a role. The female is assumed to be limited in her activities by her biological role in motherhood and child care. Most men are taller than women, with larger musculature and heavier physiques. But whether physiology is the critical determinant of behavioral differences between men and women, or whether it is cultural definitions that determine behavioral differences and assign different jobs cannot be answered in any simple fashion. Men's greater interest and demonstrated ability in abstract reasoning and in dealing with mechanical objects, and women's supposedly greater need for affiliation with others may be due to the tasks that each sex has performed over the centuries. Women, entrusted with childcare and often restricted to the company of other women, would tend to develop more sensitivity toward other people. Men, working with plow, bricks, or banknotes, had to be aware of problems that did not necessarily involve other people. Thus teaching and nursing are consistent with the traditional focus of women's attention, while engineering, mathematics, or law follow the traditional preoccupations of men.

While sex-labeling of occupations seems to be universal, there is nothing available to suggest that most jobs cannot be done by one sex as competently as by the other. In a technological society such as ours fewer and fewer jobs need be tied to any kind of physiological differences. Since the original differentiation of tasks evolved in a pretechnological age, the question now before us is whether this differentiation need continue, or whether in fact men and women would be more productive if members of both sexes were encouraged to deal with people, with things, or with ideas according to individual preference.

Does it take greater muscle to be a member of the Governing Board of the Federal Reserve Bank than to be the secretary to one of these members? Obviously not; but no woman serves as a member of this august body; many serve as secretaries. The notion that women are "by nature" unsuited to handle the weighty matters of state may still be mouthed, but we do know better. Women are not more prone to hysteria than men, nor are they necessarily more tender-hearted.

Technology has freed us from limits imposed by physiology. If cultural attitudes permit, either sex can be employed in almost any occupation. With this freedom, a whole new range of work opportunities comes into view for both men and women. How rapidly our society will shift, and begin to accept men and women in non-traditional occupations—for their sex—is an open question. We believe there will be a more rapid pressure for change than our institutions are prepared for.

Choosing an Occupation

How are occupational choices made? How are young people guided into occupations? Should boys and girls be channeled into the traditional jobs and careers of their sex?

The Constant Message

For all of us, television carries obvious messages about the role of women vis-à-vis men, and it offers direct and subtle messages about who does what kind of work. Both men and women are the victims of television advertising. Coffee commercials show the wife fussing around at breakfast, serving a husband who is either immersed in his newspaper or groggy from sleep, obviously getting ready to go out struggling with the business world while little wife cleans up the dishes.[3] The various women's liberation groups have denounced car advertisements because of their use of women as sex symbols. Advertisements using models to convey their message adhere rigorously to the traditional, stereotyped concepts of male and female roles, interests, and vocations.

Playboy magazine has been denounced by some female critics for its sexual exploitation of women. *Playboy* appears to believe that the best women are either Playboy bunnies or bedmates. That this approach is very popular with men is evidenced by the tremendous success of *Playboy* magazine, Playboy Clubs, and their imitators. Financial success is rather difficult to ignore. The message is quite clear, men want woman in her place, preferably horizontal.

And So to School

At home the child observes that fathers go to work, mothers stay home; men have careers; women have jobs. We speak of a career woman as someone special; have you ever heard of a career man? At school the child observes that women are the teachers: a man is the principal. Women are secretaries; men are custodians.

In his first textbook, the child reads about sex-appropriate activities and attitudes. In one book used in 1970 in the primary grades, children note that fathers go off to various kinds of work, mothers go off to the store to shop. At work, men obey safety rules; in the store, women obey rules about staying in line at the check-out counter.[4] Studies of children's books reveal that occupational roles are fairly consistently stereotyped and middle class: "mothers knit while dads read," and mommy and the kids beg dad for money, while he earns it.[5] A study of 134 books used in the elementary schools in a New Jersey suburban area showed that one-sixth as many occupations were shown for women as for men. Women in the stories occupied twenty-five different occupations; men were in 147 different jobs. "The women in the stories were engaged in only 'womanly' occupations, such as teacher, governess, dressmaker, and telephone operator. There were no female doctors, jurists, or college professors to be found."[6] Biographical stories reported the achievements of eighty-eight men in 119 different presentations, while only seventeen women were reported in twenty-seven presentations.

One researcher concluded that there was a great discrepancy between the work of women as portrayed in basal reading series and the actual work done by women in the real world.[7] More distressing than his conclusions, however, is a review of his article by Otto and others which states, "In discussing his findings the author did not fault the basal readers because of the discrepancy but wisely (sic) observed that they do not have as one of their purposes the dissemination of accurate occupational information."[8] Once more we find reading instruction regarded as almost contentless, or as having content of such little worth that its accuracy is unimportant. One wonders if Otto and his associates would be quite so cavalier about content if the distortions were in an area that could be criticized more acceptably, such as a distorted presentation of blacks.

Through socialization almost all boys and girls learn which jobs are appropriate to which sex, and which jobs have the most status and prestige.[9] Requests of children to give vocational choices at every age level show a typical and traditional patterning: boys choose occupations which are considered masculine; girls choose feminine occupations, including that of housewife.[10]

Vocational Mis-Guidance

Attitudes about sex-appropriate vocations are reinforced by other aspects of the school program: guidance, for instance. Many schools routinely give students a chance to study occupations at about eighth or ninth grade, when they are thirteen or fourteen years old. The Kuder Preference Inventory is often used since it is easily scored and interpreted.[11] Another popular and biased test is a readily scored version of the Strong Vocational Interest Inventory.[12] How are these tests used? Are sex-appropriate choices available, or are the scores interpreted so that boy and girl preferences are segregated? Recent analyses of both scales indicate that a sex-bias enters into the kinds of scorings that are provided, as well as the norm groups upon which scores are developed.[13]

An interesting point has been raised on a more subtle aspect of vocational mis-guidance, and that relates to the vocabulary of occupational names and activities. Many jobs have sex-specific names such as tailor-seamstress, chef-cook, janitor-maid. Other occupations such as singer or writer appear to have neutral names, but these are often feminized in standard usage to become songstress or woman writer. It has been pointed out that efforts to determine vocational interests utilize standard vocabulary, yet no study has been done to determine how gender labels on jobs may influence individual choices. A boy might find the occupation of "nurse" too feminine, but if it is called "medical aid" or "medical corpsman" he might be interested.[14]

In 1972 a film entitled "Career Education" was to be distributed through the United States Office of Education. "The film reinforces the prevailing notion that boys can select from a large array of well-paying, stimulating careers, while girls are placed in subservient, low-paying, short-term jobs."[15] This film roused the indignation of women's groups throughout the country, and it was recalled for revision.

Guidance counselors give students stereotyped advice regarding career choice.[16] A study of counselors showed a distinct bias against girls who showed an interest in "masculine" occupations, and women counselors were as biased as men.[17] Are boys treated with a similar bias, being counseled not to consider "female" occupations? The following letter in the *Washington Post* shows how the system works:

> Just last spring, my own fifteen-year-old daughter was refused admission to a course in auto mechanics at Northwood High School (Montgomery County [Maryland]) because of her sex. The principal, Mr Packard, explained that girls are excluded because "there is no bathroom in the auto shop for girls." [Blacks were denied opportunities for the same lack of facilities in the not too distant past.]
>
> When I called the County Board of Education offices and spoke to an official who handles the vocational education program, he told me that even if girls were allowed to take the course, he would still give preference to boys because "employers wouldn't hire girl mechanics anyway."[18]

If no female auto mechanics are hired, it is of course because there are no qualified ones. And there are no qualified ones because the schools do not train them "for jobs that do not exist." Before equal access to jobs is attained, many parts of the vocational education system will have to change.

Enforcement of Title IX of the Educational Amendments of 1972 may well result in effective elimination of the kinds of school programs which track boys and girls into sex-stereotyped classes and limit their choice of vocations. In many states, interested groups have conducted studies of such vocational tracking and have brought pressure on school systems to open all classes to all students.[19] The language of the Title IX guidelines specifically prohibits any sex basis in denying a student a given course.

Recently, in a print shop in a large suburban high school, the teacher proudly pointed to three girls who, he claimed, were among his most devoted students. He also stated categorically that they would have no trouble finding jobs since students trained by him were in great demand. Whether they could get into the apprentice programs, however, he did not know.

Role Models: Parents, Adults, Peers

The cultural barrage of information about sex-appropriate occupations is passed from parents to children. Mothers read stories in "women's magazines" which show how grateful the "career" girl was to leave her glamorous job for the "right man."[20] A consistent picture is provided the mother of what she should lead her daughter, as well as her son, to expect.

In today's small family, adrift from any meaningful geneological past, children are a couple's only significant stake in the future. Maybe father did not make it to the position of boss, but his son ought to. If father had to quit school to take a blue-collar job, his son can get to college and aspire to better status. If mother married a foreman, daughter can marry the boss.[21] If daughters are reluctant to admit that college is primarily a marriage mart for them, mothers are less coy.

A couple's stake in their child is a result of their feeling that the child is the product of their efforts. This is a most simplistic view. Parents can claim no control over the combination of genes that determines a child's physique or intellectual capacity; and friends, school, and experience play vital roles in what children become. However, most parents irrationally consider themselves almost completely responsible for the way a child turns out. If the child is successful, parents take most of the credit; if he is not, they may feel guilty and try to shift the blame. At deep ego levels, the child is an extension of the parent, and a public and visible extension, at that. Career and marriage choices are thus very important to parents.

The means by which children learned sex roles were relatively simple in preindustrial society, for the world of children and adults was contiguous. In nonindustrial societies the boy sees his father plowing, planting, harvesting, and butchering, and learns clearly what he will do when he grows up. The girl stays with her mother, helping with childcare, cleaning, cooking, preserving, mending; she is learning occupationally useful skills and she is learning her adult role. Specific models are available to teach the specific skills needed by each sex.

In our technological world the daughter retains an advantage because she can see what mother does at home. And even a working mother does most of the typical family maintenance chores. But what about sons? Who really knows what father does when he goes off to that mysterious place called the office? What happens at a desk? Who does he talk to on the telephone? What does the lady secretary do? Very mysterious indeed. The incredible variety of tasks and skills that men and women may need at the office is beyond the scrutiny and understanding of the child. A lawyer sits at a desk; so does an accountant, an editor, a wholesale buyer, a professor, a bank manager, an insurance salesman, a personnel administrator, and a bookie.

Having only a vague idea of the world of the office, the child of white-collar or professional workers has a less clear vocational model in early life than does the child who can see what parents do. We might ask if girls' preference for homemaking may be due to the fact that they see mom engaged in the homemaker role each day, and no specific alternative roles are suggested to them. The boy is told he will *not* be like mom, so he has to search for occupational models.[22]

Role models present a particular kind of vocational guidance. The college-bound girl who has been treated by a woman physician is not nearly as likely to reject medicine as a vocational goal as is a girl who has never seen one. The fact that few women are visible in some occupations—pharmacy, dentistry, engineering, police work, national politics—creates a self-perpetuating situation. Few women are in these occupations, therefore girls perceive them as ones to which they cannot and probably should not aspire. When boys observe that only women do certain kinds of work, elementary teaching, library work, nursing, secretarial work—they do not aspire to such jobs. Although there are male nurses, elementary teachers, librarians, and secretaries, who ever heard a ten-year-old boy say he wanted to grow up to be a nurse?

Adult friends of a family may provide occupational models, but the class-stratified society of the United States limits the range of models to those very like the ones the child has already at home. A working mother will bring home the other girls at the office; a housewife brings home the neighbor wives, or bridge friends, or church associates met through daytime activities engaged in by the nonworking woman. A man who is a truck driver is unlikely to hob-nob with professors or lawyers—and certainly not with *female* professors or lawyers!

Class differences have vocational implications for both boys and girls. Lower class youngsters may see relatively few vocations represented by persons around them: storekeeper, teacher, policeman, criminal, unemployed, farmer, migrant worker, domestic worker, factory hand, or miner. The professional persons encountered—doctors, nurses, lawyers, judges, welfare workers—may appear to be beyond the range of vocational aspiration. Many such professional persons, in fact, make it quite clear that there is a social gap between the lower class and themselves.

The aspiration levels of black youth reflect not only this restricted range of role models, but also a differential perception regarding the possibility of achieving.[23] A highly provocative longitudinal study of black and white boys revealed that one of the more crucial elements in occupational choice and achievement motivation was the availability of suitable models. The black boys were low in aspiration and expectations of success in part, the researcher concluded, because of "hero depreciation."[24] Black girls have had higher aspirations than black boys, and they have had more confidence that they would achieve.[25] The black revolution of the sixties and seventies has, however, had a considerable impact upon the achievement goals of all black youth.

The influence of peers in orientation toward school and toward future work has been documented by Coleman. The climate found in various high schools had a significant impact upon attitudes toward study or work among even very bright adolescents.[26]

The dependence of most adolescents upon their peers for validation of personal worth plays a tremendously important role in what they may make of their future. If a child's friends are studious, ambitious, motivated, and have status among the general social group with whom the youngster identifies, then the youngster is more likely to follow their model in order to gain acceptance.[27] The effect of peer group upon aspiration, particularly that of boys, has shown that "the interpersonal relationships with one's friends within the high school . . . determine high or low academic aspirations, but stratification within a school, or socioeconomic differences between schools may limit the range of friendship."[28]

Significantly, studies of ghetto black and Mexican-American

youth who finished school and obtained secure jobs showed that this was done at the cost of refusing to identify with the ghetto life-style of their peers. Instead, they looked to teachers and parents as guides.[29]

Placement in a school setting where other students are achievement-oriented may be more important than parents' ambitions and hopes for their children. In discussing the volatile subject of school desegregation, some black leaders indicate that it is the social class composition of the school that will affect achievement of black students rather than the interracial mix.

Freedom of choice? Hardly! The future of most boys and girls is programmed largely by their social milieu.

The High Price of Being Different

The individuals most likely to choose "different" occupations which have been stereotyped as belonging to the opposite sex, have traditionally come from better educated, upper income groups. Are they also among the most intelligent of these groups? Does interest in music—a feminine interest in younger children and adolescents—cause the upper class bright boy more difficult personal adjustment? Because he is more precocious than others, he would be more likely to know what is appropriate for boys, and would face a conflict as to whether he should repress his real interests and talents. Does the bright girl, who learned quite early what girls were supposed to desire, feel conflict-laden by choosing, say, to be a chemist rather than an elementary school teacher?

Parental opposition is usually accepted as one of the chief reasons why so few women are engaged in professional careers.[30] In an analysis of students' selection of teaching as a career, it was found that girls of both high and low socioeconomic status were encouraged to select teaching; boys from middle class levels received little parent or peer approval, but there was general approval at lower class levels.[31]

Parental approval is especially important when parents hold the purse strings, providing support for youngsters to stay in high school or continue to college or professional school. Parents' financial, as well as emotional, investment in children's education provides a fertile ground for parent-child trouble. A significant conflict is ahead for perceptive and educated young people when there is a gap between what they may have the ability or interest in doing and what they feel they ought to do. A boy may deeply desire to try his talents in ballet dancing, but only a very few dare run the gauntlet of parental and public dismay at such a choice. A girl may feel she has a talent for what is considered a masculine occupation, such as police-man, minister, or engineer. However, she will run into the disapproval of peers and parents, and will encounter the opposition of the men at the precinct station, in the parish, or at the engineers' desk. The girl faces even more devastating criticism if she implies that her vocational interests are more important and more driving than interest in getting a husband and having children.

Individuals of either sex whose talents and interests are not traditionally sex-appropriate may be forced into social deviancy. The aura of homosexuality which surrounds the male ballet dancer in our culture may in fact impel the boy who has ambitions to be a dancer into a socially deviant role before he can succeed.[32]

As long as nonconformity is associated with certain career choices, boys and girls with distinctive talents can use these talents only if they find sex-appropriate occupations; otherwise they run the risk of social ostracism. The role conflicts and problems with col-leagues encountered by individuals engaged in nontraditional occupa-tions is illustrated by the situation of the male nurse. One study showed that there was distinct dislocation between the expected role of the nurse and the men who were in nursing training. They could not see themselves in the subservient occupational style of the female nurses, but they were not accepted by the male doctors either. The hospital and nursing training hierarchy was geared to sex-role differentiation; male nurses in training just did not and could not fit the institutional expectations.[33]

American society provides a vast range of occupational possi-bilities, plus the promise of anonymity in metropolitan areas. Children can—and do—escape social expectations by moving to a distant city. In the large metropolis one is most apt to find groups of like-minded persons. It is no accident that occupations are geo-graphically distributed with the most deviant, in terms of sex appropriateness, found in the largest cities. Exceptions to this geo-graphic distribution can be found—there are a few women foresters, mining engineers, and oceanographers. But the farther from urban centers they are located, the more difficult it is for women to over-come male prejudice. Even superstition is against women: it took a court order to admit a woman into a tunnel or mine. The men were

"She says, 'To hell with ballet, she's going to be a jockey.'"

convinced that women bring disaster if they entered such structures. Is the male resistance Freudian or economic?

Oh Dad, Poor Dad!

The centrality of father's work as it affects family members is so obvious that it is easily overlooked. Of course a household will be upset by worry and depression when dad is out of work. When father gets a promotion, it is time for general celebration. Each income increment means more goodies all around; more household aids for the wife, better clothes for mother and children, more kinds of fun. At an early age boys begin to see their male role as one which is critical to family maintenance. And girls perceive that the family's economic well-being, as well as social status, derives from father's job.

It is an axiom that "the father's activity as breadwinner . . . [is] the chief embodiment of his self-esteem."[34] Interviews with working class families showed the occupational and economic trap which closes in on the male:

A 26-year-old man with ten years of schooling unloads and washes hogs in a meat packing business. The job is steady but he is very dissatisfied about the smells of the place "the whole set-up"—the smell nauseates him so that he is often unable to eat his lunch. But he has just bought a ramshackle bungalow and cannot afford the risk of changing to another, possibly less secure, job. A 33-year-old man, a bottler in a beer company, struggles to support his wife and three children on $3,000 a year pay. [circa 1962] He does not like his job, but he also feels that he cannot risk giving up a secure job.[35]

Most women are reported to consider the breadwinning capacity of a husband more important than his capability as a mate or parent.[36] The impact of inadequate or unpredictable income on the mother and children are so direct that men who are "poor providers" may literally or psychologically be hounded out of the home.[37] The most visible victims of this kind of valuation are black males. As one author states, "after a certain period of striving with the vagaries of the white occupational structure, black males just give up the fight to get a foot on the occupational-career rung."[38]

The greater stress and anxiety which boys demonstrate throughout their lives may have roots in their early realization that they are responsible for sustaining success at work *throughout their lives.* For the adolescent and young adult male the prospect of having to earn a living not only for themselves but for wife and children is anxiety-producing. Is the high rate of suicides among young men between the ages of sixteen and twenty-one partly due to this prospect?[39] The young male adult must prove himself in the job market or on the educational ladder leading to a career and he must also prove himself sexually, often at the same time. The double trial may be too much for a frail ego.

A man is not asked whether he prefers to stay home or go to work. He has no choice. The higher incidence of alcoholism and other stress ailments among men may be directly related to this fact. Most girls contemplate a future in which they can choose between working and staying home. The girl who chooses to work for a while, or even the one who has well-developed career interests, still has the option of quitting if the going gets too tough—providing she is married. Unmarried women who work are often looking in two directions: one is at the career potential of any given occupation, and the other is the possibility of marrying and not having to work at all. As Epstein observed, ". . . motivation for women develops in another context than the one in which men are socialized to work. It occurs within a contingency spectrum"[40]—contingent on a husband and his earning capacity.

One young married woman with a small child found her elementary school teaching assignment very difficult. After struggling with the situation for several months she resigned, and stayed home with her child until another less trying job was available. Her husband felt there was nothing wrong with this decision. Yet had he been the one with the job, and had his wife been home all alone with their child, he would not have dared give up a job in hand for a possible one in the future. Is this why employers are reluctant to hire women? If things don't work out, they expect the woman may just quit while a man would find it very difficult to give up a secure position, even if it is personally almost intolerable. Despite this, job turnover rates among women are as low as those among men.

So Who Needs to Work!

Children may have vague ideas about what men or women do, but they soon learn that whatever it is, it is not the same. More than this, children develop attitudes toward work itself. When father comes home after a long day at the office and collapses with his hand stretched out for the reviving martini he is providing a very interesting model for his children. The mother who complains bitterly, with children in earshot, of her dislike of being "trapped in the house all day with three screaming kids" is also educating her children. Mother who works, for pleasure or money, is apt to bring home an expressed or repressed message of guilt. "One result of this enforced defensiveness and guilt," says a student of sex-role behavior, "is that children perceive the whole work situation as one that is disliked and to be rejected by both men and women."[41]

In previous decades one had no choice about working. Work or starve—or beg. The work ethic has been so much a part of American culture that even the very rich man felt impelled to do some kind of work. Although many critics of welfare programs are convinced that most people on welfare are no-good bums and loafers, the truth is that most such persons would much prefer to work rather than take a hand-out. One study of unemployed workers showed that interest in work was high, and "the need for respect among our respondents [to be gained through work] appeared to surpass that encountered among employed workers in other studies which utilized the same instrument for data collection." Furthermore, this study found that unemployed women were as committed to work as men; while the men were more concerned about the loss of respect when unemployed, the women were interested in the loss of income.[42]

A somewhat different view of work prevails among a well-publicized portion of today's youth. Many middle class youth of both sexes have rejected the work ethic and achievement drive of their parents. This may be a direct result of the flowering of suburbia. When offices, factories, stores, universities, laboratories, and hospitals can be reached only by commuting, children are kept "outside the world of work, on the woman's side of the line."[43]

Should we, then be quite so surprised as we are that some middle-class young people don't take work seriously and find that an expressive, emotional way of life, seen in our social mythology as typically feminine, is the one they prefer? Should we be quite so astonished at their willingness to substitute a private, seemingly controllable drug-world where one can find satisfaction and relief at will for an unknown, external world of events and striving whose laws are strange to them, whose demands seem threatening and whose rewards have no attraction?[44]

Perhaps they have heard just once too often their father's complaints about the office, the boss, the rat race, the futility of it all.

A significant aspect of the so-called hippie culture is its lack of interest in work, careers, ambition, getting ahead. Many such youth cheerfully live on welfare and food stamps if they can get them, producing astonishment, chagrin, and hostility among their parents and the public. They seem to feel no compunction about begging, if it is necessary.

One prophet for this youth generation, Charles Reich, put forth as a goal the concept of a vocation or "non-career." What a radical idea! As Reich puts it: "the concept of a non-career requires that an individual ignore the question of whether or not this choice is one that has been defined and accepted by society; whether it represents an established occupation. Even if it does, the established outline of that occupation will probably be too rigid and general to suit a personal vocation. So the individual must define his own career."[45] Reich continues: "The question is whether one can turn the task, whatever it is, into play, art, feeling: whether one can make it a teacher and not merely a taskmaster . . . work of many kinds can be made an erotic experience."[46] What a threat to established concepts of work! Reich's view embraces a kind of community and equality of roles which effectively erases the sex-appropriate work behaviors commonly accepted. To some observers, the style of life Reich espouses appears to be a reflection of current culture, and may be an expression of alienation from the world, from others, even from one's self. Few young people today appear to have completely adopted the concept of work and community which Reich describes, but there are indications that his ideas do reflect the lifestyle of some middle class young adults. Because of their exotic and intriguing behavior these young people have been given wide publicity in the glossy picture magazines; their music is heard extensively; movies have been made about their lifestyles. As more leisure is available to those who do work, and as material needs are more easily satisfied, the concept of a "non-career" may be increasingly appealing. The new romanticism of the communal farm and the freedom to be unwashed and unbossed become more and more attractive in a work world where competition for status is cutthroat, bosses are mean or prejudiced or incompetent, and commuting to and from work is a horror.

Parental complaints about work, the bills, the boss, are falling on ears newly attuned to the message. With increased education, young people can see options which do not include working doggedly at uninspiring and demeaning jobs. As the middle and upper class youth opts for the commune in New Mexico or Oregon, the children of the blue-collar worker may well take his place. The possible consequences of such a social revolution may be far-reaching indeed.

◆   Summary

Boys and girls, men and women have many talents, abilities, and interests. Talent—an innate capacity or predilection—is distributed widely irrespective of sex. Yet cultural norms regarding sex-appropriate work lock each sex into a highly restricted track.

Boys are expected to accept the idea that they will work all their lives and face the competition of others on the job. The work available to each sex is clearly identified by the range of models available to the young in the books they read in and out of school, and in the history they study. From school counselors to television commercials the message to boys and girls is that there is man's work—and woman's work—and rarely do they overlap.

Such sex-labeling of occupations is not related to the abilities individuals are born with. Yet, depending on the range of models available, most boys and girls will accept the stereotyped sex-role work definition. To move outside the range of permissible occupations the individual must not only break with early conditioning, but move against the pressure of teachers, guidance counselors, peers, and parents. Fear of facing such a gamut of disapproval has resulted in the continuation of sex-labeling of occupations for generations.

And yet, as one astute psychologist commented, ". . . we are clearly approaching a time when there will be no kinds of valuable work that cannot be performed as well by one sex as by another. At such a time, work-role will be a thin reed upon which to depend for identity. Even now there is little reason, apart from cultural tradition, why the whole matter of who is to do what work could not be settled according to preference and convenience."[47]

In the next chapter we will examine the psychological impact of choosing a vocation if that is inconsistent with an individual's drives and abilities, as well as the hazards facing men and women as they engage in gainful pursuits. Equality? For whom? At what cost?

References

1. Harry Trimborn, "Where Women's Lib is a Nice Pile of Bricks," *Washington Post*, January 3, 1971.

2. "Fresh Air Sweat Shops: Child Labor on the Farm," *New Generation* 54 (Summer 1972): 1-28.

3. Janet Coleman, "Advertising," *You: The Magazine for the New Woman*, July 1971, p. 13.

4. Allyn and Bacon, *Cleveland Social Studies Series.*

5. Janice M. Pottker, "Female Stereotypes in Elementary School Textbooks" (Research paper, University of Maryland, College of Education, 1971); Myra McPherson, "Challenging the Books that Teach Girls 'Their Places,' " *Washington Post*, June 6, 1971, G-1+.

6. National Organization of Women, *Dick and Jane as Victims: Sex Stereotyping in Children's Readers* (Princeton, New Jersey: Women on Words and Images, P.O. Box 2163, 1972), p. 9.

7. Buford Steffire, "Run Mama, Run: Women Workers in Elementary Readers," *Vocational Guidance Quarterly* 17 (January 1971): 99-102; see also Gwyneth E. Britton, "Sex Stereotyping and Career Roles," *Journal of Reading* 10 (November 1973): 140-148+.

8. Wayne Otto et al., "Summary and Review of Investigations Relating to

Reading, July 1, 1969 to June 30, 1970," *Journal of Educational Research* 64 (February 1971): 242-268.

9. Robert W. Hodge, Paul M. Seigal, and Peter H. Rossi, "Occupational Prestige in the United States, 1925-1963," *American Journal of Sociology* 70 (November 1964): 286-302.

10. Paul H. Mussen, John J. Conger, and Jerome Kagan, *Child Development and Personality*, 2nd ed. (New York: Harper and Row, 1963), pp. 561-567; Ruth E. Hartley, "Children's Concepts of Male and Female Roles," *Merrill-Palmer Quarterly* 6 (1959-1960): 83-91.

11. G. F. Kuder, *Kuder (DD) Occupational Interest Survey General Manual* (Chicago: Science Research Associates, 1971); see also C. K. Tittle, "Sex Bias in Educational Measurement: Fact or Fiction," *Measurement and Evaluation in Guidance* 6 (1974): 219-226.

12. N. K. Schlossberg and J. Goodman, "Imperative for Change: Counselor Use of the Strong Vocational Interest Blanks," *Impact* 2 (1972): 25-29.

13. Janice Birk, "Reducing Sex Bias—Factors Affecting the Client's View of the use of Career Interest Inventories," Research paper, National Institute of Education, Career Education Project, 1974 (draft only); see also C. M. Huth, "Measuring Women's Interests: How Useful?" *Personnel and Guidance Journal* 51 (1973): 539-545.

14. Mary Faith Tanney, "Face Validity of Interest Measures: Sex Role Stereotyping" (Unpublished draft report, National Institute of Education, 1974).

15. *The Spokeswoman*, August 1, 1972, p. 4.

16. C. C. Thorensen, J. J. Krumbeltz, and B. B. Varenherst, "Sex of Counselors and Models: Effects on Client Career Exploration," *Journal of Consulting Psychology* 14 (1967): 503-508; see also Joann Gardner, "Sexist Counseling Must Stop," *Personnel and Guidance Journal* 49 (May 1971): 705-714.

17. J. Pietrofossa and N. K. Schlossberg, "Counselor Bias and the Feminine Role," in N. Glazier Malbin and H. Y. Walker, *Women in the Society and Economy* (Chicago: Rand-McNally, 1971).

18. *Washington Post*, August 25, 1971.

19. For some examples of school system studies see: Dallas Women's Coalition, *A Study of Sex Discrimination in The Dallas Independent School District* (Dallas: Dallas Women's Coalition, 1973); Commission on Women, *Quality and Equality: A Study of Sex Bias in the Fairfax County Schools* (Fairfax, Va.: Commission on Women, 1974); "Perspectives on Vocational Education and Career Education," *Inequality in Education* (March 1974): 5-58.

20. Betty Frieden, "The Happy Housewife Heroine," *The Feminine Mystique* (New York: W. W. Morton, 1963), pp. 33-69.

21. Leonard Benson, *The Family Bond* (New York: Random House, 1971), pp. 126-127.

22. Robert R. Sears, Eleanor E. Maccoby, and Harry Levine, *Patterns of Child Rearing* (Evanston, Illinois: Row, Peterson and Company, 1957), p. 369.

23. John H. Scanzoni, *The Black Family in Modern Society* (Boston: Allyn and Bacon, 1971), pp. 152-196.

24. Stuart T. Hauser, *Black and White Identity Formation* (New York: John Wiley & Sons, 1971).

25. Albert J. Lott and Bernice E. Lott, *Negro and White Youth* (New York: Holt, Rinehart and Winston, 1963).

26. James S. Coleman, *Adolescents and the Schools* (New York: Baine Books, 1965).

27. *Ibid.*, p. 24.

28. Sarane S. Boocock, *An Introduction to the Sociology of Learning* (Boston: Houghton Mifflin, 1972), p. 225.

29. Edward M. Glaser and Harvey L. Ross, *A Study of Successful Persons from Seriously Disadvantaged Backgrounds*, Final Report Prepared for Office of Special Manpower Programs (Washington, D.C.: Department of Labor, March 31, 1970).

30. Cynthia F. Epstein, *Woman's Place* (Berkeley: University of California Press, 1970), p. 74.

31. Haskin R. Pounds and M. L. Hawkins, "Adult Attitudes on Teaching as a Career," *Journal of Teacher Education* 20 (Fall 1969): 339-342.

32. Clive Barnes, "After All, Don't Men Dance Better?" *New York Times*, June 6, 1971.

33. Bernard E. Segal, "Male Nurses: A Case Study in Status Contradictions and Prestige Loss," *Social Forces* 41 (October 1962): 31-38.

34. Leonard Benson, *Fatherhood: A Sociological Perspective* (New York: Random House, 1968), p. 271.

35. Mirra Komarovsky, *Blue-Collar Marriage* (New York: Vintage/Random House, 1962), p. 281.

36. Helena Z. Lopata, "The Secondary Features of a Primary Relationship," *Human Organization* 24 (1965): 116-123.

37. Elliott Leibow, *Talley's Corner* (Boston: Little, Brown, 1967).

38. John H. Scanzoni, *The Black Family in Modern Society* (Boston: Allyn and Bacon, 1971), p. 186.

39. Jerry Jacobs, *Adolescent Suicide* (New York: John Wiley and Sons, 1971).

40. Epstein, *op. cit.*

41. Ruth E. Hartley, "American Core Culture: Change and Continuities," in *Sex Roles in Changing Society*, ed. Georgene H. Seward and Robert C. Williamson (New York: Random House, 1970), p. 145.

42. H. Roy Kaplan and Curt Tansky, "Work and the Welfare Cadillac: The Function of and Commitment to Work Among the Hard-Core Unemployed," *Social Problems* (Spring 1972): 469-483.

43. Elizabeth Janeway, *Man's World, Woman's Place* (New York: Morrow, 1971), p. 302.
44. *Ibid.*
45. Charles A. Reich, *The Greening of America* (New York: Random House, 1971), p. 368.
46. *Ibid.*, p. 371.
47. Nevitt Sanford, *Self and Society* (New York: Atherton Press, 1966), pp. 268-269.

11

Danger: Men and Women at Work

"When you ask a man who he is, he gives his occupation; when you ask a woman, she gives her name."

In some distant past fond parents could relax gracefully into old age when they had successfully launched their last son into a career and the last daughter into marriage. The son, in turn, would dutifully marry and there would be grandchildren to spoil and enjoy. This picture is still a dominant one in the all-American dream. But now instead of the dream we may encounter one of many alternative nightmares.

Some men are finding the stress of work and achievement, keeping ahead of the IRS and the bill collector, to be too great a strain. Some give up, some run away, some become drunks, some die of coronaries. Some women who ecstatically received an engagement diamond, selected the shimmery wedding dress, and welcomed the screeching red firstborn, have found the routines and entrapments of the modern home defeating and destructive. They rush back to work, or take to drink or bridge or candy, become querulous, demanding, fat, and boorish. The working woman gets backaches and headaches, is guilty over the children she has—or hasn't—and rages at the less qualified men who blithely pass her by on the promotion ladder.

So it isn't all peaches and cream. Of course, it never was. Perhaps now we just know more about it—and are less satisfied, to be less satisfied! We suffer the maladjustments of life with little patience, because we have heard and read the golden dream, and we believed in it. What's amiss? Where was the wrong turn taken?

In the previous chapter we discussed the early roots of career choice. Just as boys learn to be men and girls learn to be women, so do they choose occupations consistent with their image of themselves as men or women.

Now what is wrong with that? It seems perfectly legitimate that men and women should follow different life patterns. Obviously, men and women are different. But is it this easy? Except for their different roles in procreation and reproduction, there are few essential differences restricting either sex to a particular range of vocations. The limits on occupational choice stem almost wholly from tradition. In recent years, women's groups have begun protesting these occupational limits and the inequities resulting from them. Females are chafing at exclusion from "male" jobs, particularly those carrying prestige and higher salaries.

In this chapter we will try to learn why people feel about their work as they do, and we will examine some of the more subtle factors influencing job and career choices. We will also look at the actual distribution of jobs and income by sex and determine whether major inequities exist. Finally we will suggest some steps to provide more open vocational opportunities for both sexes.

✦   The Sexual Meaning of Money

In any discussion of who gets what job or who is refused a job or promotion, we must realize what a job really means. A job means money. And money is power. Any means of exchange, whether it be shells, cows, francs, or dollars, puts the possessor in an advantageous position vis-à-vis those without such means. Whether at the personal, corporate, national, or international level, it is men who control the money, wield the power, and dominate those around them. Waging war is a particularly male occupation—and hazard; would there be any impact upon amity among nations if women were equally in control of the power—and the money?

The transformation from the extended family to the small nuclear family has been accompanied by no real change in the power or meaning of money. Father is synonymous with breadwinner. Despite the interesting data concerning women's role in making purchasing decisions,[1] the money decisions continue to be made by men. Women may have stock and property in their name, but such listings are usually tax dodges. Concern about inheritance and keeping money within the family lies behind the desire to have sons who can carry on the family name and the family business.

Money is equated with power, control, and dominance, and this equation has many significant implications for the roles of men and women in marriage and on the job. Women are paid less. It may be discrimination, it may be a way of saving money, or there may be another explanation. How many men want their wives to earn more than they do? This is the simple—and central—question. Just as a relationship is suspect if a woman has more education or more prestige than a man, so is trouble predicted if the woman is the more productive earner in a family. Even if the woman's job carries less status, there is still concern when she earns more than her husband. However, there is little need for worry: women consistently earn less than men; this has been true in the past and it is true in the 1970s. There are many reasons why women's pay lags behind that of men, but one factor is the social pressure to keep women at a competitive disadvantage. Equal pay for women implies equal status, and this may be too threatening for men.[2]

Money is behind many marital conflicts and many divorces.[3] Money is power in the marketplace and power at home. Many wives are never told the amount of money their husbands earn. Husbands dole out household money to wives who must then use subterfuge in order to have some "free money" of their own to purchase things without permission. A good illustration of the power of money to destroy a marital relationship was portrayed by Henrik Ibsen in *The Doll's House*, written in 1879. Nora, the principal character, was not free to make money decisions, so when she wished to help her husband—who would not help himself—she had to resort to demeaning financial jugglings. And when Nora finally slammed the door on her marriage and family she was not only asserting her right to be treated as an adult, she was also reacting to the tyranny exercised by her husband by his control of the household money.

We are socialized to give generous gifts (of cash or its purchased equivalent) as a way of expressing our love for another. A child who wants to give something special to mother for Mother's Day buys a gift; it is very hard to convince the average American child that something he made himself would be equally appreciated.

The economy depends upon the high visibility of cost to keep consumers at peak levels of avidity. The advertising of many items completely irrelevant for survival—such as perfume and jewelry—emphasizes the love-gift relationship almost exclusively. A man should spend money, lots of it, on the woman of his choice, and she should spend whatever money she can lay her hands on to make herself as attractive as possible for him; both types of spending are perceived as important symbols of love. What has this got to do with occupational choice? In our culture it is psychologically essential to a man that he make more money than his spouse. Through this means men feel powerful, masculine, in charge of things. As we have suggested, this male psychological need may account in part for the fact that women consistently receive lower pay for doing the same work that men do.

Although there are more women in the work force than ever before, the gap between the earnings of men and women has widened. In 1957 full-time working women earned, on the average, 65 percent of what men earned; in 1968 it had dropped to 58 percent.[4] In 1970, women working full time earned 60 percent of the median salaries of men. This difference was not due to differences in the kinds of work done; women salespersons earned 40.4 percent of the earnings of their male counterparts, women clerical workers earned 66.2 percent and women professionals 64.2 percent of the wages of men.[5] It was estimated that in 1973 women's earnings were between 58 and 60 percent of men's earnings, with the greatest disparity between the earnings of minority women and white men.[6]

Power needs may account for women's lower earnings and slower rate of promotion to positions of leadership, dominance, and decision-making. You can't pay a person a great deal without giving him or her power. Low wages for low level jobs can be used to keep women and minorities powerless.

The fear of competition from women in the job market is so pervasive that it is readily acknowledged by both men and women. Girls are told by parents, teachers, and peers that they should not try or want to compete with men. The bright woman may deliberately act unintelligent rather than place herself in a competitive situation in which she may win against men.[7] Women even feel uncomfortable competing against other women, particularly if winning means gaining leadership. The net effect of these various pressures has been to channel women's vocational aspirations toward low status, dead-end jobs. They can aspire to be secretaries, but not administrators; to be check-out clerks but not managers; to be teach-

ers but not superintendents. It seems that women have been maneu-
vered into wanting only jobs that pay them consistently less than
men.[8]

Work is defined as labor which is paid for, and this definition is
critical to the power problems found in the American family. A
"working mother" is a mother who is working at paid labor. The
work the mother does at home is not recognized as work in anywhere near the same sense. Is the work a mother does at home any
less work because she is not paid for it?[9] This view that housework is
not real work may play a part in men's reluctance to stay home and
work while the wife is on the job. If work at home is not valued, men
cannot do it. The women's liberation movement has suggested that
wives and mothers be paid for work they do at home.[10]

A reliable paid housekeeper is treated with considerable concern
by all members of a household because such persons are relatively
rare. Yet a husband may freely abuse and exploit his wife's unpaid
labor with many kinds of inconsiderate acts. Some women feel that
only when a husband begins to pay his wife the $3,000 or $4,000 that
he would have to pay for the equivalent kind of household service
will he appreciate the value of "women's work." Few men will agree
to such a procedure, and few women have the nerve or desire to demand it. So far the only alternative for women has been to get out
of the house to do "real work" for a salary; this gives them some
semblance of autonomy. But it also creates inner conflicts, for most
women give highest priority to their work at home, even if there are
no children. As Coser and Rokoff point out, as long as there is equal
education for men and women but unequal expectations in terms of
family obligations and work commitment, women will not aspire to
nor be permitted to attain positions of prestige and status in any
fashion equal to men.[11] As Coser and Rokoff put it:

If husbands were routinely expected to be as fully responsible for the management of disruptions in the family system as wives are now, it would be much
more difficult to maintain the idea that higher-status professions have to be
wary of women as potential disrupters of the routines of occupational life.[12]

Marital serenity will profit when power conflicts are reduced, recon-
ciled, or eliminated, and this can happen only as a result of a more
realistic definition of work—one which will place a proper value on
housework.

Who Works at What

Statistics on the work force illustrate the fairly neat division between the jobs held by men and by women (Table 11.1). Trends show little change in the kinds of work men and women do, although there is an increase in the percentage of women in the labor market. More women worked in 1970 than ever before, but they worked at the same kinds of jobs they did in 1950.

The percentage of women on college and university faculties has declined. A few women have invaded such professions as engineering and architecture, and a few men have become nurses and librarians, but overall women have remained in women's professions. The most striking work shift is the increase in the number of men in public elementary and secondary schools. Prior to 1830 education was overwhelmingly a man's job. Then, as numbers increased and other jobs and professions opened up, men left and women became the school teachers of America. At one time women made up almost 80 percent of the teaching staffs of public schools. After World War II men found that teaching not only paid better than many white collar jobs, but also provided security and regular pay increases. Today there are more men than women in teaching, although at the elementary level women still predominate. Administrative posts are held almost exclusively by men. When a woman becomes a secondary school principal these days it is news.[13] Even at the elementary level, it is the men who become the principals. At one time, most elementary principals were women, but in 1972 only 20 percent were women.

The figures tell only part of the story. The career or job life of an individual is largely determined by sex. The working patterns of middle class men and women are distinctively different. A man envisions a job or career ladder stretching to retirement. A middle class woman contemplates a few years of work, then home for childrearing, then a return to work until she or her husband retires. Such expectations about life pattern certainly affect individual vocational choice. Women who are found in so-called female occupations are there not only because of tradition, but because these are jobs that can be left and returned to five or ten years later with little loss of position or self-esteem. A man who lost five years from his occupational life shortly after he had started would find that he was woefully behind his peers who kept in the occupational groove. A man must remain in the work force without major interruptions if he wants any significant career advancement.

TABLE 11-1. Employed Persons by Major Occupation Group and Sex, 1950 and 1970

MAJOR OCCUPATION GROUP	PERCENT OF TOTAL, 1950	PERCENT OF TOTAL, 1970
Men		
Professional and Technical Workers	6.4	14.2
Managers, Officials and Proprietors	12.9	14.2
Clerical Workers	7.2	7.2
Sales Workers	5.6	5.6
Craftsmen and Foremen	17.7	20.0
Operatives	20.9	19.6
Nonfarm Laborers	8.1	7.2
Private Household Workers	0.3	0.1
Other Service Workers	6.1	6.5
Farmworkers	14.7	5.5
Total	100.0	100.0
Women		
Professional and Technical Workers	10.3	14.9
Managers, Officials and Proprietors	5.7	4.4
Clerical Workers	26.3	34.8
Sales Workers	8.2	6.7
Craftsmen and Foremen	1.1	1.0
Operatives	19.1	14.4
Nonfarm Laborers	0.5	0.4
Private Household Workers	10.0	5.2
Other Service Workers	12.0	16.7
Farmworkers	6.9	1.6
Total	100.0	100.0

Adapted from *U. S. Bureau of the Census, Statistical Abstract of the United States, 1970,* (91st edition) Washington, D.C., 1970, p. 225.

Since women start in lower echelon jobs, or at the beginner ranks of professional jobs, their return after rearing their children finds them at just about the same level they left.[14] If the job is clerical-sales, there is no particular loss. Such jobs lead nowhere anyway. A check-out girl rarely if ever becomes a store manager. Salesladies may become buyers, but most do not. The woman teacher remains a teacher.

Women's household work has undergone unprecedented changes in the last century. With the coming of technology to the home, housework has been revolutionized. And the new technology produced an urgent demand for clerical workers and salespersons, offering women and girls for the first time semiskilled but "ladylike" or "clean" tasks. In the last three decades many middle class women who had never worked before have entered the work force. The whole orientation of middle class women to work has shifted.

The increased consumer demands of children tempt middle class women to reenter the job market. If the family were to depend on the husband for all income, then many things—necessities as well as luxuries—would be unobtainable. It may seem to be only a modest shift from the two car family to the three television home, wall-to-wall carpeting, automatic dishwasher, clothes washer and dryer, walk-in freezer, and garbage disposal. But all these things cost money. If these things are worth getting—and television says they are—then a working wife is indispensable to the good life. In talking about the lifestyles of young suburbanites, Riesman and Roseborough comment:

. . . they have re-arranged somewhat the career commitments both of the husband and the wife. The latter agrees to earn money only to support the family in the manner to which it has, in anticipation, become accustomed; she enters the labor market to bring home a new car, a new room, a vacation canoeing in Minnesota, but not to "have a career" in the sense of seeking status and satisfaction in job advancement and enlarged work horizons. The former, the husband, agrees to earn enough money to keep the standard package away from the repossessors, and, since the standard package grows in size as new products come on the market or old ones develop new angles (as cars have done), to keep up with this elaboration. For this, he needs merely to get on a seniority ladder—and the recent survey of young people made by the Social Research Service of Michigan State College, indicated that they think seniority the fairest way of distributing promotions. That is, seniority plus fringe benefits from the wife's working will keep the family up with the rising standard of living.[15]

If consumer drives do not motivate a woman to return to the job market, her own restlessness and boredom at home will. The relatively nondemanding modern apartment, townhouse, or detached home is a silent prison for the young, educated wife. The loneliness of separated living where relatives are across the continent and only strangers live down the hall or across the street propels many women to seek the instant camaraderie of the office or shop. Just as men find many of their social needs met in the office, so do women.

The traditional work patterns of women have interesting implications that are ignored by most guidance personnel, vocational planners, husbands, and psychiatrists. Girls become typists or teachers, possessing almost guaranteed moveable skills. No matter where their husbands may find work, someone will need a good secretary, and where there are families there are children and a school. Nurses can get jobs any place; so can beauticians and check-out girls.

Many bright, ambitious career women say that a major barrier to returning to full-time work is the difficulty of finding competent domestic help. But one traditional female occupation, that of domestic, is among the least desired of all jobs. If domestic workers cannot be found, who then will take care of the homes and children of professional women? Employers of large numbers of women will probably establish day care centers in or near the place of employment. Many are already in operation. Numerous private day care centers or nursery schools are opening. In some areas commercial firms are replacing domestic help with trained crews who clean on contract. As this is combined with convenience foods and prepackaged dinners, the working wife is almost freed of home and child care. Increasingly, too, middle class husbands are expected to assist with the few chores that remain.

Despite the great demand for them, domestic workers remain in short supply. Lower class women find factory openings for unskilled and semiskilled workers more attractive than domestic work, for such factory jobs offer steady employment, a minimum wage, a feeling of belonging to a work force, and self-respect. The domestic worker, on the other hand, must face indignities and financial insecurity:

In no other industry is the modern day worker so completely at the mercy of her employer. What can a worker do when a woman she normally works for once a week calls that morning and says it is not convenient to have her that day? She is stranded—without pay, of course! To whom can a worker appeal when her employer decides to "bargain down" the pay rate previously accepted? What can an employee do when each of the six housewives who employ her every week tells her to go about her job in a different manner?[16]

The financial security offered by a job is extremely important to the lower class woman. Unlike middle class and professional women who work for their own fulfillment or in order to purchase luxuries, lower class women work in order to support their families. *In fact, the majority of working women provide their families with income that means the difference between starvation and subsistence.* These women are not eager to work, but the working mother is the norm for the urban poor. For these families, the goal is achievement of sufficient financial security to allow the mother to stop working and stay home with the children.

Women who support the women's liberation movement are primarily middle and upper class women seeking equal access to opportunity and equal recognition of talent. They are ambitious and have demonstrable talents. For the rural and urban poor these goals are unreal. They are neither ambitious nor skilled. Their chief objectives are freedom from unfair exploitation in the labor market and job security for their husbands so that the wife and mother can stop working outside the home.

Out of Work

Employment is so intricately tied up with a man's self-esteem that fear of loss of job, or technological displacement, is one of the overwhelming anxieties of males.[17] To be out of work can be *the* most devastating event in a man's life; for a woman loss of her job may mean some belt-tightening at home, but her primary identification as wife and mother is retained. The resistance of male workers to new machinery, ranging from the violence of the Luddites to the featherbed contracts of today, is better understood in this context.

The heavy burden of work and responsibility produces some men who cannot or will not sustain the pressure. The population of the Skid Row districts of big cities is almost strictly male.[18] In the United States, Skid Row originated with the massive dislocation of thousands of men as a result of the Civil War demobilization.[19] Economic depressions in the nineteenth century and the great depression of the 1930s brought new recruits and perpetuated the Skid Row districts.

Why is Skid Row inhabited almost exclusively by men? In an earlier era, desertion was the poor man's divorce. Even today when divorce is relatively inexpensive and no longer a major personal or social disgrace, desertion is still common, particularly at lower class levels. Women, tied down with children, rarely run away from home alone. And the laws which provide welfare to a single woman with children not only contribute to male desertion, they also reduce the likelihood of women "floaters."

The fact that most men do not end up there does not reduce the symbolic significance of Skid Row in the male work and life pattern. Are the men who end up on Skid Row dropping out of life and relationships with others or are they escaping the pressures of work and achievement? Probably both. The interrelationship of these phenomena is a subject which rarely if ever is discussed when vocations and work are analyzed. Interestingly, Skid Row areas are populated almost wholly by white males; black males may cluster in areas of a city, but most black males have a family to stay with. They do not typically live alone in rooming houses or flop houses. The greater affiliation socialization of blacks appears demonstrated in a significantly positive fashion by this social phenomenon.

While loss of a job may not entail any psychological crisis for a woman, it may cause considerable financial distress. In general, women's jobs are not as secure as men's. Women are apt to be fired first unless they are protected by civil service or union regulations. With massive unemployment as in the 1930s, a married woman was expected not to work, and policies were enforced to keep her from doing so. These policies reflected the idea that since a married woman had someone to support her she should not compete against men for jobs—particularly when jobs were scarce. They also reflected the notion that married women ought to stay home.

For a man unemployment is considered a major personal and family crisis, and unemployment insurance provides interim support for his family while he is looking for another job. The assumption is that his unemployment is the result of factors beyond his control. Even if fired for incompetence he can claim unemployment benefits. In the past, a woman could not claim similar insurance benefits if her unemployment was due to pregnancy. Until March 1972, the loss of a job due to pregnancy or a delay in return to work caused by complications of pregnancy did not entitle a woman to unemployment compensation. The wife's salary might have been greatly needed for family support, but she was in effect being punished for having children. A pregnant woman may lose her job permanently.[20] The woman may not wish to be pregnant, but in many areas abortion is not available or, if it is available it may be too expensive.[21]

A man receives unemployment benefits if his wife is working or even if she is able to work but won't. However, a woman may have difficulty obtaining unemployment benefits if there is an able unemployed male at home.

Work, Age, and Race

Employment rates for boys and girls reflect a market preference for males. In 1968 white males aged sixteen to nineteen had an unemployment rate of 9.7 percent; white females, 13.1 percent. For nonwhites the unemployment rate for males was 20.6 percent, for females 28.9 percent. In both groups, females have a poorer chance of obtaining a job.[22] In 1975 the data are even more dismal, and the pattern is the same. The teenage girl who seeks part-time work may get a traditional female job as a secretary or waitress. The teenage boy has many more options open to him. The problem is not whether it is boys or girls who deserve or need jobs more, but whether the job market is so organized that girls have less chance of getting work—and money and power—than boys. If at first job entry boys and girls are differentially employed, they will gain different views of themselves as workers, and this view will permeate their adult decisions. These initial encounters with the world of work establish expectations which are very hard to change. Boys expect to have the best chance of getting jobs and they develop beliefs about who should get jobs accordingly. Girls are less likely to expect jobs and thus have little expectation that there will be jobs for them if they want and need them. Girls are less apt to have an opportunity to develop work attitudes and skills for later competition with men in the job market.

The job discrimination facing women applies also to minority groups, that is, blacks and the Spanish speaking. As noted previously, unemployment rates are high among blacks—much higher than among white males. Like white women, blacks obtain many marginal jobs, and consequently their job expectations and job skills often remain low. The establishment of all-male daytime social groups, the inability to find or keep steady work characterize the work patterns and work life of many marginal black males. Black women and men are considered expendable: last hired, first fired.

The language barrier introduces an extra job hazard for the

Puerto Rican, Cuban, or Chicano. Among these groups, cultural pressure against women working outside the home is intense, and only great necessity forces Spanish-speaking women into jobs. Few of these women work beyond the minimum to maintain the family, and even fewer make an effort to enter professional ranks. This is particularly true in the United States. In their countries of origin, a few women are making significant and daring contributions to political and professional life.

Even women on welfare who would like to obtain training so that they could work fare less well than men. One training program designed to get persons off relief provided job placement for men and women, but at very different wage rates. Even if the trainees had been able to get employment, few of the women could earn enough to be financially independent. Almost 40 percent of the male trainees obtained jobs at $2.00 an hour or above but only 9 percent of the women did.[23]

Are the work patterns and expectations that we have described inevitable? Is it socially necessary that men see themselves as productive workers outside the home to have adequate self-esteem? And if women work, is it necessary that their work be intermittent and subject to economic restrictions? Men and women are allocated different jobs and expected to work at them. If there are any major shifts in women's view of the world of work, or in men's attitudes toward the pressure of career and vocation, then many aspects of personal life will be influenced. If the schools educate youth to function in a work world which no longer exists, then confusion, conflict, and alienation will result. Youth's ideas about work are influenced by the market, peers, and the media. Again and again the world outside school is perceived to be far different from that presented in and approved by the school. But what kind of working world is best? As Toffler said, imaginative and creative understanding of the possible future may be far more necessary in today's education than a careful and objective view of either the past or the present.[24]

What Makes Women Mad

"White males hold 96 percent of America's over-$15,000-a-year jobs; women and blacks divide the remaining 4 percent."[25] This fact, headlined in the introduction to the lead article in the *New York Times Magazine*, makes women mad and blacks furious. White men have a clear monopoly over jobs, money, and power. This condition was long accepted, but those who were subject to such discrimination are no longer powerless and no longer mute.

The Federal legislation which made it illegal for any employer to discriminate on the basis of race, religion, or ethnic origin was amended to include sex. Though this amendment was introduced originally as a cynical ploy to defeat the equal employment opportunity legislation, it did not serve that function. Instead the whole legislative package was approved by Congress and the president. For a number of years the main emphasis in enforcing the act was on the employment of racial and ethnic minorities. Suddenly in the late 1960s women began to publicize the inequities they suffered and demanded that the law be applied to them, too. In 1964 women were included under the provisions of the equal pay for equal work law provided by the Fair Labor Standards Act of 1938. Between 1964 and 1972 more than 350 suits were filed under this law.[26]

Women have not always benefited from the efforts of organized labor, even though some early union activities were among the exploited immigrant women of the garment industry. Much so-called protective legislation—defining the jobs individuals can have, restricting the amount of overtime they can earn, and promoting job classifications by which only males can proceed to higher echelon positions—has been challenged recently. Union contracts have been questioned when the contracts have included limitations on women's jobs.[27] Some unions are in active opposition to the Equal Rights Amendment.

Study of the professional world has revealed that women are told they are not promoted or rewarded as much as men because they are "less productive." However, inspection of the gatekeepers for professional publication, the boards of reviewers and editors for professional journals, shows that many contain no women and a large number include only one or two women among fifteen or twenty men. A study of reviewers who assess articles for publication in a professional education journal revealed a sharp prejudice against women authors. Articles were far more likely to be accepted when submitted under male authorship.[28] Recognition of the bias against women is reflected in the recent decision by the American Psychological Association that all articles submitted for publication to their journals must be read "blind," with author's name and institutional affiliation removed before reviewers read it.[29] Despite the handicaps facing women, the notion that women academics are less productive than men is not well substantiated. At least one study of male and female Ph.Ds in the natural sciences, social sciences, humanities, and education showed that between 1958 and 1963 there was no difference between the sexes in publishing productivity.[30]

Inequities are visible at other levels in the occupational structure. The governmental bureaucracy, while employing thousands of women, has very few in the upper grade levels; women remain to retirement at lower paying grades. Reports by women attest to the fact that they may perform the same work as men but are not given the title or salary that goes with the work. When promotions are made a man will rise faster than an equally qualified woman, who may not rise at all.[31]

Women's protests over such discriminatory treatment are already having an effect. Suits have been threatened in universities and colleges to enforce the equal pay law, and institutions are scrambling to comply. Similarly, universities have promised to accept men and women in graduate programs in proportion to the number receiving B.A. degrees; women are monitoring graduate schools to see that this happens.

One interesting and significant trend must be noted. The first year since the 1930s in which the job market for teachers was unfavorable was 1971. The traditional haven for bright women, public school teaching, is no longer a guarantee of a safe job. As jobs become scarce at all professional levels, more men will apply for teaching positions. Able women, meanwhile, will seek other professional goals. Already—and quite suddenly—the number of women applying to professional schools has increased markedly. More women are being admitted to all professional schools. As men find themselves pushed out of law and medical school slots, there may be pressure to increase the number of doctors and lawyers being trained. The increase in facilities, extremely costly in the health professions particularly, will require considerable subsidy from Federal sources. The male vote in Congress for such a purpose will undoubtedly be forthcoming.

Another development may be the proliferation of paraprofessionals or semiprofessionals. Instead of becoming doctors, some will become doctor's assistants or associates. Lawyers can be helped by legal aides. Master teachers can supervise teacher aides. Who then will occupy the superior positions—that will be the new battleground between men and women. We predict that for some time to come women will be "helped" into the lesser roles.

The tax structure is so developed that women are not encouraged to seek work if they have children and a husband. If both husband and wife work, income tax rates are higher than if only one works. Minimal tax benefits are available to a woman for childcare when she is working, but only at very low income levels. A man who is left a widower may get a tax deduction for the housekeeper he needs to keep at work. In typical retirement programs women pay less than men at a younger age of employment, but they must pay more the older they are at entry. In some plans, men and women pay the same amount into the retirement fund, but women get less per month after retirement. These policies reflect actuarial data which indicate that most women have a shorter work life than men, while those who retire at the same time as men have a longer life expectancy. Some women's groups are asking whether these actuarial tables reflect contemporary trends and current statistics or whether they are actually discriminatory. In one retirement plan, women may contribute as much as $4,000 more than men, but would receive yearly benefits of $1,000 less. In a challenge to these inequities, it was pointed out that thin people live longer than fat people, and whites longer than blacks, but sex was the only basis being used for differential scales.[32]

How will the new occupational patterns affect social life? When the power base in the home shifts, with the male no longer necessarily the superior wage earner, more significant role shifts can be expected.[33] At present, a man can stay home while his wife works outside only if he is a writer, artist, or otherwise his own employer. The competitive pressure remains heavy. If they were given the same choice that women now have—work or stay home and be supported—men would be released from the strain of being forced to compete in the work world. With such an option for men, it is possible that Skid Row would disappear; the man most vulnerable to job stress could withdraw and survive as father and husband for many more years.

The groundwork has been laid for such a shift, with most middle class fathers doing many household chores considered typically female by previous generations: food shopping, dish washing, scrubbing, feeding baby. The young marriages of today are characterized by much more sharing of home tasks by husband and wife. There is no stigma attached to a man changing baby's diapers or taking the laundry to the laundromat. The hostility some men feel for the "easy life" of the housewife, expressed in punitive withholding of money and demeaning of the work women do, may in time be seen for what it really is: envy. In time, men may acknowledge it might be fun just to stay home, too!

Many individuals view such a shift in roles and role behavior with alarm akin to panic. The change is considered sexually damaging, blurring male and female into "uni-sex."[34] Whether viewed favorably or unfavorably, it is undeniable that shifts in work and work roles inevitably affect other social roles and social relationships.

Anatomy of the Resistance

Segregation of jobs by sex is more widespread than segregation by race. "Most men work in occupations that employ very few women and a significant fraction of women work in occupations that employ few men."[35]

Although women's lib is making headlines, the barriers against integrating women into the general work force are holding firm. In a proposal for increasing the employment of women and minorities, John Kenneth Galbraith forecasts that by 1980 there will be enough women with training and experience to compose from thirty to thirty-five percent of the work force at every level of business, industry, government, and education—*except* at the very top levels.[36] Galbraith states categorically that only tradition has prevented women from doing the tasks any man can do. But why then is there so much resistance to female occupational change and mobility? Why do both men and women view with unease and distaste attempts to change the power relationship?

One factor in the male resistance to female coworkers is the kind of male group life which Lionel Tiger explores in *Men in Groups.*[37] He traces the evolution of all-male work groups from prehistoric all-male hunting groups. Women, he argues, were a liability on a hunt because they could be slowed by pregnancy and the caring of infants, or they could distract men for sexual dalliance.[38] Through the thousands of years during which civilization evolved, tribal custom as well as the exigencies of survival produced a ubiquitous sex-work cleavage. Every society has designated some work exclusively male, some exclusively female (see Chapter 2). Thus the "racial unconscious," which the psychoanalyst Jung developed into a complex theory to explain contemporary behavior, restricts shifts in role relationships. Considerable doubt has been cast on Jung's theory, and Tiger is careful not to make too much of precivilization experience. He argues that what civilization has done, however, is to codify through law and sanction through religion those sex-role separations whose roots can be traced to more simple social organizations.

The typical resistance to the inclusion of women in many all-male occupations or managerial levels is justified on the grounds that men at work use language which would not be fit for a "lady" to hear. Such reasoning was used to justify restricting the floor of the Stock Exchange to men. Tiger comments:

One of the formal excuses for this curious condition is that during hectic trading Stock Exchange members may utter curses from which as a gentleman they should presumably desist in the presence of ladies. Gallant as this and similar reasons may be, it seems more likely that the floor of any stock exchange is really an arena for highly skilled predatory behaviour which rests on an overall co-operative pattern, and that this mixture of predation and co-operative professional bonhommie, men fear, will be significantly altered by the participation of females. If men are right in this assessment, it would no doubt be the final argument of women that if the system depends on the exclusion of women for its operation it is an unacceptable system given contemporary notions of sexual equality.[39]

An economic system which depends on exclusion of females could not be a viable system in the world of high finance and international exchange. It is spurious to argue that including women would make one iota of difference in the way the Stock Exchange functions.

In one Federal agency, prior to the Federal policy of admitting women to all levels and grades, certain assignments were considered off limits for women. The "real work" was done in groups and conferences; it was explained that the men just could not relax enough to do business if women were present. The concepts of work as play, work as relaxation, and work as an arena for realizing interpersonal satisfactions unrelated to those derived from getting a job done, are implicit in this kind of exclusion. The work game has one set of rules for men only, and another when women enter.

It is possible that men resist a wife's interest in a career, particularly one which would place her among many men, because of fear of rivals. Just as some wives have viewed their husband's secretaries or female colleagues with jealousy and suspicion, so husbands now respond to a wife's interest in the working world of men. The pervasive inability of men and women in our culture to see each other as persons first and sexual objects only incidentally is a major ingredient in the job-career conflict.

As currently perceived, what women add to a work situation is a sexual dimension. A study of the interaction of men working in an agency in their relations with the one female secretary is instructive. All the agents had to make complicated final reports, but use of the stenographer for dictation of this report was related to the status of the individual: "An agent found the presence of the stenographer disturbing if he worried about the impression he made on her—for instance, when he had to tell her to correct a mistake he had made. . . ."[40] Agents with high status appeared not to care how the stenographer viewed them.

Agents who felt insecure in the peer group, on the other hand, were probably more eager to receive, at least, the respect of the stenographer, and were at the same time less confident of doing so. Their consequent preoccupation with the impression they made on her prevented them from concentrating their thoughts upon composing the report. This disturbance often induced the less advantaged agents to forego the advantages of dictating.[41]

Certain jobs are held by women primarily because of their sex. Attractive women are selected as airline stewardesses.[42] Beautiful women are more apt to become fashion models or night club entertainers than scientists or mathematicians. A beautiful woman is encouraged to exploit her physical attributes and need not bother with her brains; does this explain the greater number of relatively unattractive women in highly intellectual jobs?[43]

Recognition of the role that sexual attraction plays in interpersonal relations may underlie the objection many women have to working for another woman. Both men and women teachers prefer a male principal. In the informal social system of the school women find it easier to "use" men to manipulate the system to maximize their own rewards; women principals cannot be appealed to in the same way. Men resist women principals because they dislike this power relationship and they do not want to have to play the male-female game in such a work situation. The work game and the sex game do not mix well. The inclusion of women in work groups may produce a situation in which men who gain leadership and power will do so through a combination of work skills and sexual skills.

In an interesting study, the impact of a lone woman on work groups of professional men was studied.[14] In none of the groups was the woman allowed to participate freely or equally without undergoing a significant period of isolation. Only after she had remained silent and unobtrusive for some time could she gain entry into the work group, particularly if the group leader tried to make the men realize their hostility toward her.

A woman can observe the impact of her presence upon males in a working group. The men will show "preening" behavior when she enters—adjusting a tie, shifting their jackets or sleeves, patting their hair. Once in the group, however, she will have difficulty being accepted as an equal. Many professional women note that their male colleagues do not hesitate to interrupt or contradict them, and they ignore women's bids to be heard, behavior which they demonstrate less often with male colleagues. It is not uncommon, women report, for males to appropriate their ideas without credit, or for others in the group, men and women alike, to attribute women's contributions to male members. Women who use "feminine wiles" rather obviously in a work situation are less apt to be criticized than women who do not flirt, wear "sexy" clothes, or otherwise accentuate their femaleness. Evidently, male colleagues feel more comfortable with a "real woman" than with a professional female who may seem to be more like a male competitor.

A factor that has militated against women with career aspirations is a phenomenon termed the "Queen Bee syndrome."[45] The lone woman who has attained a position of eminence among male peers has been found to be peculiarly anti-feminist. That is, she has no sympathy for other women struggling several echelons below her in the hierarchy. "If I can make it, so can they," is an attitude implicit in her refusal to espouse their cause. She tends to deny any evidence of discrimination. After all, she is a living symbol of the absence of discrimination, isn't she? These women feel that women should blame themselves for lack of success. They do not favor preferential treatment to make up for past discrimination against women, they do not support collective action by women to fight discrimination, do not feel that they have been subject to discrimination, they moderately support the women's movement, and they place a high estimation on the values of traditional family life.[46] However, with the women's movement of the 1970s there have appeared many women in high level positions who make it quite clear that one of their priorities is to be alert to barriers to achievement for other women. It is possible that the Queen Bee syndrome may soon pass into history.

In many occupations, professional organizations exist to promote group interests and to serve as an arena for exchange of ideas and information. Women have been excluded from some of these organizations or else restricted to minimal participation. Professional associations for women lawyers, dentists, and engineers were long necessary because the men's groups excluded them.[47] Separate honorary associations were the rule in professional education. Most men seem to be uncomfortable treating a woman colleague or superior as nonsexual, despite the fact that there is conflict between proper work behavior and the kind of behavior appropriate to "courting." The sex-role dichotomy has educated men and women to see each other first in a sex-role and then in any other role they may hold—doctor, lawyer, supervisor, secretary. As long as this holds true, sex-separated groups and intersex competition will remain barriers to job equality.

Traditionally, girls were taught to defer to men's wishes. This engrained respect for men permitted women to accept them as superiors. In the so-called semiprofessions filled with women—nursing, social work, library work, and teaching, Simpson and Simpson noted "deference to men" as a cultural norm. In most professional relationships, women respected their male superiors. According to the research, women "accepted" subordinate roles "better" than men.[48] The Simpsons' data were obtained in 1950, when it was felt that women were "more comfortable" taking orders, not being too ambitious, and having low career commitment.[49]

Today, women are asserting that deference is not a comfortable posture; many women have strong ambitions and vital career commitments.[50] They will not defer to men; instead they will compete with them to determine who is more qualified.

The Working Parent: Myths and Realities

The mother who works at a full-time job has long been regarded with sympathy if she were poor or widowed. She is viewed with suspicion and hostility if she has a husband with adequate income and she works because she likes to. All men and most women have believed that children can be reared properly and adequately only by their mothers. The woman who works because she wants to has been considered selfish and irresponsible.

Studies of working mothers and their children do not support this view. If a mother wishes to stay home with her children but has to work, she will provide adequate mothering. If she stays home but wishes she could work, she will be a poor mother. If she is at home and wants to be there, she will be good for her children. What is crucial is the quality, not the quantity, of the mother's relations with her children.[51] As Bowlby and others point out in *Maternal Care*,[52] it is the quality of care, not the source of care, that is significant.

These findings are not new. Yet the mother-child relationship is surrounded by an aura of sentimentality and fear, and most women and men believe fervently in the "sacred" mother-child twosome. Some cynical viewers, such as Philip Wylie in his popular commentary *A Generation of Vipers*, have suggested that mom was not always benign.[53] But this view has been submerged beneath the sticky ooze which covers middle class motherhood. The incredible mother in Philip Roth's *Portnoy's Complaint* is seen as an outrageous caricature.[54]

The research on women, work, and motherhood provides a fairly objective account of what actually happens. Women who stay home— and do not want to—can indeed become devouring moms, who engulf, or neglect daughters and sons and drive husbands to drink, divorce, or desertion.[55] Women who work may find satisfactions in work which neither husband nor children can provide.

Our main point is that the myth that childcare can be provided only by the natural mother has served to keep women out of the labor market and out of competition with men, and it has placed a major handicap upon them when they do return—later and older—to careers.

The hypocrisy of the mother cult is revealed when policymakers discuss mothers on welfare. Then it becomes a very important matter to get the mothers off welfare and into jobs. If mothers ought to stay home and care for children, then welfare policies should be adjusted to make this possible. Instead, policy discussions center on how to get these women back to work by offering such incentives as a tax relief or subsidy. That these mothers must leave infants and young children in the care of others is not considered a significant issue. The debates over daycare for preschool children, or after-school care for elementary school children are not concerned with the effects of such facilities on children. The social critics who deplore the ambitions of middle class mothers who want to work as a kind of self-indulgence seem to have no such qualms when chiding women in poverty for being "unwilling to work." In fact, such women may be denied welfare if there are jobs available, although such work may require that they leave their youngsters. It is clear that the sentimentality surrounding motherhood is reserved for those who can afford it. The discrepancy inherent in welfare policies is not lost upon the poor, who are understandably bitter and impatient with the kind of social planning that makes them the continued victims of inequality.

Why is there a cult of the mother in the United States? The reasons are many and intricate. For one thing, it serves to keep women out of competitive work relations with men, and effectively keeps many women out of the job market for many years, if not all of their lives. Galbraith predicts that even in 1980 only 34 percent of the work force will be women, and he assumes that at least two-thirds of all women will be at home with children.[56]

In an economy of labor oversupply there is significant utility in keeping a portion of able-bodied workers from actively competing for jobs. In times of unemployment and economic recession it is the patriotic duty of women to stay home and raise children.

In our society women must be wives and mothers first, career women second. But men are expected to give their work first priority. The idea that a large number of men might be just as happy to be relieved of the job-work pressure is rarely mentioned by social policymakers. The middle class father who commutes to work from his suburban home may see his children only on weekends. For such commuters, the work day may be more nearly ten to twelve hours—portal to portal—than the eight hours for which they are scheduled. Children need fathers who take an interest in them. As women take more interest in careers, some men may assume a larger parental role.

The differential values currently placed on career versus parental roles by men and women are well illustrated by the following letter, printed in the *Saturday Review:*

We pay equal pay for equal work. But I ask a woman assistant if she would like us to send her to a three-month training course in banking. She exclaims, "Oh I couldn't possibly be away from my husband and children *that* long!" I offer it to the man at the next desk—same pay. He jumps at it, scenting recognition and promotion. He kisses his wife and children, and he's off. Has the woman, for "equal pay," been rendering a truly equal service to the bank?[57]

Is an employer justified in taking either father or mother away from home for a three-month training program? The fact that a man would jump at the opportunity demonstrates not only the higher priority that men put on work, but also a lack of awareness of the effect of prolonged absence of either parent on growing children. The employer who wrote the above letter gave no thought to the family problems he might have created. His attitude reflects the low valuation placed on a man's family role.

◆   Summary

Discrimination against women in the job market is rooted largely in a tradition that says men must be stronger, richer, more powerful, more intelligent, and more aggressive than women. As women achieve success in their careers, such myths must die and relations between men and women must be more open and equal.

The changing aspirations of women are creating new competition for men at every occupational level. But more importantly, they are causing major alterations in family patterns and in patterns of interaction between men and women. Women are no longer programmed exclusively for the wife-mother role, and men are discovering alternatives to the fiercely competitive career world.

References

1.   Maryann Suelzle, "Women in Labor," *Trans-Action* 8 (November-December 1970): 50–58.
2.   Leland J. Axelson, "The Working Wife: Differences in Perception Among Negro and White Males," *Journal of Marriage and the Family* 32 (August 1970): 457–464; see also Margaret M. Poloma and T. Neal Garland, "The Myth of the Egalitarian Family: Familial Roles and the Professionally Employed Wife," in *The Professional Woman*, ed. Athena Theodore (Cambridge: Schenkman Publishing Company, 1971), pp. 741–761.
3.   William J. Goode, *Women in Divorce* (New York: Free Press, 1956).
4.   U.S., Department of Labor, Workplace Standards Administration, Women's Bureau, *Underutilization of Women Workers*, rev. ed. (Washington, D.C.: Government Printing Office, 1971).
5.   U.S., Department of Labor, Women's Bureau, *Facts on the Earnings Gap* (Washington, D.C.: Department of Labor, 1971).
6.   U.S., Commission on Civil Rights, Staff Report, *Women and Poverty* (Washington, D.C.: 1974), pp. 15–16.
7.   Matina Horner, "Fail: Bright Women," *Psychology Today*, November 1969, p. 36+.

8. David Riesman and Howard Roseborough, "Careers and Consumer Behavior," in *Consumer Behavior*, ed. Lincoln H. Clark (New York: New York University Press, 1955), Vol. 2, pp. 1-18.

9. Walter S. Neff, *Work and Human Behavior* (New York: Atherton Press, 1968), pp. 39-42.

10. Betty Roszak and Theodore Roszak, *Masculine/Feminine: Readings in Sexual Mythology and the Liberation of Women* (New York: Harper and Row, 1969), pp. 251-276.

11. Rose L. Coser and Gerald Rokoff, "Women in the Occupational Worlds: Social Disruption and Conflict," *Social Problems* 18 (Sept. 1971): 535-554.

12. *Ibid.*

13. "Rare Move in Fairfax: Woman Named Principal," *Washington Star*, June 27, 1971.

14. Richard Simpson and Ida H. Simpson, "Women and Bureaucracy in the Semi-Professions," in *The Semi-Professions and Their Organization*, ed. Amitai Etzioni (New York: New York Free Press, 1969), pp. 196-265.

15. Riesman and Roseborough, *op. cit.*

16. Darry A. Sragow, "Taking the 'Mammy' Out of Housework," *Civil Rights Digest* 4 (Winter 1971):34-39.

17. Myron Brenton, *The American Male* (New York: Coward McCann, 1966), pp. 193-213.

18. Samual E. Wallace, *Skid Row as a Way of Life* (Totowa, N.J.: The Bedminster Press, 1965), p. 18.

19. *Ibid.*

20. Katherine Auchincloss, "Unemployment Benefits," *Women's Rights Law Reporter* 1 (Spring 1973):38-47.

21. U.S., Congress, House, Special Subcommittee on Education of the Committee on Education and Labor, "Are Women Equal Under the Law?" in *Discrimination Against Women* by Gene Boyer, 91st Cong., 2nd sess., H. Rept. 16098, part 2, July 1 and 31, pp. 1089-1090.

22. U.S., Department of Labor, Manpower Administration, *Assessing the Economic Scene* (Washington, D.C.: Government Printing Office, 1969), p. 11.

23. U.S., Department of Labor, Manpower Administration, *The Potential for Work Among Welfare Parents* by Leonard J. Hausman, Manpower Research Monograph number 12 (Washington, D.C.: Government Printing Office, 1969).

24. Alvin Toffler, *Future Shock* (New York: Random House, 1970).

25. John Kenneth Galbraith, Edwin Kuh, and Lester C. Thurow, "The Galbraith Plan to Promote the Minorities," *New York Times Magazine*, August 22, 1971.

26. Kathryn G. Heath, "Support to Eliminate Sex Bias in Education," mimeographed (Washington, D.C.: Office of Education, April 29, 1972).

27. *Ibid.*
28. Henry Walbesser, research in progress, University of Maryland.
29. *APA Monitor*, August 1972.
30. R. J. Simon, S. M. Clark, and K. Galway, "The Woman Ph.D." *Social Problems* 15 (1967): 221–226.
31. U.S., Congress, House, *op. cit.*
32. *New York Times*, February 4, 1973.
33. Robert O. Blood and Robert L. Hamblin, "The Effects of Wife's Employment on the Family Power Structure," *Social Forces* 26 (May 1958): 347–352.
34. Charles S. Winich, *The New People* (New York: Pegasus Books, 1968); Lawrence H. Fuchs, *Family Matters* (New York: Random House, 1972); Erich Fromm, "Mother," *Psychology Today*, March 1971, pp. 74–77.
35. Victor R. Fuchs, "Male-Female Differentials in Hourly Earnings," National Bureau of Economic Research, 1970, p. 12, quoted in Barbara R. Bergman, "The Economics of Women's Liberation" (Paper presented at the American Psychological Association Meeting, Washington, D.C., September 1971).
36. *New York Times Magazine*, August 22, 1971.
37. Lionel Tiger, *Men in Groups* (New York: Random House, 1969).
38. *Ibid.*, pp. 93–125.
39. *Ibid.*, p. 112, fn.
40. Peter M. Blau, "Patterns of Interaction Among a Group of Officials in a Government Agency," *Human Relations* 7 (1954):337 348.
41. *Ibid.*
42. *New York Times*, September 1, 1969.
43. David P. Campbell, "The Clash Between Beautiful Women and Science," in *The Professional Woman*, ed. Athena Theodore (Cambridge: Schenkman Publishing Company, 1971), pp. 135–141.
44. Harold H. Frank and Carol Wolman, "The Solo Woman in a Professional Peer Group" (Paper presented at the Annual Meeting of the American Psychiatric Association, 1973).
45. E. Jayaratne, "The Queen Bee Syndrome," *Psychology Today*, January 1974, pp. 55–60.
46. *Ibid.*
47. Cynthia F. Epstein, "Encountering the Male Establishment: Sex-Status Limits on Women's Careers in the Professions," *American Journal of Sociology* 75 (May 1970): 965–982.
48. Simpson and Simpson, *op. cit.*, p. 225.
49. *Ibid.*, pp. 226–229.
50. Karen de Crow, *The Young Woman's Guide to Liberation* (New York: Pegasus-Bobbs Merrill, 1971), pp. 128–137.
51. Eleanor Maccoby, "The Effects Upon Children of Their Mothers' Employ-

ment," in *Work in the Lives of Married Women*, ed. National Manpower
Council (New York: Columbia University Press, 1958), pp. 150–172.

52. John Bowlby *et al.*, *Maternal Care and Mental Health* (New York: Schocken
Books, 1966).

53. Philip Wylie, *A Generation of Vipers* (New York: Holt, Rhinehart and
Winston, 1942); see also Edward A. Strecker, *Their Mothers' Sons* (New
York: J. B. Lippincott, 1946).

54. Philip Roth, *Portnoy's Complaint* (New York: Random House, 1969).

55. David Levy, *Maternal Overprotection* (New York: Columbia University
Press, 1943).

56. Galbraith, *op. cit.*

57. *Saturday Review*, July 3, 1972, p. 22.

12

Surviving

The Sexual Revolution

The truism "knowledge is power" is worthy of the attention of those who wish to understand the contemporary revolution. Basically, the revolution rests on:

...the knowledge women have acquired regarding their sexuality;

...the knowledge of effective means of birth control available to women, and the spread of this information;

...the knowledge of access to free or inexpensive legal abortion for women of whatever age or marital status;

...the knowledge that equal rights are legally enforceable;

...the knowledge among men that traditional sex-role expectations limit human potential.

Revolutions occur not when the dispossessed are desperate, but when those without power gain a sufficiently close view of those in power to make a confrontation potentially successful. Through legal means, some of which imitated the more dramatic methods tried and tested by the black revolution, women have been able to challenge male power, and have rebelled against a lifestyle and tradition which is male oriented.

Two Sexes or Uni-sex?

The more dramatic and excessive aspects of the women's liberation movement make front page news. The marchers and Freedom Riders of the black revolution were taken seriously enough to be attacked;

militant women are laughed at, caricatured, and demeaned by name-calling. They are called lesbians, bra-burners, castrators or just silly females.

However, the verbal attacks on women militants point up a fact of contemporary life: there is indeed a sexual revolution in process whether many people know it, like it, or approve of it, and women are the new revolutionaries. One perceptive historian noted that the verbal abuse encountered by feminists during the 1960s was hardly proportionate to what they did. The media revealed that among ordinary middle class people antifeminism seemed the only remaining respectable prejudice; to take feminism seriously might be disastrous.

Feminism might well be the most truly radical proposition of them all, one that threatened to reach into secret and intimate places which politics had scarcely touched. Hence, along with all the other problems they had to deal with, liberated women had to confront this widespread, if seldom admitted, anxiety. And they had to resist the other pathologies to which radical movements were prone in the sixties. They all succumbed to sectarianism, fissioning, rhetorical extravagances, posturing, and obsessiveness. But if liberated women could avoid imitating them they might go far indeed.[1]

The culturally important point about the women's movement is that men as well as women are its potential beneficiaries. When women demand equal chances for promotion, equalization of pay and working benefits, access to career education, and repeal of discriminatory legislation, traditional ways are under attack on a wide front. The necessary adjustments, which balance female expectations against male prerogatives, may temporarily dislocate some men and women and threaten their self-concept as well as their livelihood. But this is only the short run impact of the women's movement.

As was noted in previous chapters, there is a vast amount of human misery, much of it due to inappropriate sex-role expectations. Men are expected to shoulder all the burdens of family support; to maintain their self-esteem they must show drive and ambition, and be willing to wage war and kill. Otherwise, they may crumble into alcoholism or impotence. Many well-educated women, socialized to give priority to marriage and childrearing, find that the nuclear family is stifling, providing them with a blurred sense of identity and a very shaky basis for existing. They too crumble. When fathers and mothers provide weak support, children cannot thrive. All values seem relative, education seems meaningless and materialistic goals unrewarding, so youth drift into apathy or passionless violence. Although most of us are familiar with only a few of these problems, enough of us are dogged by anxieties, frustrations, and fears that the possibility of personal collapse is too close for comfort.

The sexual revolution may redefine or rather extend the definition of what is sex appropriate for males and females. Men will no longer have to be aggressive: those not wanting to push will be able to feel adequately masculine. Similarly, women will be free to decide whether to have children, to exercise their talent or ability, and to accept reward for achievement without guilt. Aggression and independence in women will be as acceptable as dependence and passivity in men, and there will be no loss of sexuality or self-esteem for either sex.

The doomsayers attack the sexual revolution out of fear that sex-role redefinitions will feminize men and masculinize women. Yet, as physiologists point out, sex is sex. Changes in psychological characteristics do not change the sex act itself. There cannot be a reversal of sexual roles in procreation.

People marry those who are accessible, and they are socialized to be supportive of such choices. As a result of the sexual revolution there will be a wider range of personality expressiveness so that males and females will be more able to find mates who satisfy their personality needs. The able, ambitious girl will not have to hide her talents to "get a man," because she will find a man who values these traits and feels that they are needed in building a marriage where the burdens and parental roles can be shared equally. Males and females with high dependency needs may find life more satisfying when both are free to admit such needs.

However, some believe that such changes will lead to a condition of "uni-sex." Says the headmaster of a private school:

> I look at the present tendencies toward "unisex" with some horror. It is not so much that girls affect male clothing and act like males and that boys affect increasingly feminine clothing and hair styles and behave like females, especially toward work, defense, and leadership. Rather it is the suspicion I have that sex is being stripped of its emotional ritual, deprived of its division of labor, isolated, and degraded to a matter of physiological drive reduction. Humane sexual relations require a masculine principle and feminine principle. Without these, sex is merely a form of release, a way of discharging tension, a means of self-gratification, a technique of solipsism.[2]

Another commentator is concerned about sexual "depolarization." Winick feels that youth are growing up in a culture which has "blurred sex roles almost hopelessly," forcing Americans to drift toward sexual "neutering."[3] He concludes: "If our age of electronics and computers continues to drift toward depolarization of sex, there is indeed a possibility that men and women will ultimately be able to produce nothing together and each will become a less appropriate audience for the distinctive performance of the other."[4]

Some women view the changing definitions of sex-appropriate behavior with alarm and dismay. Women who have actively opposed the Equal Rights Amendment have stated repeatedly that they fear that such a constitutional change will cause women to be drafted into the army, expose them to new kinds of exploitation, and leave them defenseless in marital situations. Some consider it irreligious to support the drive for women's equality: "A truly Christian woman could care less about equality. She is her husband's helpmate. He is her pride and joy."[5]

Except for a few remarkable early dissidents, such as Mary Wollstonecraft, John Stuart Mill, George Bernard Shaw, Havelock Ellis, Virginia Woolf, Mary A. Beard, and Karen Horney, most commentators on the roles of men and women in Western society have proclaimed without any fear of effective contradiction the desirability of traditional sex-role relationships. There is a considerable body of literature which insists that male domination is required for adequate adjustment of both men and women, and that changes in traditional role relationships are impossible. In a recent (1972) book Payette says that "Woman feels profoundly the imperative need to be completely taken in charge of by a man. He must do this with firmness, constancy, passion, compassion, sympathy, and in no uncertain manner."[6] After an extended discussion on the nature of the human animal, Jonas and Klein conclude that men are becoming infantilized in part due to the emancipation of women and in part due to the effects of technology upon the basic family structure, so that man, his woman, and indeed all of civilized society faces extinction.[7] Fuchs says that the only way to save the troubled American family is to restore the father to his role of authority in the home, and to counter super mothers who will not let children grow up. While pleading for a humane family based on the reciprocity of love, Fuchs sees this as possible only within traditional sex-role relationships and behaviors.[8]

A Few Minor Changes?

Man is behaviorally polypotential—he is capable of anything within his individual genetic limits, but he is not predetermined to be anything particular. What he becomes, he learns on the basis of potentialities that are biological and influences that are social. His heredity is not what he is biologically endowed with at conception or what he is born with, but the expression of the interaction between his genetic potentialities and the environmental influences that have acted upon them.[9]

Through study of other cultures we are reminded of the infinite variety of behaviors, etiquette, mores, and attitudes which human association can produce. Anthropology provides us with a long view into the human potential for social variety. In anthropological terms, "The appropriate or correct behavior varies from culture to culture; exactly which one is appropriate is arbitrary. This sort of behavior is known as 'context-dependent behavior' and is, in its learned form, pervasively and almost uniquely human. So pervasive is it, indeed, that most of the time we are unaware of the effects of context dependence on our behavior."[10]

Most of us prefer what is known and familiar. When traditional behavior and attitudes are challenged, we feel uncomfortable. The sexual revolution is providing many challenges to tradition, and they are met by suspicion, fear, and distrust.

The fear that males and females will be indistinguishable from each other is a particularly interesting objection to contemporary trends. It is somewhat like the anger whites feel when a black has successfully "passed" and then reveals that he has duped the whites into accepting him as one of them—as good as a white. Men seem to resent the long hair of young men and the blue jeans worn by males and female alike. "How can you tell them apart?" How can a man know which to treat as an equal, and which to treat as a woman? Socially prescribed labels of dress, hair style, and adornment have served the very useful purpose of transmitting an instant message: male, female. The conduct code can be immediately operational: males can use obscenities in front of other males, and hold the door open for females. The driver of the car ahead can be cursed for being a "stupid woman driver." There is a gut-level shock when one comes abreast of the car and finds that the long-haired driver has a beard.

Distinctive garb has been evident in all times and places. Jews in medieval society (and during Hitler's reign) wore the yellow J. Hester wore the Scarlet Letter. Nurses wear little caps; doctors wear white jackets. We do not want to make too much of the changes in dress in relation to the sexual revolution, but they are symptomatic of deeper and more significant changes in the way persons perceive themselves, and how, through their appearance, they desire to communicate this to the observer. The similar garb of youth today may be their view that sex differences are far more than skin deep; that it is not clothes but feelings that produce sexual response.

Feminists see marital name change as a symbol of the way in which women are deprived of an enduring identity of their own. A woman may experience a loss of a sense of self when she marries and must change her name from Barbara Brown to Barbara Jones, and to Mrs. Harry Jones. As Blackstone stated in the eighteenth century, upon marriage a woman ceases to exist as a separate entity; the change of name formalizes this process. Understandably, some women do not like it, and have been protesting since the time of Lucy Stone, in 1855. Name change is a cultural invention. In Japan, it is possible for a man to adopt the name of his wife's family in order to keep property within the family.[11] Even English tradition permits males to take the name of their spouse when it is a matter of inheritance and lineage.[12]

The courtesy titles which women are given immediately identify their marital status. A Mr. is a Mr. no matter whom he marries, or when, or how often. The marital history of a woman is recorded upon employment records and school transcripts, since these will show maiden name, first married name, and second or third married names if there are such. Rarely are these records expunged, for the individual would be "lost" in the files. Some advisers at universities warn graduating women that if by any chance they are married during their last semester they should not change their names with the registrar or their records may never be found again. The marital history of a male is invisible. Feminists are advocating the use of the title Ms. for all women, married or not. This seemingly minor change has polarized advocates for women's equality. Some feel it is essential to achievement of the goal of equality with men, others feel it is an unnecessary if not subversive tampering with role relationships. Chairman or chairwoman or chairperson? Symptoms or trivialities?

These social distinctions have kept people in their traditional

"I just can't get used to calling her a chairperson—it makes me think she's in the upholstery business."

places. Do such distinctions rob an individual of his or her uniqueness? Our society is struggling with the basic idea of a "person." That is, we are trying to accept the notion that abilities, talents, personality characteristics, ambitions, and feelings, are similarly distributed in the male and female populations. A male or female is to be treated not according to sex, but on the basis of other attributes such as skills, attitudes, needs, interests, and ambitions. The important—and consoling—fact (and one which those who fear "uni-sex" have not really comprehended) is that physiological sex differences will not and cannot change or fade away.

Many who advocate changes in sex roles argue that physiology does not determine destiny. As pointed out in Chapter 3 of this book, the data indicate that human beings are very flexible, and that chromosomal differences place very few, if any, limits upon that flexibility. Males can develop every aspect of female personality (or vice versa) and yet retain the sexuality that is inherited. Current concepts of sex-appropriate behavior almost force those who develop what society considers nonappropriate behavior into homosexual relationships. There is no evidence that with social support these people could not have perfectly satisfying heterosexual relationships. One observer of current trends in sex-role behavior who is particularly alarmed by homosexuality states, "This trend towards neutrality of the sexes is taking place at a time when evidence is mounting that many of the most serious ills of society stem specifically from a lack of clear distinction [between the sexes]."[13] Instead of identifying social ills as deriving from a *too-rigid* definition of what is sex-appropriate, this author wants to stop the clock, if not turn it back. We would argue that a less rigid sex-role norm would in fact reduce the incidence of homosexuality among both male and female.

Social indicators point to an ever accelerating process of social change. Although women's incomes remain significantly lower than men's, women are aware of discrimination and inequality and are fighting it. It will be increasingly difficult to keep discriminatory practices covert and unchallenged. Successful and secure men agree that talent rather than genital differences should be the basis for advancement and remuneration.[14]

◆   What Is To Be Done?

Our goal in this book has been to identify and report the findings about sex differences and spell out implications for parents, educators, and social planners. Who has the harder time growing up in America? Pick your expert. Some claim that the male sex role is so fraught with dangerous contradictions that it is a wonder that any boys survive to maturity.[15] Others feel that girls have the hardest time.[16] The published data were collected prior to most of the developments connected with the women's movement. It will be several years before the impact of the new sexual information and sexual freedom upon men and women and their children can be studied. Two conclusions seem warranted: 1) there is occurring a shift in women's views of themselves and of life's offerings, and 2) this shift will cause readjustments in occupational, family, and child-rearing relationships. In our view these trends are positive, and can contribute to the enhancement of personal potential if they are supported by our institutions and by individual men and women.

What Can the School Do?

Schools have been such an important socializing agency for our multicultural nation that their practices should be scrutinized with care. The school is one of the few institutions which is amenable to deliberate policy changes and adjustments.

—School personnel need to assess school programs for sex bias for or against either sex.

—Teachers must be sensitized to the ways in which sex-appropriate behavior can limit the self-expression and intellectual development of boys and girls.

—Texts and other material should be assessed to determine whether they reinforce outmoded stereotypes. Approaches to the study of sex roles must be developed.[17]

—Counselors and others involved with students' career decisions should support individual inclination without regard to sex.

—Career opportunities must be equally available to men and women in the educational system.

—Schools need to interpret these policies to parents and educate parents to help them allow children to fulfill their unique potential without rigid sex role limitations on their behavior.

—Colleges of education must include in teacher, counselor, and administrator training understanding of sex-role problems. These individuals should be sensitized to their own socialization regarding sex roles, and should be helped to overcome these limitations. Just as whites and blacks need to become color blind, so do educators need to see children not as typical boys or girls, nor as sexless students, but as unique individuals who are also boys and girls.

—Children need adequate and sensitive education about family life in order to understand that sex roles are socially defined. Instructional materials which present a balanced and nonsentimental view of interpersonal relations in families are needed.

—Colleges and universities must provide access to professional and scholarly careers on the basis of talent alone, so that students can see male and female role models performing academic and professional activities with competence, serenity, and creativity. Colleges can also support the parental role of these professional men and women so that parenthood is perceived as a significant and equal part of personal life—for those who choose to be parents.

—Universities accepting a research function as a major objective must regard research in sex roles as a priority. In many disciplines there is minimal support for the study of sex roles and specifically the study of women. Colleges and universities must take the view that women's studies are a legitimate scholarly endeavor—in history, literature, physiology, sociology, anthropology, or any other area of investigation that can contribute greater insight. The greater the effort to fill the gaps in research the more rapidly the study of women or sex roles will move into the mainstream of the discipline and influence the interpretation of other facts. Specialists in women's studies or in sex-role research will be needed even after the gross errors and misinformation has been cleared away, and this focus should be accepted for any level of scholarly analysis.

—Colleges and universities should provide continuing education for men and women of any age who wish to renew their skills, broaden their vision, gain an understanding of the changing world, and be supported as they seek to understand the several revolutions through which we are living, of which the sexual revolution is only one.

What Can the Family Do?

THE family can do nothing; individual families can do a great deal. Concerned parents have asked each of the authors, throughout the development of this book, for help in avoiding traps in the rearing of sexually secure boys and girls. What can parents do?

—Parents can attempt to understand their own sex-role identity, with an honest appraisal of their views of what is appropriate for each sex. This is not an easy task. Most of us are bound by twenty-five or more years of socializing by the time we produce children; we have acquired many facades. Sometimes it is difficult to know what is real. Consciousness-raising groups have been formed in many communities, sponsored by churches, colleges and universities, and groups related to the women's movement. These groups serve both men and women, and can provide support and assistance. That some such groups may be difficult to deal with and cause unhappiness should also be noted.[18]

—Before one has children it is essential to know clearly what the sex of a child implies to each parent. Where there is confusion, doubt, even possible rejection, counseling is advised. Boys and girls are seriously damaged in personality development by a mother or father who really wanted a child of the other sex. We cannot damage the innocent by imposing our sexual preferences on them.

—Parents should examine their childrearing practices to see if they are promoting overaggressiveness in their boys, and dependence and lack of initiative in their girls. Are they labeling some toys for boys only? Are some activities only for girls? A child's preferences can be fostered and supported without in any way confusing the child as to his or her sex or gender. Yes, boys can bake cakes and girls can play baseball, and neither will be less male or female as a result. It is the valuation placed on the behavior by the parents that makes for gender confusion and eventually sexual confusion.

—Parents must be careful to assess the degree of tolerance of differences among the children's potential peers. Parents can go just so far in providing a less sexist upbringing without running the risk of having their children labeled peculiar or sissy. Wise parents identify "things we do in our house which are good for our family," and tell children that "other people do things differently, and that is ok for them, too."

—Providing a peer group of children with like-minded parents is perhaps the most valuable addition to nonsexist childrearing that parents can employ, particularly during the crucial early years, and again during early adolescence. Some cooperative and public nursery schools and day care centers, are attempting to establish a nonsexist atmosphere, and other groups such as the Liberal Religious Youth of the Unitarian-Universalist Church give guidance to young people so that sexist biases can be faced.

—Parents are children's most important models. It is obvious that fathers and mothers must practice what they preach. Father cannot say, "See, you got into that accident because you drive just like a woman;" Mother cannot say, "You just wait until your father comes home, and he will see that you get punished." In typical middle class homes where mothers must often fix household appliances, deal with difficult salespeople, and respond to emergencies of all kinds, the children see a resourceful and adequate woman, who is not less feminine for such "masculine" competencies. Similarly, a father whose physical strength is used in pushing a pencil or holding a telephone is not less masculine because he engages in no big-muscle activity. Both parents can engage in fishing, bowling, crafts, gardening, hiking, bicycling, breadmaking, reading aloud to the children, dancing, and mourning.

—Unknowingly, parents often make career decisions for their children. Many people struggle with inappropriate projections of a parental ambition throughout their lives. Parents need to learn to love—and let go. The best nonsexist child guidance regarding careers is to provide a wide range of experiences on which the child can test his or her interests and talents. Parents can support these activities which the child finds most enticing and where ability is most apparent.

What Can Society Do?

Society, like family, is not a monolithic entity which can make rational decisions. However, those of us who work within major social institutions can provide assistance in molding the small piece of society where we labor to make it more possible for boys and girls to grow up to be fulfilled adults, regardless of sex.

—Laws which interfere with optimizing human potential should be reexamined and revised. There is both negative and positive discrimination which makes it difficult for men and women to cope with the pressures and problems of today's social order. Prisons which brutalize men are outmoded. Laws which make prostitution a crime for women and not men are remnants from our sexist past. Social institutions of all kinds need a thorough examination to see to what extent they perpetuate socially destructive notions of male and female. In this regard it is gratifying to note that many state legislatures are systematically reviewing their statutes and removing sex-discriminatory phrases and words.

—Occupational opportunities must be available at every level for each sex according to interest and talent. Women might prefer to be carpenters rather than domestics. Men might prefer to be nurses rather than miners. The sex-labeling of occupations has restricted the creative contributions of many talented individuals, and talent and creativity are always in scarce supply in any society.

—Youth-serving agencies should continue with their studies and research into the motives and concerns of their clientele. Major shifts in the programs offered by Campfire Girls, Boy and Girl Scouts, YMCA and YWCA, and 4H indicate their willingness to experiment with new ways of reaching youth so that influence can be exerted through accepted peer group involvement, and with sensitized adult guidance. The organizations might do a better job of monitoring messages conveyed by advertisements in their own publications that blatantly and consistently utilize audience-appeal based on sex-role stereotypes which the associations themselves claim to be working to dispel.

—The mass media, particularly television, need a thorough and continuous critical evaluation to eliminate the distortions in sex roles which are part of so-called entertainment fare. We cannot expect nonaggressive males to feel sexually safe when television presents violence as an inextricable aspect of the male image, and one that pays well psychically and financially. So-called situation comedies which caricature family members are socially subversive. The bumbling idiotic father is no model for anyone's son, nor is the silly dim-witted female someone to emulate or marry. All mass media need to include more women in policy and production. All media personnel must be alert to distortions that support inadequate sex-role perception. Even comic books and "harmless" Saturday morning television cartoons too often provide boys and girls with inappropriate models.

—Religious bodies have been run by men, and theological doctrine has helped uphold male supremacy. Biblical pronouncements on the proper roles of males and females hold sway in our nuclear age; this is clearly a case of cultural lag. The bible is invoked to keep women in a weak, dependent, and subservient position, and to reinforce men as aggressors and warriors. Changing attitudes toward sex roles are consistent with religious tenets and beliefs, since the Judeo-Christian tradition is also the root of our belief in the value and uniqueness of each individual and the right of each person to live in peace with others. Religious groups can provide support for persons seeking insight into their own sexuality. This job is too often sidestepped by nervous or uninformed religious leaders.

—At all levels, government can provide a model of law enforcement, dispensing justice, jobs, and rewards without regard to gender. By example, governments can show business and industry that men and women, of all races and creeds, are equally competent at dealing with affairs of state when access to training and experience is open. The experience women now lack in administration excludes them from managerial roles. Such opportunities can be provided by government agencies. Government legal agencies often provide the first job to minority and female lawyers, who are not accepted by law firms until they have "proven themselves"—unlike their white male peers. Commissions on the Status of Women, now established in a number of states and cities, are useful fact-finding bodies whose activities have resulted in progress for women, their children, and their husbands.

Conclusion

There is much to be done. We need more facts, more understanding, more vision, and, of course, more time. Never before have we had as good an opportunity to look with objectivity at the most significant fact about each of us—our sex.

We have attempted to report what is known and conjectured regarding sex differences, and by this means to provide some information for those who want to alleviate some of the unnecessary suffering and deprivations which arise from confused or distorted sex-role perceptions and expectations. We have left many topics untouched, and some were barely mentioned. There is far more data than any one volume could begin to assess. We have been surprised that so little synthesizing of the available research has been done in an objective and useful fashion. There are enticing bits and pieces of data lying around which if examined by creative minds could help us understand the puzzle of human sexual identity in a complex society.

We believe that each person is unique. We believe that our society is on the verge of a new and more satisfying understanding of the role of sex and gender in life decisions. We believe people are trying to determine how to change their sex-role image to make their lives more fulfilling. This book is an effort to help them along the way.

References

1. William L. O'Neill, *Coming Apart: An Informal History of America in the 1960's* (New York: Quadrangle Books, 1971), pp. 198–199.
2. Donald Barr, *Who Pushed Humpty Dumpty?* (New York: Athenaeum, 1971).
3. Charles Winick, *The New People* (New York: Western Publishing Company, 1968), pp. 356–357.
4. *Ibid.*, p. 358.
5. *Washington Post*, March 7, 1973.
6. G. C. Payette, *Understanding Woman Bahavior: or, How to Deal With Women* (Montreal, Que.: G. C. Payette, 1970); see also Wallace Reyburn, *The Inferior Sex* (Englewood Cliffs, N.J.: Prentice Hall, 1973).

7. David Jones and Doris Klein, *Man-Child: A Study of the Infantilization of Man* (New York: McGraw-Hill, 1970).

8. Lawrence II. Fuchs, *Family Matters* (New York: Random House, 1972).

9. Ashley Montague, review of *The Human Imperative* by Alexander Alland, Jr. in *Natural History* (1972): 93-94.

10. David Pilbeam, "The Fashionable View of Man as a Naked Ape Is: 1) An Insult to Apes, 2) Simplistic, 3) Male-Oriented, 4) Rubbish," *New York Times Magazine*, September 3, 1972, pp. 10-11+; see also Suzanne Little, "You Can Fool Mother Nature: Sex Roles in Faraway Places," *Ms* 3 (February 1975): 76-79+.

11. John Singleton, *Nichu: A Japanese School* (New York: Holt, Rhinehart and Winston, 1967).

12. Priscilla R. Macdougall, "Married Women's Common Law Right to Their Own Surnames," *Women's Rights Law Reporter* 1 (Fall/Winter 1972-73): 2-14.

13. Robert P. Odenwald, *The Disappearing Sexes: Sexual Behavior in the United States and the Emergence of Uni-Sex* (New York: Random House, 1965), p. 172.

14. Marianne A. Ferber and Jane W. Loeb, "Sex Discrimination Among Faculty," *American Journal of Sociology* 78 (January 1973): 995-1002.

15. Nevitt Sanford, *Self and Society* (New York: Atherton Press, 1966), p. 201. According to Sanford, the male "is forced to deny or put aside large aspects of himself—his own biological and psychological feminine dispositions as well as any interest or activity that he believes to be 'feminine'—and thus is prevented from being a whole person." G. C. Griffith, "The Penalty of Being a Male," *Annals of Internal Medicine* 55 (1961): 166-168; Roy G. D'Andrade, "Sex Differences and Cultural Institutions," in *The Development of Sex Differences*, ed. Eleanor E. Maccoby (Stanford: Stanford University Press, 1966), p. 202; Peter Blos, "The Child Analyst Looks at the Young Adolescent," *Daedalus* 100 (Fall 1971): 961-978; "The Male Sex Role: Keeping the Man in the House," *Civil Liberties* (May 1972).

16. Bruno Bettelheim, "Dialogue with Mothers," *Ladies Home Journal*, August 1927, pp. 24ff.; see also Paul Schwaber, "Women and Freud's Imagination," *American Scholar* 41 (Spring 1972): 224-237; James O'Toole *et al.*, *Work in America* (Cambridge: MIT Press, 1973); Nancy Frazier and Myra Sadker, *Sexism in School and Society* (New York: Harper and Row, 1973); Judith Stacey *et al.*, eds., *And Jill Came Tumbling Down* (New York: Dell Publishing, 1974).

17. Outstanding examples of such approaches are: *Today's Changing Roles: An Approach to Non-Sexist Teaching* (Washington, D.C.: National Foundation for the Improvement of Education, 1974); Phyllis T. Greenleaf,

Liberating Young Children from Sex Roles (Somerville, Ma.: New England Free Press, 1972).

18. Catherine Breslin, "Waking Up From the Dream of Women's Lib," *New York Magazine*, February 1973, pp. 31-38.

Index

Abortion: 62, 63, 85, 86, 199
Adelson, Joseph: 108, 109, 110
Advanced degrees, 183
Althus, William D.: 148
American Federation of Teachers: 159
Anthony, E. James: 123
Anttonen, Ralph G.: 124
Arithmetical skills. *See* Numerical skills
Athletic competition: 19, 104, 105, 106, 127–129, 187–188; women and, 105, 106, 132, 188
"Atomized society": 56
Austin, David: 138

Backman, Carl F.: 166, 167
Bard, Joseph F.: 132, 137
Barr body: 33
Barr, Donald: 257
Beard, Mary: 60
Bellamy, Edward: 70
Benson, Leonard: 87, 219
Berger, Brigitte: 91
Berger, Peter: 91
Berman, Edgar: 45
Biller, Henry B.: 167
Blacks: 60, 126, 151, 180, 181, 187, 195, 196, 216, 239, 240
Blackstone: 60, 260
Blau, Peter M.: 246
Block, James H.: 194
Body types: 37–38
Bolton, Charles D.: 186, 192
Boocock, Sarane S.: 167
Bowlby, John: 249
Boys: athletics and, 19, 104, 105, 106, 107, 108, 109–111; behavior in school, 123, 139–140; college admissions and, 127; creativity of, 158–159; employment rates for, 239; fathers and, 86–87, 88; friendships and, 111–112; grades and, 125–127, 156, 158; groups and, 102, 103, 104, 105, 106, 107, 108, 109–111; impact of school on, 123–129, 162, 163, 167, 168; learning and, 146–152; male teachers and, 167, 168; mental health of, 48–51, 69–70, 150; metabolic rate of, 37; non-sexist rearing of, 91–94; numerical skills of, 124–125, 147, 148, 149, occupational choice and, 212–214, 216, 218; physical maturation of, 128; reading skills of, 124–125, 137, 147; test-taking and, 152–159

Bragdon, Henry W.: 136
Bride-price system: 25
Buddeke, Sr. Rita: 151
Burr, Elizabeth: 137
Byers, Loretta: 137

Campbel, John D.: 81
Campus protest: 193–197
Chesler, Phyllis: 49
Child, Irvin L.: 134
Children: abuse of, 83; choosing sex of, 6–7; education and, 122–141; fathers and, 78, 81–82, 86–91, 91–94; first-born, 3–6, 79–81; gender identification of, 82, 87, 90, 91, 152; later born, 80–81; learning and, 146–152; mothers and, 76–79, 82–26, 91–94; naming of, 2–3; non-sexist rearing of, 91–94, 265; occupational choice and, 212–219, 265, 266; peer group and, 99–118; sex roles, learning of, 99–118, 264–266; test-taking and, 154–159; treatment by parents according to sex, 7–11, 82, 83, 254. *See also* Boys; Girls

271